Built on a Lie

By the same author

Barbarians in the Boardroom: Activist Investors and the Battle
for Control of the World's Most Powerful Companies

Built on a Lie

*The Rise and Fall of Neil Woodford and
the Fate of Middle England's Money*

OWEN WALKER

BUSINESS

PENGUIN BUSINESS

UK | USA | Canada | Ireland | Australia
India | New Zealand | South Africa

Penguin Business is part of the Penguin Random House group of companies
whose addresses can be found at global.penguinrandomhouse.com.

First published 2021

001

Copyright © Owen Walker, 2021

The moral right of the author has been asserted

Set in 12/14.75 pt Dante MT Std
Typeset by Jouve (UK), Milton Keynes
Printed and bound in Great Britain by Clays Ltd, Elcograf S.p.A.

The authorized representative in the EEA is Penguin Random House Ireland,
Morrison Chambers, 32 Nassau Street, Dublin D02 YH68

A CIP catalogue record for this book is available from the British Library

ISBN: 978–0–241–46819–7

Follow us on LinkedIn: https://www.linkedin.com/company/penguin-connect/

www.greenpenguin.co.uk

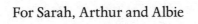

For Sarah, Arthur and Albie

Contents

Made in Maidstone

From the Medway Room's open window in the Grade II listed Sessions House, inmates from HM Prison Maidstone could be heard exercising in the yard outside. Grandly designed in the Greek Revival style, Sessions House had seen better days. The musty rooms were freezing in winter and sweltering in summer. It began life as a court in 1824, dispensing local justice and disposing convicted criminals into the jail next door. Kent County Council later moved into the imperious building and throughout its nearly two centuries as a civic centre it had been the setting for plenty of life-altering deliberations. On the morning of 16 November 2018, hundreds of millions of pounds were at stake.

The motley crew of councillors, local government staff, retired council workers and union officials gathered and nervously shuffled their meeting packs. Old books lined the walls, while black-and-white photos of mayors from years gone by looked down on the congregation. The smell of damp filled the air. While meetings of Kent County Council's Pension Fund Committee usually began with idle gossip about local politics and town hall affairs over weak coffee and cheap biscuits, on this occasion one topic dominated discussions. The fourteen committee members and four council officers present were about to decide whether to sack their favourite fund manager.

Neil Woodford was the most celebrated British investor of his generation. For more than three decades, the savers of Middle England had entrusted him with their hard-earned nest eggs and he had made them rich with years of blockbuster returns. He was lauded in the press as much for his daring bets and bull-headed conviction as for his fleet of fast cars and his ostentatious mansions: the rock-star fund manager with a lifestyle to match. He not only was the biggest name in the investment industry but also held sway over Britain's largest companies. In boardrooms up and down the country his fierce temper and strong-arm approach to getting his own way were the stuff of nightmares.

But things had not been going his way of late. It had been a shocking eighteen months for Woodford's business, with his investment portfolios pummelled by the collapse of some of the companies he had backed the hardest. Among the businesses Woodford had helped prop up with Kent's retirement savings were the A A, Provident Financial and Capita, all of which had been hobbled by individual problems. Meanwhile, many of the other companies in his fund were suffering from the malaise in Britain's economy brought on by uncertainty over the direction of Brexit negotiations. His fund had lost nearly 17 per cent that year and other clients were giving up on him. Kent's pension board summoned him to their November meeting to explain his dire performance.

Yet, as Woodford strutted into the Medway Room, accompanied by his top salesman, Will Deer, he was far from repentant. With a broad chest, thick neck and close-cropped white hair, Woodford had the swagger of a bulldog as he burst through the doors. A natural sportsman and an amateur rugby player in his youth, Woodford was still a fitness fanatic. The cocky investor had abandoned his preferred getup of a tight-fitting black sweatshirt and jeans – which gave him the appearance of a menacing nightclub bouncer – in favour of a blue suit, crisp white shirt and burgundy tie. But the famous fund manager showed no sign of discomfort. If anything, he was in his element. There was nothing Woodford liked better than being put through his paces on his knowledge of the companies he had invested in and his predictions for the markets and economy. With no attempt at small talk, Woodford got straight down to business.

In unscripted comments, delivered in his trademark down-to-earth style, Woodford gave a spirited defence of his investment record. Displaying supreme confidence in his own ability to pick companies, Woodford was unflinchingly supportive of the businesses he had poured money into. He insisted that, despite their recent blow-ups, they would eventually come good. He had had periods of severe underperformance at several points in his career, he conceded, but always emerged stronger for them. All Kent needed to do was stick by him and their patience and loyalty would be rewarded. Members of the board quizzed Woodford on his expectations for Brexit and how the portfolio would respond. Again, Woodford was bullish, insisting that once Britain left the EU, money would flow into UK companies from overseas and his fund would rebound. He was dismissive when asked about the scale of the withdrawals from the fund, hubristically insisting that those who left early would regret doing so when it bounced back.

The cocksure performance worked. Kent's trustees were persuaded that Woodford was suffering a short-term blip, and that as soon as the UK left the EU – an event scheduled for the following March – confidence would return to the markets and Woodford's fund would surge. The investor was given a reprieve. Perhaps against their better judgement, Kent's trustees continued to support Woodford – a decision they would later bitterly regret.

What was so concerning for the Kent trustees was that they had £263 million tied up in Woodford's fund. This was money they had handed over to the investment guru that was meant to pay the retirement benefits of the more than 135,000 street sweepers, librarians and local government workers who were members of the scheme. The more fellow investors in the fund asked for their money back, the harder it would be for Kent to get its cash out. Just like with runs on a bank, when lenders are in distress and account holders queue round the block to take out their savings, funds that allow investors to withdraw their money daily are vulnerable when customers become skittish.

Kent's pension board knew all too well about the perils of a bank run. Just over a decade earlier the council had handed £50 million of taxpayers' money and retirement savings to three Icelandic lenders, seduced by the promise of high interest rates on deposits. But when the banks – Glitnir, Landsbanki and Heritable – all buckled under the weight of the global financial crisis in 2008, those deposits were jeopardized. A damning report from the UK government's now defunct Audit Commission said Kent had been 'negligent' over its Icelandic investments. It revealed how, even after the credit ratings of Glitnir and Landsbanki were downgraded below a level acceptable for local authorities to do business with them on 30 September of that year, Kent continued to hand over money. Kent made two deposits on 1 and 2 October totalling £8.3 million. Within a week the banks had collapsed, trapping Kent's cash. The Audit Commission, which was set up to monitor public sector finances, found that the final deposit was made after council officials had received but failed to open an email warning them not to continue doing business with the struggling banks. It was an embarrassing revelation that showed up the council's finance department as incompetent.

It took more than three gruelling years of fighting through the Icelandic courts before Kent finally recouped its money. The charge was led by the council's head of financial services, Nick Vickers, an accountant by training. The bespectacled Vickers had led the team under which the Icelandic deposits were made, but he emerged from the crisis emboldened, having successfully conducted negotiations on behalf of the 123 UK local authorities that had deposits in Icelandic banks.

Kent's history with Neil Woodford was a long one, going back to his days managing money for Invesco Perpetual, one of Britain's biggest investment groups, in the early 2000s. Vickers, who had spent much of his career working in humdrum finance roles within Kent's council, was initially drawn to Woodford's strong performance and unconstrained style, and soon became seduced by the showbiz stock picker. In 2007 he convinced the pension fund to invest £240 million, around a tenth of Kent's entire portfolio at the time, in Woodford's Invesco Perpetual fund. When institutional investors such as pension funds make large allocations to investment managers, they usually structure them through so-called segregated mandates, where the money is handled in the same style as the manager's main fund but is ring fenced in a separate pot. Pension funds pay more for this structure, but have some say over how their funds are managed. Crucially, they also have more flexibility over withdrawing their money, which is especially important in times of stress. But Vickers and the Kent pension board decided to save on fees and place their whole allocation in the main fund. That decision to scrimp on costs would prove hugely expensive in the long run.

Kent stuck with Invesco Perpetual for several years as Woodford comfortably beat his benchmark. By February 2014, Kent's initial investment with Woodford had grown to £520 million, with the fund returning 20 per cent in the previous year. It was then that Woodford decided to leave Invesco Perpetual and go it alone in one of the investment industry's most stunning defections. The Kent trustees took their cue, withdrawing their investment from Invesco Perpetual and giving Woodford's new venture, Woodford Investment Management, £200 million to manage. This time the allocation was around 5 per cent of Kent's total pot.

According to previously unreported meeting notes, Nick Vickers met Will Deer in March 2014 to discuss the allocation to Woodford's new business. Vickers told Deer, an athletic Australian with thinning hair, he had been delighted with Woodford's performance since he'd started managing money for Kent seven years earlier. Vickers was so keen to continue the relationship that he once again offered to lump the entire investment in Woodford's main fund rather than taking the safer route of a segregated mandate. Vickers explained that if they went for a segregated mandate, the scheme's rules meant it would trigger a competitive tender process, wherein other fund managers could pitch for the business. This would potentially block Woodford from winning. Vickers stressed this was something he wished to avoid. Vickers's admiration for the great fund manager and his determination to stick with him was bypassing the council's business safeguards.

Initially, the decision to stick with Woodford paid off. Kent's investment returned 2.7 per cent in its first full financial year, compared to a 3.9 per cent expected loss in the market. Yet even during this honeymoon period for Woodford's new venture, there were signs that the relationship would not last. In November 2015 Vickers wrote a report for the pension board outlining the ramifications of the UK government's plan to merge local authority schemes. He said Kent was the only local authority pension fund in the UK that had invested with Woodford and that the relationship would probably not survive when Kent's retirement pot was pooled with other schemes. 'Given the style of investing it is unlikely that Woodford would be selected to manage a UK equity pool and so we could potentially be forced to end the mandate,' he warned.

Kent's allocation to Woodford reached £317 million in January 2017. Soon after, the fund manager's performance took a drastic turn for the worse. Other institutional clients began to abandon ship, but still Kent's pension board stayed loyal to their prized stock picker. His self-assured performance in November 2018 convinced the board to stick with him a little longer, but when the Brexit deadline was further extended past March 2019 and Woodford's fund continued to shrivel, it became clear to all that the relationship was coming to an end. To make matters worse, several stories were appearing in the press that showed Woodford's business in a bad light. Clearly under pressure, he had tried ever more creative ways to contain the dangerous effects of the run on his fund. These included moving stakes in companies to different portfolios within his business. Elsewhere, some private companies he had invested in took the highly unusual step of listing in Guernsey's tiny stock exchange. While the moves were not illegal, they were attracting negative attention. Woodford's company was suffering so badly that he was forced to bend the rules to stay in business. Even Nick Vickers, one of Woodford's biggest devotees, could no longer summon the enthusiasm to convince Kent's trustees to stay with him. The board instructed Vickers to write to Woodford and ask for an explanation for the odd and questionable actions taken by his business. They also put the fund formally on watch, and would decide in June whether to sack the manager.

Vickers and Deer were in touch regularly throughout the spring of 2019. Vickers led Deer to believe the trustee board would pull the plug on Woodford at its 21 June meeting. By this point, Kent's allocation represented about 7 per cent of Woodford's flagship fund. Knowing what a shock losing such a large amount of money all at once would be to the business, Woodford's team suggested to Vickers that they might move Kent's money into a separate account. This would mean that, when they did withdraw the cash, it would have little impact on the other investors in the main fund. This seemed a tidy solution to both Kent's and Woodford's problems. Yet Vickers inexplicably rejected the proposal. A worried Woodford and his team began planning for the June decision, building models for how they would cope with the loss of such a large client.

All their planning was in vain. On Thursday, 30 May, the headline plastered across the front of the *Financial Times* read: 'Woodford fund shrinks by £560 million in a month as investors jump ship'. The story, picked up and covered by the rest of the UK's national media, exposed the extent to which Woodford was struggling against the tsunami of client desertions. Investors were withdrawing an average of £10 million every business day from his main vehicle, the £3.7 billion Equity Income fund. It was simultaneously being battered by the market, losing 8.3 per cent of its value in the previous month alone. As the *FT* story first revealed, the alarming shrinkage of one of the country's most popular funds had not gone unnoticed by the City regulator. The Financial Conduct Authority was so concerned about the fund's plight that it had secretly demanded regular updates about its ability to cope with the escalating withdrawals.

Even for Woodford's most ardent supporters in Kent, this was impossible to ignore. When the trustees met the following morning, the twelve committee members present made the unanimous decision to fire Woodford and ask for their money back immediately rather than waiting for the June review. The decision would have profound consequences, both for hundreds of thousands of savers across the country and for Britain's £9 trillion investment industry.

Later that day, Nick Vickers, who had attended the morning's committee meeting, emailed Will Deer to give him the bad news. Though the termination was anticipated, it had occurred three weeks earlier than Woodford's team had planned for. Vickers tried to reassure Deer that the Kent board would not expect their money to be returned for at least a month, and that they favoured a staged withdrawal, where the money would be refunded in instalments. This suited Woodford, as the fund did not have enough available cash to pay back Kent's £263 million investment as a lump sum. Over the weekend, Woodford, his top lieutenants and Link Fund Solutions, an important though under-the-radar service provider to the fund, considered how they could rejig the investment portfolio to raise enough short-term cash to pay Kent back without affecting other clients. They modelled shedding various combinations of assets to hit their target. The plan involved raising £85 million from selling the fund's stake in Sabina Estates, a luxury property developer that built private villas in Ibiza for the super-rich. Sabina was the brainchild of one of Woodford's long-time allies, Anton Bilton, the flamboyant multi-millionaire property mogul, who is married to the American singer and model Lisa B.

But on Monday, 3 June, the plans fell apart. Vickers was out of the office on holiday. His stand-in for the week, unaware of the frantic discussions Vickers had had with Woodford's team on the Friday afternoon, decided to be proactive. He made an official request to Link to return Kent's £263 million investment with Woodford in a single transaction, the money to be transferred immediately. Although Link had been involved in the discussions with Woodford throughout the weekend which had planned for a staged withdrawal, the company decided to follow Kent's instructions to the letter. As Woodford did not have enough cash available to meet its obligation to Kent, Link decided it had no other option but to suspend trading in the fund, thereby preventing Kent and more than 400,000 individuals invested in the fund from reclaiming their money. Europe's biggest investment scandal for a decade had begun.

This book tells the full story of the rise and fall of Neil Woodford – the superstar fund manager who fell to earth. Once described as 'the man who can't stop making money', he was forced in October 2019 to close his business, which once managed £18 billion, after trapping hundreds of thousands of savers in his flagship fund. There is more to the story of his dramatic downfall than simply a high-powered financier losing his Midas touch. Woodford's ruination is a tale of greed, obstinate conviction, betrayal and misplaced loyalty. It exposes the flaws of a timid regulator and an industry in thrall to its star performers. But most of all it reveals what happens when ordinary people hand over their savings to financial advisers and fund managers. Just how is their money spent and how effective are the safeguards intended to ensure their trust is not abused?

More than 400,000 people had their savings stuck in Woodford's stricken Equity Income fund for well over a year, as did the 135,000 members of Kent Council's pension fund. But this story is not just about the direct victims of the Woodford scandal. It encompasses the more than 700,000 clients of wealth manager St James's Place and 1.1 million savers with accounts at fund supermarket Hargreaves Lansdown – two of Britain's largest financial companies – who are ensnared in the affair. Three-quarters of British households use fund management services – whether they know it or not – and more than 4.5 million UK adults employ a financial adviser to help them protect and grow their hard-earned savings. The Woodford scandal has crushed consumer confidence in one of Britain's most important sectors, one that is critical to the financial security of its ageing population. Was Woodford solely to blame or was he just one of many weak links in a chain that ultimately disintegrated into dust? How did Neil Woodford's career collapse so spectacularly? Was the hype surrounding him built on a lie? And what is the fate of Middle England's money?

2

Follow the Money

Pauline Snelson and Fred Hiscock had always planned for a long and comfortable retirement. The couple, who met later in life, had nine grandchildren between them and hoped to have enough savings spare to leave a meaningful inheritance. Pauline, sixty-seven, had run a patisserie in the Midlands for twelve years and then went on to manage a restaurant for another twelve. After that she relocated to Salcombe, a picturesque waterfront town in Devon, to open a bed-and-breakfast. 'I never liked managing people – by setting up on my own I could work by myself,' she says. Throughout her working life she had done the right thing: saved a little each month in the hope of building up a decent nest egg.

Fred, four years Pauline's senior, had started out in construction as a civil engineer, but ended up working in the motor industry, eventually becoming a senior manager at Jaguar. He took early retirement and invested his pension lump sum in property. He also drove a shuttle bus for elderly Salcombe residents to supplement his pension.

By the mid-2010s Pauline and Fred had enough put by to start to look forward to a more sedate retirement. It was then, prompted by Pauline's financial adviser and their own research, that they made one of the biggest mistakes of their lives: they decided to entrust their savings to Neil Woodford. Over the years the couple would invest a combined £75,000 in Woodford's funds, money that was earmarked for their future wellbeing. But the scandal that brought a crashing end to Woodford's business and career has had even worse consequences for Pauline and Fred. 'I really feel like I don't want to work any longer, but after the money we've lost, I'll probably be doing this for ever,' says Pauline. 'I was hoping to retire, but I can't any more. The money is gone, and so is the grand-children's inheritance.'

The tragedy of Pauline and Fred's circumstances is as much about the failings of the multi-billion-pound financial advice industry as it is about the even more profitable investment sector. Pauline's relationship with her financial adviser will be familiar to millions up and down the country. Once a year she would call in at his offices for an hour-long meeting. Over mugs of tea, they would discuss how her investments had fared over the previous twelve months and he would suggest other savings and investment products she might like to consider.

More than 4.5 million Britons rely on financial advisers or wealth managers to help them decide where to keep their life savings. The dizzying array of investment funds – with more than 3,000 standard products in the UK alone, in addition to myriad convoluted schemes and complex vehicles also on offer – has made personal investing a daunting task for even the most avid market watcher. Yet, at the same time, changes to the pensions market have forced individuals to take on more responsibility for how they finance their retirement. Gone are the days when workers could simply trust their employer to provide for them in old age through pater-nalistic final-salary pension plans. Individuals are having to take matters into their own hands, deciding which funds to invest in, or consider whether their money would be better served buying property or other assets. Thanks to the powerful nature of compound interest, mistakes can be amplified decades down the line. Various studies have shown that the difference between paying 0.5 per cent a year and 1 per cent in fees could result in tens of thousands of pounds' difference in a saver's eventual retirement pot. Deciding to back the wrong fund manager or pay over the odds for a type of product can be hazardous. The demand for trustworthy and trans-parent financial advice has therefore never been greater.

The UK government has long been concerned about the crucial relationship between saver and financial adviser. Following a series of mis-selling scandals in the 1990s and early 2000s, the industry regulator unleashed ground-breaking market reforms that sought to upend the financial advisory industry, making it more professional and better designed to serve customers' interests. The changes banned commissions paid to advisers by investment managers for selling their products, forced advisers to be entirely open with their clients about whether they were offering independent or restricted advice, and required advisers to undertake tougher professional qualifications.

While the reforms were widely seen as a success in limiting conflicts, they had the unintended side effect of reducing the number of advisers in the market. Banks and building societies found it less profitable to sell their own products, so several cut back their advisory arms. Meanwhile, older independent advisers chose to retire from the industry rather than retrain or change their business models. The result was that between 2011 and 2014 the number of financial advisers dropped by a quarter to just over 30,000. This reduction had a disproportionate impact on poorer customers, as they were the cadre more likely to use services offered by their banks or building societies. Less wealthy customers were also unlikely to be able to pay upfront fees for advice.

Fred Hiscock was one such customer. He had used a financial adviser for a while, but eventually found the charges too high. 'It was costing me about 3 per cent a year and I was only getting 4 per cent myself. It was ridiculous, so I sacked him,' he says ruefully. 'I was fed up of paying consultants. But unfortunately, without a financial adviser, I made mistakes myself.' Fred's decision to buy property with his pension lump sum initially seemed a sound one, but an ill-fated decision to sell several properties and invest in banks in the run-up to the financial crisis would decimate Fred's savings.

As demand increasingly outstripped supply, the remaining advisers concentrated their businesses on attracting richer and more profitable clients. As a result, those with less than £50,000 of savings are finding it harder to source affordable advice. Though one in ten UK adults use financial advisers, what is more concerning is the 18.2 million people, or 36 per cent of the adult population, who have £10,000 or more in savings but do not receive professional financial advice. They are more susceptible to making the sort of investment mistakes that Fred made, with life-changing consequences.

The rich, however, are well catered for, even if the service they receive is not always what they might expect, considering what they pay. The wealth manager synonymous with Middle England is St James's Place, a FTSE 100 company whose network of 4,300 advisers looks after £117 billion on behalf of more than 700,000 customers. The group would play a crucial role in helping Woodford set up his own business when he left his long-term employer, Invesco Perpetual, in 2014.

SJP, as it is widely known, targets the mass affluent – the 11 million individuals in the UK with between £50,000 and £5 million of investable assets – by hiring function rooms at country houses and luring potential customers with offers of free advice seminars. The thirty-year-old business is astoundingly successful, raking in close to £1 billion of pre-tax profit a year. But its financial success has been marred in recent years by a spate of damaging revelations about the company's business practices.

In 2019 an anonymous former SJP adviser gave an eye-opening account to the *Sunday Times* of the high-pressure and rewards-heavy practices the company used. The whistle-blower looked after 700 clients, who on average had £100,000 of savings. For this he was paid £250,000 a year before bonuses, funding a large house and private education for his children. He not only owned a Porsche but also had a Mercedes as his second car. It was a lifestyle few of his clients experienced, yet it was funded by the fees taken from their savings. And that was before factoring in his rewards for hitting sales targets. Successful SJP advisers were awarded diamond-encrusted, 18-carat white-gold cufflinks that were worth £1,200. Other perks included Mulberry bags and Montblanc pens.

Each year SJP's advisers from across the country descended on London to a huge venue, either the Royal Albert Hall or the O2, for a sales conference at which the best performers were lauded. The whistle-blower described it as resembling a scene from *The Wolf of Wall Street*. Spouses were also invited to London, to stay in five-star hotels and attend dinners. A succession of sports stars and politicians provided the entertainment at the lavish events, with speeches from the likes of Bill Clinton, Tony Blair, David Cameron, Vince Cable, David Beckham and Lance Armstrong. Compères included TV personalities Jonathan Ross and Fiona Bruce. At one event, the then *Top Gear* presenter Richard Hammond joked that his own supercar was hard to spot among all the Ferraris and Bentleys in the car park belonging to SJP advisers. But the most extravagant rewards were reserved for the advisers who brought in the most revenue. They were invited to the company's annual week-long overseas conferences where no expense was spared. SJP chartered flights, hired luxury cruise ships and treated guests to safaris in Zambia, camel rides around the pyramids in Egypt and sumo wrestling in Japan. All the while, expensive booze flowed freely.

'Despite the rewards, I grew to hate the job,' the former adviser confessed to the *Sunday Times*. 'I found I couldn't keep pretending to customers that they were getting the best value. I felt we were not advisers; we were salespeople, and I felt I was not acting in their best interests. It was clear many investors simply had no understanding of the long-term impact of the charges they paid – or how lucrative they could be for the likes of me and SJP.'

Pauline and Fred fell just below SJP's radar, but there were plenty of other financial intermediaries willing to take them on as clients and charge for advice. In recent years the UK has seen a rise in popularity of low-cost fund supermarkets, also known as investment platforms. These direct-to-consumer websites allow investors to pick their own products from a broad range of fund managers, removing the need for expensive advisers. It was here that Woodford found the bedrock of his support.

There are more than twenty such brokers in the UK. At the no-frills end of the market, providers have the most basic of platforms, offering just a cheap way of accessing a variety of funds. In addition to her financial adviser, Pauline used a low-cost broker to invest in Woodford's funds, as did Fred. But further up the scale, some fund supermarkets offer detailed analysis of the various funds, recommendations on which are likely to perform well and even the option of taking advice from in-house specialists. Between 2008 and 2015 the amount of money invested through fund supermarkets ballooned from £100 billion to £500 billion. The sales channel now accounts for half of money flowing into British investment funds.

The undisputed king of the British fund platform market is Hargreaves Lansdown – the business that did more than any other to convince individuals to park their savings in Woodford's funds. The company began in 1981 in the spare bedroom of co-founder Peter Hargreaves. He and Stephen Lansdown built the business up from having a single phone and a borrowed typewriter at launch to listing on the London stock market for £800 million in 2007. It is now firmly entrenched in the FTSE 100. The Bristol-based business has 1.2 million customers, who have £100 billion of savings on the platform, from which Hargreaves Lansdown makes more than £300 million a year in pre-tax profits. Throughout the 1990s and 2000s, the Hargreaves brand grew into a household name via a combination of heavy advertising and indirect marketing. The latter relied on a band of Hargreaves spokespeople who would be on hand to provide expert commentary to journalists on any finance-related news story going. Chief among them was Mark Dampier, the group's head of research and Woodford's most ardent follower.

Peter Hargreaves described Dampier as the 'thorn in his side' while Dampier worked for a rival Bristol intermediary and constantly featured in news stories owing to his willingness to make himself available to the press. Envious of Dampier's coverage, Hargreaves convinced him to join. 'It wasn't long before, thanks to Mark's efforts, it was Hargreaves Lansdown that was being quoted in all of the newspapers,' Hargreaves wrote in his autobiography, *In for a Penny*. 'I think I can safely say that we have rarely had a bad piece of press since he summoned up his courage and opted to join us.' Yet Dampier would generate headlines for all the wrong reasons following Woodford's demise.

By the 2010s, Hargreaves Lansdown's website had become Britain's best-known and most used fund supermarket. Part of its success was its so-called best-buy list, which was a selection of funds it recommended to clients. Best-buy lists made investors' lives much easier as the funds they featured were touted as the cream of the crop. But the problem with such lists was they trod a fine line between advice and advertising. From a regulatory perspective, they were not classed as financial advice or guidance, and therefore were not monitored to the same extent. But the way the lists were promoted on the platforms often left customers confused about whether they were being recommended the products or not. This obfuscation would cause deep anger among Woodford's many victims who had been convinced to go with the fund manager based on his inclusion on HL's best-buy list.

Whether customers use expensive wealth managers, mid-range financial advisers or DIY investment platforms, their money eventually finds its way to investment managers. Three-quarters of British households use fund management services through their pensions or personal savings products. These businesses play a pivotal role in the British economy, channelling the savings of millions of citizens into businesses that need funding. They identify companies they expect to grow and provide steady dividend payments. These proceeds are transferred back to the investor – but not before the fund managers take their cut. Their investment choices have a direct impact on the financial wellbeing of the UK population, while their decisions over which companies are deserving of the capital injection have a bearing over whether they can prosper, expand and hire more workers. This means fund managers hold considerable sway over Britain's biggest companies, giving them a powerful say in how the businesses are run and by whom.

The investment sector's clout and prestige have grown significantly in the past two decades. The UK industry is the second largest in the world, controlling more than £9 trillion, and its influence is felt throughout the corridors of Westminster. So much so that it has become a rite of passage for British chancellors to take up well-paid advisory roles at investment groups after leaving office. Nigel Lawson, Norman Lamont, Ken Clarke, Gordon Brown, George Osborne and Philip Hammond have all accepted such positions. Former prime ministers John Major and David Cameron have also taken similar roles. Several other sitting MPs have supplemented their parliamentary income by working in lucrative jobs at fund managers, including Jacob Rees-Mogg and John Redwood.

Despite its importance to the British economy, the asset management industry has managed to portray itself less like a utility and more as an elite service where it dictates the terms. Funds are run so that all the investment risk is borne by the end investor. Investment manager fees are charged as a percentage of the size of the fund rather than a fixed sum, meaning the more money that goes in, the bigger the profits for the managers – despite the fact the workload and resources needed do not grow at the same rate. Fund managers are paid fees even when they lose their clients' money. This 'heads I win, tails you lose' model is embedded in the industry.

It is no wonder that investment management is one of Britain's most profitable industries. The best-known fund managers and executives of investment groups can expect to earn millions of pounds a year, affording them lifestyles akin to Premier League footballers. Huge country mansions, fleets of sports cars, exotic holidays and expensive leisure pursuits are all paid for by the annual fee taken from the British public's savings. But unlike top footballers, whose peak earning period is just a few years, fund management careers can stretch for decades. The amount of money sloshing around the investment industry has inevitably made it one of the most competitive. Every year, graduates from Britain's top universities give up on careers in medicine and engineering to seek their fortunes working in fund management.

It is an industry that has turned fund managers such as Neil Woodford into multi-millionaires, but has severely failed the likes of Pauline Snelson and Fred Hiscock, the very people it is supposed to serve.

3

Big Bang

Neil Russell Woodford was born on 2 March 1960 in the affluent Berkshire village of Cookham. His parents, Victor and Pamela, lived at 75 Westwood Green, an unassuming semi-detached house two minutes' walk from Cookham station. The home, which looked out onto an expansive village green and backed onto the railway line, was where Woodford and Simon, his older brother by two years, grew up. Perched on the banks of the Thames, at a particularly leisurely bend, Cookham served as the inspiration for Kenneth Grahame's *Wind in the Willows*. The historic village had been made famous through the paintings of its one-time resident the artist Stanley Spencer. Its tranquillity and proximity to London – being just under an hour's drive from the capital – made it a favoured spot for wealthy commuters. The *Daily Telegraph* once named Cookham the second-richest village in England (behind East Horsley in Surrey).

The Woodfords were not well off by local standards. Neil's father, Victor, had served as an RAF pilot as a nineteen-year-old in the final few months of the Second World War. But by the time he married Pamela seven years later, Victor had followed his own father into the publishing trade, working as a production manager at a postcard printer's. It was a profession he would continue with for much of his working life. 'He wasn't terribly successful,' Woodford later told *The Times*. 'I think he wanted to own his own publishing business but he wasn't very ambitious. Things were tight, but we got on.' The Woodfords lived in the same modest home throughout the future fund manager's childhood. His humble upbringing gave Woodford a yearning for the finer things in life.

Unlike his father, Woodford was very driven. He was urged on by his mother, who instilled in him the mantra of 'he who gets there first, gets most'. It was a maxim which he would both live by and carry into his future business dealings. Young Woodford was smart and very much his parents' blue-eyed boy. He sailed through the eleven-plus exams before taking a place at Maidenhead Grammar School in September 1971, where he was inevitably christened 'Woody' by his classmates. Maidenhead was an all-boys school and a typical grammar of the time. Masters wore gowns, referred to pupils by their surnames and were always themselves addressed as 'sir'. The school prided itself on taking local lads and pushing them on to better things. Among Woodford's contemporaries at Maidenhead were the authors Nick Hornby and John O'Farrell, while Dire Straits keyboardist Guy Fletcher was in his year.

Broad-shouldered, even as a teenager, and with curly blond hair, Woodford was easily recognizable and well known among the 150-odd other boys in his year group. 'He had charisma about him – he was definitely someone you would notice,' recalls Nick Stein, who started in the same class as Woodford. 'He had quite a sarcastic manner at times and was good at banter. He certainly gave as good as he got. It was a boys' school in the 1970s, so there was a fairly laddish and macho culture.'

Woodford excelled academically. Maidenhead was a high-achieving school and it 'hothoused' its brightest pupils, pushing them to take certain O-levels a year early. Even in such a pressure-cooker environment, Woodford made the top stream for most subjects throughout his seven years at the school. But it was on the sports field where he really shone. Maidenhead was very much a sports-driven school. The domineering head of PE, George Griffiths, was a die-hard rugby fan who believed 'football' was a dirty word. The beautiful game was therefore banned from the premises. Woodford and his classmates would defy the rules and kick a tennis ball about at lunchtimes. Despite having a soft spot for Tottenham Hotspur, Woodford's real passion was also for rugby. He played in the 1st XV for the school, and for the county throughout his time there, as well as for the school hockey team, which benefited from his aggressive play and goal-scoring ability. Woodford was also accomplished at athletics and competed at county level in javelin for Berkshire. His strong shoulders, fast arm, explosive speed over a short distance and good technique made him an excellent thrower. He was Berkshire schools javelin champion in 1977 and was selected for the All England Athletics Championships. 'He was an outstanding sportsman,' recalls Gavin Coventry, his teacher for several years. Such was the importance of physical activity at Maidenhead that those in the first teams were expected to give up several evenings a week as well as weekends for practice sessions and matches. Sport, in particular rugby, became the centre of Woodford's life, with his social circle dominated by fellow 'egg-chasers'.

Not all Woodford's contemporaries remember him fondly. 'My overriding memory of him was he was a thug and bully,' remembers another ex-classmate. 'He didn't like me as I once stood up to him during a chemistry lesson when he was belittling me. He actually punched me! It wasn't a tough school. Very little bullying went on, but Neil thought he was hard and liked to take it out on people he thought were weaker than him. We never got on as I was a bit too left field for him. He was someone you avoided unless you were part of his clique.' Those who later crossed Woodford during his investment career would find out about his quick temper for themselves.

Still, Woodford proved popular with his teachers – not least owing to his sporting prowess. In the sixth form he was selected as a prefect by the headmaster, Leonard 'Rover' Reynolds, a celebrated former motor gunboat captain and military historian. In this role Woodford helped keep discipline within the school and was given a special tie. In his final year he was awarded the prestigious Headmaster's Prize, thanks mainly to his sporting achievements. The sixth-form common room had a record player and students would bring in their latest purchases to share with friends. The music was eclectic, ranging from heavy metal and punk to obscure soul imports. Woodford's favourite band was Led Zeppelin. While studying, his first summer job was cleaning machinery at the Maidenhead Beecham factory. Beecham would go on to become part of the pharmaceutical giant GlaxoSmith-Kline, a company Woodford would later be a major investor in.

Though most of the sixth-formers learnt to drive, Woody was one of the few to own a car. His beaten-up Fiat 850 became his circle's de facto taxi. On one occasion, Woodford and three friends loaded up the car and headed down to Bournemouth for a weekend of swimming and drinking on the beach. The vehicle doubled as their sleeping accommodation. The pubs in Cookham and nearby Bourne End and Marlow were the drinking dens of choice for Woodford and his adolescent friends. They set themselves the 'Cookham thirteen' challenge – a pub crawl taking in many of the local drinking establishments.

Other than sport, Woodford's other great obsession was flying. He had heard his father's old war stories and developed a keen interest in a career in the RAF. He joined the 155 Maidenhead Squadron Air Training Corps, along with several other classmates, including Nick Stein. Between 7 p.m. and 9 p.m. on Monday and Friday evenings, the air cadets would meet in a hut behind Maidenhead Leisure Centre. They would go through drills and receive lectures on the principles of flight. The *Maidenhead Advertiser* once sent down a photographer to capture 'cadet N. Woolford' [sic] being shown by an instructor how to fasten the harness of an ejector seat. In the photo, Woodford – dressed in a khaki uniform with shiny boots and a beret – appears to be weighing up the merits of bailing out or crash landing. At weekends, the squadron would travel to RAF training camps and test their skills on two-seater Chipmunk light aircraft. Being near the Heathrow flightpath and with White Waltham airfield nearby, Maidenhead was a hotbed for interest in aviation. Three of Woodford's schoolmates would go on to become pilots.

After leaving school, Woodford studied economics and agricultural economics at Exeter University. Exeter was academically challenging and also had a strong reputation for sport. Woodford turned out for the university rugby team, playing as flanker. He still harboured aspirations for a career in aviation, but as the university did not have its own air squadron, he fell behind his peers. On gaining his degree, he attempted to join both the RAF's graduate scheme and the much harder BA one, but without success, failing the aptitude test at Biggin Hill airport in south London owing to his slow reflexes. Stein is surprised that such an able sportsman, with obvious innate hand–eye coordination, would have failed on that measure. 'Neil had the right character to have been very successful in the air force,' says Stein, who went on to join the RAF. 'I was always surprised he didn't make it.'

By the time Woodford graduated from Exeter in 1981, his parents had relocated to the Cotswolds. Short of money, and with his dreams of becoming a pilot shattered, he sought his fortune in London. His brother Simon was working in an administrative role at Foreign & Colonial, an investment group with Victorian origins, and Woodford slept on his floor while looking for his break. Armed with an economics degree but with little understanding of how the City operated, he bummed around for a few months, taking a low-paid job as an admin clerk at a commodities trader. 'It was unbelievably boring and tedious,' Woodford later informed *The Times.* 'They told me that only a few years previously they had been taking on recruits just with CSEs, but now they were receiving applications from graduates. It was depressing.' Britain was in the throes of a recession and the unemployment rate was heading to 12 per cent nationally, with 3 million out of work. Margaret Thatcher had swept to power two years earlier following the Winter of Discontent on the promise of cutting inflation, improving efficiency and crushing the powerful unions. But her economic policies were taking time to bear fruit, with inflation peaking at 22 per cent in 1980. The worst effects of the disruption were felt far from the City, but even so there were few attractive opportunities available to graduates.

As luck would have it, Woodford stumbled into his first role in the investment industry at the depth of the crisis. Bill Seddon had been in place as fund manager of a small insurer, Dominion, for just a year when he realized he needed an assistant. Having never hired anyone before, he placed a small advert in the *Financial Times*. Of the half-dozen applicants who responded, Woodford was chosen. 'He was a very pleasant young man,' Seddon recalls of the strapping graduate who turned up on his first day in autumn 1981. 'He was polite and respectful. He had a good eye for detail and was someone you could rely on – the perfect assistant, really.' Dominion was a general insurer that sold its products through a network of independent intermediaries across the country. Since its founding in the early 1900s, it had always been a bit-part player in the wider industry. Even in car insurance, where it wrote most of its policies, it had a sliver of market share.

The group's London offices were situated at the busy junction of Cornhill and Gracechurch Street, just next to the historic Leadenhall Market, which traced its roots back to the Middle Ages but which by the 1980s had become one of the City's main drinking spots. Dominion was so small that the investment department consisted of just Seddon and Woodford, who together occupied the building's cramped eyrie. Looking back, Seddon describes the investment approach as basic, consisting mainly of dollar- and sterling-denominated bonds, with a few equities thrown into the mix along with cash. It was Woodford's first taste of managing money, but he was hooked. 'I stumbled into fund management, but once I'd stumbled into it, I realized that I enjoyed it, really enjoyed learning about it,' he later said. Within eighteen months, Woodford had learnt the ropes and was itching for a new challenge. Dominion's size meant there was nowhere else for him to go internally – he was literally at the top of the business in the eyrie – and so it was a natural time for the fund manager's assistant to find his own feet. 'We spent a lot of time working closely with one another and went for a few beers too,' remembers Seddon. 'I can't say I ever thought to myself, "I've got a young Warren Buffett here sitting opposite me." But I suppose he never thought the same about me.'

Woodford's next stop was the Reed International pension fund, where he got a job as a trainee equity analyst. It was a much bigger operation than Dominion and while not a pure investment group, it allowed Woodford to take on more responsibility and had the potential for promotion. Becoming an equity analyst was a tried-and-tested route to becoming a fund manager, a role by now Woodford had set his heart on achieving. The job involved learning how to study and value listed British companies, working through reams of financial data to try to estimate a business's growth potential. The analyst's research would then help inform the investment managers about which stocks to pick. Such a role at an investment group offered good career prospects, but Reed's pension team sat within its corporate finance department, where a would-be fund manager would find few roles to aspire to. Woodford lasted just two years before he was on the move once again.

Though short lived, Woodford's employment at Reed was during a pivotal time for the group. The business had its roots as a paper manufacturer, but by the 1970s it had followed a similar path to many of its contemporaries and established itself as a sprawling conglomerate. The rationale was that if it operated in many different business lines it could diversify income streams and spread risk. Growing bigger through acquisition also ensured the stock price continued to rise. In doing so, Reed mopped up a range of businesses, from the Crown Paints and Polycell DIY brands to the *Daily Mirror* and a swathe of trade journals and consumer magazines. By the 1980s the biggest conglomerates were increasingly seen as bloated and many came under shareholder pressure to shed under-performing divisions. For several years Reed tried to shift its newspaper brands in a bundle it named Mirror Group Newspapers. After considering a float, Reed eventually sold to Robert Maxwell in 1984, much to the chagrin of the papers' staff, the print unions and Labour politicians. One of the pension department's biggest operations during Woodford's time working there was deciding how to apportion the savings pot in preparation for the split.

Maxwell would later plunder £460 million from the Mirror Group scheme in one of Britain's most brazen corporate frauds.

While living in London, Woodford had continued to dedicate his spare time to rugby. Former colleagues recall it was his main interest outside work. During sixth form, Woodford played for Maidenhead RFC's under-19 team. The town's rugby club and grammar school were closely intertwined, with several teachers and ex-pupils involved in playing and coaching for both. In late 1984 Woodford made his debut for Maids, playing as a flanker in a 12–9 victory over Banbury. He even managed to score a try. The win kept Maids, who were Berkshire champions the year before, just a point behind league leaders Henley. While Woodford was developing his career in finance, he played regularly for the team over the next few years as the club was placed in the newly formed South West Division 1, at the seventh tier of the national league system. Woodford's time with Maids reached a pinnacle in 1990 with promotion to National League 4, the next division up. But the flanker's season was blighted by knee injuries that would eventually bring about the end of his playing days.

After leaving Reed in 1985, Woodford took a job working in the corporate finance division of TSB Group, the recently formed amalgamation of Britain's various regional trustee savings banks. While the job was once again a step removed from his chosen career as a fund manager, Woodford undertook a postgraduate finance course at London Business School in his spare time. He joined TSB during a period of seismic change. Over the previous decade, more than seventy regional savings banks had gradually been merged into a single entity. The Tory government was hell bent on upending the British economy through a swathe of privatizations. Savings banks had been formed more than a century earlier as non-commercial institutions to encourage the poor to put some money aside. In 1985 the TSB Act was passed, which restructured the merged group and set it up for flotation on the stock market the following year. The lender also launched its highly successful advertising slogan, describing itself as 'the bank that likes to say yes'. After becoming a public company, TSB continued to expand, setting up a network of estate agencies and buying up small banks.

It was while working at TSB that Woodford began dating Jo Mullan, who was PA to the chief executive and five years his senior. Within two years they were married and living at 6 Knowsley Close, a detached house on the outskirts of Maidenhead. By then, Woodford had already got itchy feet again and applied for a job as an investment analyst at Eagle Star, an insurer with a growing investment business. Eagle Star was a similar vintage to Dominion, having started as a marine insurance specialist in the 1900s, but, unlike Dominion, it was a big player, and throughout the 1980s had been courted as a takeover target by overseas companies. First Allianz, the German insurer, made an unsuccessful hostile bid, then BAT Industries – a conglomerate that owned British American Tobacco – bought the company for £968 million in 1984. Just as BAT's customers were addicted to its products, Woodford would become hooked on investing in the tobacco company throughout his career.

The year 1986 was a momentous one for Britain's financial services sector and the peak of Thatcherism. Having been re-elected in 1983 on a wave of national support for her exploits in the Falklands, Thatcher and her new chancellor, Nigel Lawson, set about recasting the British economy with renewed vigour. At the centre of the white-collar revolution was a pact made with the London stock exchange to end fixed commission charges and remove the distinction between stockbrokers and stockjobbers. While these changes were technical and related specifically to the trading of assets like shares and bonds, the consequences were huge. The distinction between brokers, who dealt with outside clients who wished to buy and sell shares, and jobbers, who carried out the trading, dated back to the Boer War. Ensuring the two roles did not overlap was a means of protecting jobs for those working in the stock exchange, but it meant added costs for customers. The Labour Party had originally planned to break up the cosy public-school club atmosphere, but when Thatcher came to power she took on the project and embraced it with zeal.

The agreement with the stock exchange, which came into force in 1986, was known as the Big Bang and fundamentally shifted the balance of power in financial markets from New York to London. For decades, Wall Street had been the centre of global finance. But the Big Bang made the City more competitive and opened the market up to international banks. The reforms sparked a wave of mergers and acquisitions in the Square Mile, as overseas investment banks swooped in to buy out ageing partners of traditional London firms. American and Japanese banks were especially attracted to London as its time zone, which bridged Tokyo and New York market hours, meant the City became the heart of a twenty-four-hour global trading network. The flood of money washing into the City drew a new generation of recent graduates, drawn by the exciting career opportunities and riches on offer. For centuries, London's financial capital had chiefly been the domain of blue-blooded former public schoolboys, but Thatcher's Big Bang went some way towards democratizing and regenerating the historic institutions.

At the same time, electronic trading was introduced to the City and brought London kicking and screaming into the modern age. Previously, trades had been carried out between jobbers, barking prices to one another face-to-face across the exchange floor in a system known as open outcry. Under the new system, computers allowed real-time data on market prices to be shared electronically. Over time, the hollering of frantic traders would be replaced by the hum of data-processing centres as trillions of dollars' worth of trades moved lightning-quick along fibre-optic cables.

Thatcher's privatization drive was getting into top gear. The first sign of intent was the 1984 sale of British Telecom, and the government was soon offloading a rash of state-owned businesses onto the market, including British Airways, Britoil and British Gas, which was heavily promoted with the effective 'Tell Sid' advertising campaign. As individuals heeded the message and rushed to buy up shares, investment companies offering unit trusts had a field day, giving amateur stock pickers an easier way to diversify their investment holdings. The government too tried to foment the public's craze for investing in privatized companies. If individuals owned personal stakes in the newly listed businesses, the theory went, they would feel closely connected to the government's market reforms and less inclined to boot it out at the next general election. Thatcher herself summed up what she described as her 'popular capitalism' crusade at the 1986 Tory Party conference in Bournemouth. 'Millions have already become shareholders. And soon there will be opportunities for millions more, in British Gas, British Airways, British Airports and Rolls-Royce. Who says we've run out of steam? We're in our prime!' Many of the big privatizations had been funded by workers buying shares in their own employers, but for the upheaval to be a success, they would need to be persuaded to buy shares in other companies as well. In the 1986 budget, chancellor Nigel Lawson unveiled the personal equity plan, or Pep, which offered investors tax incentives to build their own portfolios of shares in public companies or invest in unit trusts. The reforms were a boon for the investment industry and would later set Woodford's career on its stellar trajectory.

Thatcher's government also pushed through the 1986 Financial Services Act, which brought in a lighter regulatory environment for the City, following the US Reagan administration's policy of self-regulation for the industry. In response, Eagle Star, the BAT-owned insurer, separated its investment division into a new company called Eagle Star Asset Management, which Woodford joined in 1987. Eagle Star's main administrative body had moved from London to Cheltenham, but the investment team still occupied the company's historic headquarters at 1 Threadneedle Street, in the heart of the City, just yards from the Bank of England and opposite the Royal Exchange. While the address was prestigious, the building was anything but. Of concrete, with its rectangular-windowed facade, it was a prime example of the buildings thrown up in the 1960s in the modernist architectural style. By the mid-1980s, the building was already falling apart and its canteen, where most workers socialized at lunchtime, was situated in the rat-infested basement.

The two dozen fund managers worked on an open-plan floor, with more senior staff in surrounding private offices. The Tory government's financial reforms brought an influx of younger work-ers to the City, with many from middle-class backgrounds. Half of Eagle Star's investment team at the time were under thirty. The company was on the lookout for up-and-coming investors who were trying to get their break in the industry but without demand-ing too high a bonus. Woodford fit the mould. 'The City was very youthful and vibrant – a lot of us were given pieces of portfolios to manage when we were quite young,' recalls a fund manager who worked at Eagle Star in the late 1980s. 'All the managers were mid-dle class, there was no one there from Oxbridge and no double-barrelled names.' Unusually for an investment business at the time – and indeed since – half the investment team were women, including several team leaders. Given the age profile, there was plenty of after-work drinking among the young Eagle Star investment staff and office romances were common. But workplace socializing was far removed from the traditional City image of long boozy lunches and nightcaps at private members' clubs.

Working for BAT had its benefits. Staff were allowed to smoke in the office after 5 p.m. in an era when no-smoking policies were becoming more strictly enforced elsewhere. Among BAT's wide web of businesses were the US high-end retailer Saks Fifth Avenue and Britain's more prosaic offering of Argos. Staff were entitled to discounts, which meant work trips to New York invariably fea-tured a visit to Saks's flagship Manhattan store. One of the first things BAT did when it bought Eagle Star was to introduce the sort of marketing flourish that had made its cigarette brands such as Lucky Strike household names. The tobacco giant saw insurance as a market that had traditionally avoided glitzy advertising cam-paigns, and its products were seen as suitably dowdy. Emboldened, Eagle Star's marketing team set about trying to make its products more appealing to everyday customers. It introduced an evocative rainbow theme to its investment products, with different colours denoting various levels of risk. It also employed the comedian of the day, Rowan Atkinson, to front a national television advertising campaign promoting its investment products.

On the night of Thursday, 15 October 1987, Britain was hit by its worst storm in almost 300 years. The cyclone was widely unexpected, and few traders made it to work the following morning. After a couple of false starts, the stock exchange was closed for the day at 12.30 p.m. But that afternoon, as Wall Street got into full swing, the Dow Jones Industrial Average suffered its biggest ever daily sell-off as investors responded to poor economic data and a new tax bill. When London's traders returned to work on Monday morning and the market reopened, they reacted to New York's plunging market by selling whatever they could. The result was that nearly a quarter of the value was wiped from the FTSE 100 index within days. It took two years for the market to recover its losses from what would later be known as Black Monday.

Despite the tectonic events during his time at Eagle Star, Woodford appears to have breezed through the company without provoking much attention. One near contemporary who joined the business weeks after he left says she was not aware he even worked there until about ten years later. 'I don't think he made much of an impression – no one mentioned his name the entire time I was there,' she says. 'I get the feeling he was a bit of a nonentity.' Woodford by this time had fallen out of love with London and spent little time getting to know his colleagues, who were mostly young and very social. His work at Eagle Star was also not as grand as he would later make it out to have been. In subsequent interviews throughout his career, Woodford claimed to have started as a fund manager at Eagle Star, but his wedding certificate from the time describes his role as an investment analyst, a more junior position. Eagle Star enticed bright recruits into investment analyst roles by offering them the chance to oversee small pots of money on the side of their main roles to gain experience.

Woodford had settled into married life in sleepy Maidenhead, but his four hours of daily commuting were taking their toll. The intensity, speed and noise of the Square Mile – an atmosphere he would later describe as 'bullshit' – were also starting to grate. He began to detest the hustle and bustle of the City, with its gossipy culture and – as he saw it – herd-following mentality. Despite being early in his career, he had already developed a fierce independent streak. He needed to find something closer to home that would nurture his increasingly headstrong temperament. The seeds of Woodford's obstinate conviction – a character trait behind his heady rise and ultimate downfall – were already being sown.

4

Taking a Punt on Henley

Martyn Arbib had always stood out from the crowd. Despite founding one of Britain's most successful investment businesses, he bore little resemblance to the hordes of pinstripe-suited men with tidy haircuts who swamped the City. Forthright and self-confident, he commanded attention whenever he entered a room. What he lacked in stature he made up for with his deep tan and an opulent white bouffant. He had the appearance of a man who, rather than being stuck in an office, was much more at home watching his horse running at Newbury or Ascot – places he would typically prefer to be.

Born in 1939, Arbib spent his early childhood in the affluent north London suburb of Hendon before attending Felsted School in Essex. Felsted's public schoolboys gave Arbib the puerile nickname of Snurge, which stuck. After training as an accountant, and while working for the firm Spicer and Pegler, Arbib fixated his analytical brain on picking winning horses – a skill he quickly developed. In 1962 he placed a few pounds on Golden Fire and Hidden Meaning in the Cesarewitch and Cambridgeshire handicaps at Newmarket, and scooped £3,000 in winnings – the equivalent of more than £60,000 today. His bookie closed his account and Arbib used his winnings to fund a two-year excursion to Australia.

By the early 1970s, Arbib was living in Henley-on-Thames, a genteel town to the west of the capital that was best known for its annual Royal Regatta rowing event. He soon realized that he not only had a talent for picking fast horses, but also could identify promising companies. Following the old stock-picking adage of 'only invest in what you know', his first big investment was to buy shares in a recently listed chain of bookmakers called Ladbrokes. Arbib had spent enough time at the racecourse to know as well as anyone that bookies rarely failed to make a profit. Professional investors and stockbrokers tended to steer clear of the gambling sector, which had been legalized off-course only a decade earlier, seeing it as a grubby industry that was beneath them. Arbib, on the other hand, recognized it for a highly profitable business that, when managed well, could grow significantly. His early investment in Ladbrokes turned out to be one of the best of his career, with the company's stock price rising more than 2,000 per cent throughout the 1970s.

Arbib decided that his new-found hobby of investing could actually be turned into a career in fund management. After initially setting up portfolios for friends, he turned his attention to unit trusts, investment funds aimed primarily at individual savers. 'A good racing-form student could make a very good fund manager,' Arbib once told *Investors Chronicle*, the amateur stock picker's bible. 'Winning at racing is all about calculating odds and assessing risk. It's the same as picking shares. But you have to be meticulous. The last thing you need to be is a wild gambler.'

Beginning in his spare bedroom, with two telephones and a secretary, he started the Perpetual fund management company in 1974. His first fund was launched in September, at the depths of the worst bear market for four decades. The fund was one of the first on the market that offered British investors exposure to what it presented as a global mix of stocks – though it mainly invested in large UK companies with a few US and Japanese shares thrown in. Most of the money he had raised at launch came from friends and acquaintances, and despite some early wobbles, Arbib loaded up on cheap UK shares in early 1975 as Britain's stock market hit its lowest point since the Second World War. As the market rebounded, Arbib's fund soared while more established fund managers dithered about whether the bull run would last. It did, and Perpetual was off to a flying start.

Arbib was not inclined to spend three hours a day commuting between his home and London. As the business grew, he set up its first office at 48 Hart Street, Henley, a timber-framed Grade II listed house opposite the thirteenth-century St Mary's church in the centre of the town. The fledgling Perpetual shared the building with an optician. Initially just four people worked at Hart Street – Arbib, his assistant fund manager, an office clerk and a secretary, who would bring along her two dogs to the office. Roger Cornick, who started working at the business in 1979 as employee number five, remembers it having the feel of 'a high street accountancy firm'.

Perpetual's base in Henley literally set it apart from rivals, which were mostly concentrated in either London's Square Mile or Edinburgh. Such distancing played into Arbib's view of himself as an outsider. At the annual dinner for the Unit Trust Association in the early 1980s, by which time Perpetual was already established as a top performer in the industry, Arbib stood at the back of the packed hall talking to an *FT* journalist. 'I have nothing in common with these people,' he confided, talking with his lower lip curled and, as usual, from the right side of his mouth. 'I only come here to keep up appearances. In Henley, at least, I'm away from the herd and I don't need to go to brokers' lunches every day.'

Arbib's strong performance began to attract the attention of financial advisers, some of whom convinced their clients to take a punt on the quirky start-up in the investment backwater by the Thames. But as his fund drew in more money, Arbib struggled with its size. He was much more comfortable running a small fund that invested in a concentrated portfolio of stocks. Arbib and Cornick recognized that in order to allow the business to flourish they needed to recruit more managers to launch other funds. As a self-taught investor, Arbib knew his own limitations and targeted people who had learnt the ropes at much bigger businesses.

Arbib began to build a coterie of like-minded non-conformist fund managers. The self-made Arbib found kindred spirits in investors who did not want to be part of the old boys' club that dominated the City, where getting on was as much about whom you knew as what you knew. Those drawn to Henley were keen to make their own way. An early recruit was Bob Yerbury, a cautious actuary by training who specialized in US stocks. Bearded, with a neat side parting and large glasses that took up half his face, Yerbury had the appearance and temperament of an avuncular academic. He had been poached from insurer Equity & Law by Arbib in 1983, when the latter sensed an opportunity to buy up US stocks at rock-bottom prices.

Another early recruit was Scott McGlashan, head of Asian investments, who would run five miles into the office each morning before taking calls with Japanese brokers at his desk, rarely bothering to change out of his tracksuit before lunchtime. Leading the UK team was Stephen Whittaker, a law graduate with a piercing stare and volatile nature that unnerved colleagues. He had cut his teeth in the City, starting as a stockbroker and then a fund manager at one of Britain's oldest investment management companies, Save & Prosper. In 1987 he heard Arbib was looking for a UK equities manager to join his close-knit team, and Whittaker took a chance on the small but growing business. 'The establishment viewed us as a somewhat eccentric bunch down in Henley,' remembers Yerbury.

The company grew rapidly throughout the 1980s and attracted a cult following of financial advisers who wanted to offer their clients something different from the blue-blooded investment groups and life insurers based in the Square Mile. Arbib had already forged a strong reputation as an accomplished stock picker, and Yerbury, McGlashan and Whittaker were among the other Perpetual fund managers whose performance was getting noticed. The more investors and financial advisers heard about the group of misfit managers generating stellar returns on the banks of the Thames, the more money rolled in. By 1987 the company's seven UK funds and five offshore trusts managed £500 million between them – and its pre-tax profits had tripled in a year to £4.35 million. Having run the business from a standing start almost a decade and a half earlier, Arbib decided it was time to cash in. He floated Perpetual in

March on a £45 million valuation, making £10 million for himself and still retaining 74 per cent of the company.

Newly enriched, Arbib set aside £250,000 of his windfall for his first great love – racehorses. He spent £32,000 on a chestnut Irish thoroughbred, to which he gave his old public-school nickname of Snurge. The horse had a less than impressive pedigree and Arbib's trainer warned him it would amount to little owing to its under-developed hindquarters. But by the time of Snurge's retirement, the animal held the record for the most prize money won by a European-trained horse at more than £1.2 million, its crowning achievement being victory in the St Leger classic in 1990. Arbib commissioned two bronze sculptures of Snurge, costing twice as much as he originally paid for the stallion, to be displayed under floodlights in the gardens of two of his homes.

At his Henley residence, a Grade II listed farmhouse with 200 acres of land just outside the town, Arbib had built, at a cost of £250,000, a swimming pool in an outhouse connected to the main building by a covered walkway. For several years he fought a legal battle with HM Customs and Excise over whether the pool build-ing was an extension to the main house and therefore exempt from VAT. Arbib eventually won the case, saving himself £43,000. The eight-bedroom main house had six reception rooms, and on an adjoining plot of land was a separate four-bedroom house and vari-ous farm buildings. The estate was the scene of a great deal of entertaining over the years.

Perpetual had surfed the stock market waves throughout the 1980s, but all that was to change on 19 October 1987, when the Black Monday market crash sent Perpetual's share price, and its equity funds, into a tailspin. The FTSE 100 index plunged 23 per cent in the days that followed and was down 36 per cent from its pre-crash peak by November. US markets were similarly roiled. For the first time since the business had launched, shocked investors fled Per-petual's funds. Arbib decided that, to help rejuvenate the business and bring back investors whose savings had been scorched by the downturn, it needed to redouble its efforts on funds that were less focused on growth but could provide steady returns from dividends. These vehicles – known as income funds – were popular with UK savers, especially those whose appetite for risk had been rocked by the crash. Whittaker, Perpetual's head of UK equities, needed an assistant and he agreed with Arbib to look for someone who could eventually step up to manage the company's sole and somewhat neglected UK Income fund. Of the handful of applicants who were shortlisted for the role, one stood out head and shoulders above the rest – a cocksure and ambitious twenty-eight-year-old called Neil Woodford. Though Woodford had been managing money for only a year at the time, Arbib believed his independent streak would fit right in at Perpetual. Within a few months Woodford was running Perpetual's Income fund and a year later he launched the High Income fund, which was like the first product but with a slightly more aggressive performance target.

By this point Perpetual had graduated from Hart Street to the seventeenth-century Old Rectory, another Grade II listed building nestled next to Henley Bridge in the centre of town. The handsome three-storey riverside structure with tall sash windows boasted commanding views of the gently flowing Thames. It was a world away from the characterless glass towers shooting up across the City of London and Docklands. The building had been derelict and crumbling when Arbib took possession of it, promising the town council he would bring it back to its former glory. The large rooms with high ceilings on the ground floor were left intact, as was the imposing staircase that greeted visitors as they walked through the main entrance, but much of the original detail was stripped back. At the rear was a walled garden, dominated by a fine oak tree, which would later be burnt to ashes after being struck by lightning.

Some saw Perpetual's base in Henley as a competitive disadvantage. Without nearby investment groups to poach from, it was harder to recruit talented investment professionals. Anyone considering joining the business from elsewhere in the industry would almost certainly have to relocate to the local area. Henley lacked a direct train service to London. This meant only the most dedicated brokers and bankers – the lifeblood of the investment world, who introduce fund managers with capital to businesses that need backing – would make the eighty-minute journey from London, changing trains at the tiny Berkshire village of Twyford. Perpetual's money managers were also cut off from the gossip of the Square Mile, where industry chatter about potential deals filled the pubs and restaurants every working day from lunchtime into late evening.

But for Arbib, all these deficiencies were seen as positives. Only the most committed managers – those who bought into his ethos – would be willing to up sticks and move to Henley for a job at Perpetual. Their reward would be a life in and around one of England's most picturesque towns, complete with good schools and the possibility of strolling along the banks of the Thames to work or taking a riverside jog at lunchtime. Once settled, they would become unpoachable – after all, who would give up that quality of life for the drudgery of long commutes into congested London? Henley's inaccessibility meant only those brokers keenest to attract Perpetual's investment would make the trip – time wasters tended to stay away. As for his managers being out of touch with rivals in London, Arbib again saw this as a positive as it allowed his team to act independently without succumbing to the groupthink and herd mentality so common in the rest of the industry.

Arbib and Roger Cornick, his second in command, who took charge of the sales and marketing side of the business, set about building a brand to match the company's bold and idiosyncratic style. For a logo, Cornick chose an outline of Nepal's Ama Dablam mountain, known as the Matterhorn of the Himalayas. Perpetual sponsored an expedition to the peak, which left an advert for the business on display halfway up the mountain. But as Perpetual became better known outside the UK, it attracted the attention of Prudential Inc., a much larger US insurance group. The American company's lawyers complained that Perpetual's name was too similar to their own, and that the two companies' logos looked too much alike – Prudential used an image of the Rock of Gibraltar. Cornick dismissed the allegation in his characteristically no-nonsense way. He wrote back to the American lawyers, claiming they must be dyslexic for confusing the names, and insisting Perpetual had the 'moral high ground' as at 22,494ft, Ama Dablam towered over the 1,396ft Rock of Gibraltar. It was enough to kill off Prudential's protests.

Woodford's and Whittaker's UK equities team gradually grew. The managers huddled together in the rectory's former drawing room, elbow to elbow on desks piled high with stockbrokers' research notes, competing for space among phones, screens and keypads. From the open windows came the sounds of quacking ducks and the passing pleasure boats cruising along the river. Woodford sat opposite Whittaker, who managed the UK Growth fund. While Woodford's income-oriented funds were geared more towards finding strong-performing companies that would deliver chunky dividends whatever the market conditions, Whittaker was charged with discovering which companies would expand rapidly.

Relationships among Perpetual fund managers became close both inside and outside the office. Sport was key to bonding. Ever the accomplished sportsman, Woodford shone in the games of tennis, cricket, golf and five-a-side football that pitted the investment managers against the sales team. Perpetual also sponsored several local sports clubs, including Henley's rugby and cricket teams, and staff would often meet up at matches. A favourite spot for socializing during the week was Villa Marina, a family-run Italian restaurant, sited between the Old Rectory and Henley Bridge. The menu offered hearty food and a selection of palatable wines, while the tables covered in white linen provided one of the best views of the river idling by. It was here that the fund managers unwound after a stressful few hours trying to outwit the markets.

A salesman who worked at Perpetual at the time remembers no great personal bond between Whittaker and Woodford, but the simplicity of offering financial advisers' straightforward growth and income funds helped build the company's brand, especially when it came to British stocks. 'If a client wanted income, they went for Neil's fund. If they wanted growth, they went for Stephen's fund – it was as simple as that,' he recalls. Personal equity plans, or Peps, had been introduced by chancellor Nigel Lawson in the 1986 budget to encourage equity ownership within the UK. By the early 1990s they were big business for investment managers. These tax-privileged investment accounts, a precursor to today's ISAs, allowed individuals to invest up to £6,000 a year in funds, with at least half in UK-focused products, free from capital gains and income tax. Perpetual's simple offer of growth or income to UK-focused investors soon propelled it to become the leading provider of Pep funds in the country. In the run-up to the end of the tax year, financial advisers and newspaper personal finance pages would be awash with recommendations for where to invest any leftover annual allowance. Woodford's and Whittaker's funds always featured on the lists. Perpetual's success at exploiting this sales channel led it to be dubbed the 'king of Peps'. This increased exposure helped put Woodford on the same platform as the country's leading investment professionals – the much-revered star fund managers.

Throughout the 1980s and 1990s, investment groups competing for clients spent heavily on promoting their individual fund managers. They chose investors whose performance records set them apart from rivals, but who would also play well in meetings with clients and in media interviews. Soon, a cadre of elite investors emerged. Known as star managers, they were marketed heavily by their employers and were in turn recommended by influential financial advisers to their clients. The strategy was aimed at tapping into the prehistoric human trait of preferring to follow leaders over teams, and it worked. Funds managed by these galactico investors received plenty of press attention as business journalists – always on the lookout for a human angle to spice up otherwise potentially dry financial stories – competed with one another to interview and profile the best-known managers. Investors put their faith in managers who not only could evidence their stellar returns but also spoke with conviction about why their views on the direction of the market would bear out.

The more companies fired up the profiles of their brightest stars, the more they relied on them to attract and retain clients. Just as in a team of popular and talented footballers, the balance of power soon shifted away from the executive owners and towards the most accomplished performers. Successful fund managers were able to demand higher and higher pay, with annual bonuses in the millions for those at the very top. Executives knew that if they were to lose such high-profile staff, who were integral to their business's juicy profits, it could jeopardize the future of their company. A cult of personality developed around the best-known managers, who lived rock-star lifestyles with their new-found wealth, buying fast cars and palatial mansions.

One of the pioneer star managers was Peter Lynch, at Boston-based outfit Fidelity Investments. Lynch first caught the eye of Fidelity's president, George Sullivan, while caddying for him at the Brae Burn Country Club in Massachusetts. He joined the company in 1966 and in 1977 was given the reins of a small and relatively unknown equities product called the Magellan fund. Over thirteen years Lynch grew the fund from $20 million to $14 billion on the back of one of the investment industry's best winning streaks. Lynch averaged 29 per cent returns a year over that time, more than double the return of the S&P 500 index of the biggest US listed companies. It was not only his investors who did well. *Boston Magazine* once put his personal wealth at £352 million. Another much-vaunted US investor, Bill Miller, who ran Baltimore-headquartered Legg Mason's Capital Market Value Trust, attracted a large following of advisers and customers by being the only manager to beat the S&P 500 index over a fifteen-year period. In the UK, the contrarian bargain-hunter Anthony Bolton was the industry's leading light throughout the 1980s and 1990s. Managing the Special Situations fund for Fidelity's international business, he produced an average 19.5 per cent annual return for clients over a twenty-eight-year period.

The most ardent devotees of the star fund manager cult were the legions of financial advisers, especially those who sought a high profile for themselves. Soon a small group of advisers began to become as prominent as the fund managers they lauded. Promoting themselves as independent experts on the investment industry, they spent as much time schmoozing with the managers whose funds they would recommend to clients as they spent courting attention from the financial press. Investment companies knew the value of receiving a strong endorsement from these powerful middlemen and expended large portions of their marketing budgets on hosting social events and jollies to build closer relationships.

Chief among this group of self-publicists was Mark Dampier, head of research at Hargreaves Lansdown, the UK's biggest investment intermediary, who once described himself as a 'media tart'. Floppy-haired, with a tight-cropped beard, Dampier looked more like a geography teacher than a financial adviser. But he could always be relied upon to offer his opinions to the press about which fund managers were in or out of favour. Dampier began to strike up a relationship with Woodford in the mid-1990s. The adviser saw a kindred spirit in the investor, someone who had strong views on the market and stuck to his convictions. Dampier became besotted with Woodford, recommending his funds to anyone who would listen, even describing himself as a 'Woodford groupie'. 'In my opinion Neil Woodford is the best fund manager currently working in the UK,' Dampier wrote in his 2015 book *Effective Investing*. 'What makes him stand out from the average run-of-the-mill fund manager is that he is prepared to stick his neck out and make high-conviction bets on the companies and sectors he believes in, while areas he doesn't like . . . he avoids completely.' Dampier added: 'I have been investing in Neil's funds for nearly twenty years and have never regretted it.'

To promote Perpetual's own galaxy of stars, the sales team organized roadshows. Top investment managers and sales staff would travel the country for weeks at a time, meeting clients in hotels and speaking to larger gatherings of financial advisers at sales conferences and seminars. Woodford, with his frank views and plainspoken delivery, soon became the star attraction, regularly attracting audiences of up to 250 at venues including the luxurious Savoy hotel in central London. But speaking to large crowds was not Woodford's strong point – he much preferred intimate gatherings of advisers. Perpetual regularly hosted lunches with a dozen or so of its favourite clients – those who could be relied upon to bring in most business – at Rules in Covent Garden, London's oldest and one of its most opulent restaurants. It was here that Woodford came into his own, wooing the advisers over chateaubriands and venison with off-the-cuff commentaries on his portfolio and the wider investment markets.

Woodford typically arrived at the office just after 8 a.m. and spent the morning taking calls from analysts and brokers, discussing the companies in his portfolio while monitoring the markets on his screens. He stuck to a straightforward strategy of identifying industries he expected to do well over three to five years, and then picked the best companies in the field. It was less about identifying cheap companies that would grow rapidly and more about choosing strong businesses that would continue to prosper. 'Make sure you are investing in companies, not in stock prices,' he would say. 'The key to performance is often not so much what you have got, as what you have not got,' he once told an *Observer* journalist. 'It is important to miss the problem stocks and the corporate black holes in the market.' Unfortunately for his investors, this was advice he would later ignore.

One of Woodford's favourite sectors was tobacco, an industry that had become toxic to most mainstream investors owing to its undeniable links to deadly diseases and the mounting litigations that were stacking up against the biggest producers. In 1997 an insurance analyst at Schroders Securities called Paul Hodges wrote an influential paper, arguing that big tobacco companies were much less exposed to potential litigation than was widely believed, and therefore were undervalued. Woodford lapped up the argument and began to see cigarette makers as highly profitable businesses with captive customer bases. He also believed the market had such a high barrier to entry that there was little chance of the biggest companies being disrupted by new players. Woodford was one of the largest shareholders in his former employer, British American Tobacco, maker of Lucky Strike and Benson & Hedges, and only railed against the company's executives when they failed to increase the company's dividend for the first time in more than twenty years, leading to a 4 per cent fall in its share price. 'A company that says [it is committed to shareholder value] decides not to spend £24 million increasing the dividend and, as a consequence, the shareholders are now £621 million worse off. It is one of the most bizarre decisions I have ever experienced,' Woodford moaned to *The Times*.

Perpetual's base in Henley offered the company another advantage besides a comfortable rural surrounding away from the London rat race. During the first week in July, the town played host to the Royal Regatta, the world's most celebrated rowing festival. A key event in the British social season, the regatta was a magnet for the country's well-to-do, and somewhere the attraction was as much about seeing and being seen as it was about the sport. The event was also hugely popular among thousands of business executives enjoying corporate hospitality on a sunny day out of the office. Along the nearly two-mile course, the riverbanks overflowed with attendees observing the regatta's strict dress code: men in chinos, striped blazers and boaters, women in floral dresses and extravagant hats, with everyone quaffing champagne and Pimm's. The river itself was crowded with hospitality boats, bobbing along next to the racing craft.

Though the members-only Stewards' Enclosure that overlooked the finish line was the most exclusive section of the course, the hottest ticket was to attend Perpetual's annual bash at the Old Rectory, with one of the best views of the river. 'It was an opportunity that was too good to miss,' remembers Roger Cornick. Guests began the day with drinks in the walled garden, before a boozy silver-service lunch, and were then offered access to the Stewards' Enclosure. Top clients and the company's shareholders would all be invited, rubbing shoulders with leading industry figures and Perpetual's team of star fund managers, all the while knocking back champagne and gobbling up lobster. For many IFAs (independent financial advisers) up and down the country, it was the highlight of the year.

By the mid-1990s Perpetual's assets had swelled to more than £4 billion and the company was valued at around £400 million. Yet Arbib's interest in the business he had built from scratch was beginning to wane. He started to become preoccupied by outside distractions. In 1995 Arbib sold off £5.3 million of Perpetual stock and bought three adjacent houses on the west coast of Barbados, knocking them down and replacing them with a grand colonial-inspired villa known as Four Winds. The six-bedroom beachfront property – designed in the Palladian style and with classical columns supporting a pagoda roof – included a courtyard as well as a wide double staircase into the vast hallway. A first-floor veranda looked out onto a pool, while the white sands of Gibbes Beach were just steps away. His neighbours included dancer Michael Flatley as well as the entertainer Cilla Black.

Arbib continued to indulge his passion for racing, owning a string of eighteen horses: twelve in training and another six for breeding. He also took a greater interest in philanthropy, becoming one of the UK's biggest donors and giving away money to a range of institutions, from the Conservative Party to local schools and charities. In 1994 he donated £4 million to Henley's River and Rowing Museum and later funded a statue of Olympians Steve Redgrave and Matthew Pinsent.

Arbib knew that Perpetual's strength lay in its ability to produce strong returns. As a small, independent business, it lacked the distribution networks and marketing budgets of its much larger rivals. Without Perpetual's reputation for outperformance, IFAs had little reason to promote the company's funds. Arbib introduced a sophisticated computer system to measure fund performance and analyse which trends and managers were contributing to it. Rather than assess a fund's returns in absolute terms, the system categorized them according to the fund's underlying drivers. Armed with these insights, Arbib would chair a monthly meeting with the investment team where he would grill each investment manager on their funds' performance. 'There was no hiding place for the fund managers,' recalls a regular attendee at the meetings. 'Martyn would be there with his sheet of paper with investment performance on it for each fund. What was fascinating was Martyn would probe fund managers far more if they outperformed than if they underperformed. He wanted to know whether they had achieved that by taking too much risk. It was an effective way.'

The monthly get-togethers became an important part of the Perpetual culture, where each manager knew they would be held accountable for their investment decisions in front of their peers. The investors appreciated being able to run ideas past each other and mine the collective wisdom, even if discussions could get a little heated when managers took exception to their portfolios being picked apart. Arbib kept a close eye on what each manager was up to. But, acknowledging he had prioritized hiring independently minded investors, he gave them free rein to run their funds as they wished. Arbib encouraged an entrepreneurial culture among his investment team and expected them to take individual responsibility for their own funds.

With Perpetual riding high in the sales charts as king of Peps, the Woodford and Whittaker double act continued to flourish. The pair were by now Perpetual's prized assets and the marketing team promoted them heavily through roadshows and advertising campaigns. Woodford, in particular, was winning fans for his strong performance, but also for his strong views. He gradually emerged as one of the leading managers, not just at Perpetual, but across the UK investment sector. His opinions were regularly courted by the financial press and he discovered his recent fame and the platform it brought not only helped promote his funds but also allowed him to influence the decisions at the companies he invested in. When Conrad Black, owner of the Telegraph Group, attempted to buy out minority shareholders in the British newspaper publisher in 1995, N. M. Rothschild, the merchant bank advising the company, declined to pass on the offer of 470p a share to its investors, claiming it was worth at least 500p. Using his new-found pulpit, Woodford – who was a Telegraph Group shareholder – gave an interview to the *Independent on Sunday*, criticizing Rothschild's refusal to discuss the offer. Later, as a large shareholder in two insurers, United Friendly and Refuge Group, he threatened to block their £1.5 billion merger. 'I am seriously considering voting against the merger,' he told the *FT*, a day before meeting the executives and advisers of each company. 'This deal strikes me as having been put together in haste and with too little recognition of the asset position of Refuge shareholders.' Following months of wrangling, Woodford eventually gave his blessing to the merger after terms of the deal were sweetened. UK investment managers rarely publicly criticized companies in which they invested – with most preferring to voice their concerns in private meetings with the businesses' executives. It was a tactic more often used by the growing band of abrasive activist investors who were finding their voice in the US. But Woodford realized he was becoming an influential force in corporate Britain – and he was not afraid to make his feelings known.

Another of Woodford's favourite industries was pharmaceuticals. He especially liked the largest players, which could be relied upon to sell products to needy customers whatever the economic conditions, allowing them to pay generous dividends consistently. Two of Woodford's cherished companies, British groups Glaxo Wellcome and SmithKline Beecham, had spent years considering a merger to create the world's biggest pharmaceuticals business. As one of the largest shareholders in both companies, Woodford was only too aware that the combined group could make hundreds of millions of pounds in savings, which could be reinvested into researching and developing new drugs. The merged company would also have an enviable portfolio of profitable drugs and vaccines – as well as a range of much-loved consumer products, from Aquafresh and Sensodyne toothpaste, to Ribena and Lucozade soft drinks – that would continue to sell well and provide tasty dividends. But when initial talks between the two sides stalled over which executives would end up running the new business, Woodford groused to the *Wall Street Journal* that 'management egos [had] grown so great that they can stand in the way of £20 billion of shareholder value'. He added that he was dismayed 'the non-executive directors have not bashed some heads together – which is really what they're there to do'.

The more Woodford waded into corporate deals and picked up press attention for his outspoken views, the more he saw himself not so much as a sideline investor but as a powerful player in the cut-and-thrust world of mergers and acquisitions. Where once he would receive calls from investment bankers pitching companies to invest in, now he would call the intermediaries, lambasting them for failing to negotiate satisfactory terms in a takeover or suggesting they arrange a deal he felt would bring his portfolio huge rewards. City bankers began to dread calls from Henley, where an increasingly aggressive and forceful Woodford started to see himself as corporate Britain's puppet master. He also railed against other fund managers for failing to impose themselves on the companies they invested in as much as he did. As an investor in several insurance companies, he openly talked about the benefits of banks buying them up, which could increase their market value by as much as a third should the buyer be forced to pay a hefty premium.

By 1998 Perpetual was worth more than £1 billion and employed 400 staff. It had long outgrown the Old Rectory and had spread into several other buildings in the town, where it was becoming the largest employer. To accommodate the growing staff, with the need for increased technology and a modern working environment, the company built Perpetual Park, a vast new campus in the town. It also developed an office complex round the corner from the Old Rectory, opposite Henley station. The new red-brick building with broad archways was a bold design and the sign of a company on the up. The new head office called for a glitzy, attention-grabbing opening – and Arbib knew just how to deliver. Queen Elizabeth was due to visit Henley in November 1998 to cut the ribbons at the new River and Rowing Club. Never one to miss a trick, and having been involved in planning the monarch's visit to the club, Arbib managed to arrange for her to stop by at Perpetual House after lunch and formally open his company's new headquarters. She then attended a reception at the offices, meeting staff, local residents and members of voluntary organizations. Arbib the outsider was becoming part of the establishment.

Though Perpetual as a business was expanding, its funds were sputtering. Many of the Henley managers – including Woodford, in particular – had shunned telecom stocks and tech companies, which were soaring to unprecedented valuations. The managers felt many of the new businesses were too expensive and would ultimately crash – but the performance of their funds suffered as a result. While Perpetual's funds led the way in the early 1990s, as the decade drew to a close they lost ground to rivals. The sales team had also been rocked by the New Labour government's decision to replace Peps, which had brought in billions of pounds of business for Perpetual, with ISAs. Savers were slow to pick up the new products, especially the ones designed for investing, and Perpetual's sales team found its most important income stream had dried up. The king of Peps had lost its realm.

Arbib saw rival mid-size manager and Pep specialist M&G sold to UK insurer Prudential in March 1999 for £1.9 billion, representing a 40 per cent premium to its share price and just over 10 per cent of the £18.5 billion of assets it managed for customers. The deal was expensive by any measure and showed Arbib how much appetite there was in the market among large financial service providers to buy investment management businesses.

Arbib was also starting to look towards his retirement. He had built up Perpetual over a quarter of a century, becoming Britain's forty-third richest person in the process. To celebrate his sixtieth birthday, Arbib hosted a lavish party at his Henley home – one of many big bashes he hosted over the years. Among the 500 guests were local MP and former Conservative leadership contender Michael Heseltine, Michael Ashcroft, the Tory treasurer, and Gary Lineker, the former England football captain and presenter-in-waiting of *Match of the Day*. Perpetual's top performers Woodford, Yerbury, Whittaker and Cornick were also invited. As Arbib passed between guests and took in the performance by Kit and the Widow, a cabaret duo who belted out Noel Coward ditties, he wondered whether he still wanted to spend his days running an investment business. He soon let it be known that Perpetual was up for sale.

Despite the company's strong growth, Arbib became less engaged with the business. He promoted Yerbury, the US equities manager, to chief investment officer, and handed over responsibility for keeping the fund managers on their toes. He sold down his stake further and spent more time with his beloved horses, as well as at his beachside villa in Barbados and property in Australia. His philanthropy was also taking up more of his energy. It was through his work with the NSPCC children's charity that he got to know Prince Andrew, the Duke of York. In January 2000, just before the prince's fortieth birthday, Arbib paid for him to fly out to Barbados and put him up at his beachside mansion so that the prince could enjoy two days of golf at the exclusive Royal Westmoreland course.

There were several suitors for Perpetual, but Amvescap, a large London-listed fund manager that was mainly based in the US, emerged as the keenest. The group had a big presence in Atlanta and its chief executive, Charles Brady, was looking to expand its operations in the UK. The heavy-set Georgia native had spent most of his career at Amvescap, having spun the business out of Citizens and Southern Bank in 1978. He had a vision of creating an international investment management powerhouse made up of strong local businesses across the globe. A relaxed boss around the office, he never wore a jacket unless meeting guests. But he was also a tough negotiator who loved to do deals.

Perpetual's 800,000 retail customers were a tantalizing proposition for Amvescap, which owned a rival UK fund manager called Invesco. For a long time, Invesco struggled to compete with Perpetual, but it had adapted to the switch from Peps to ISAs much the better of the two. Arbib began negotiations with the Anglo-American group over a sale, but a persistent thorn in his side was the performance of Woodford's High Income fund, now the business's most popular product. Woodford's decision to avoid what he felt were bloated technology, media and telecom stocks during a period of surging growth for the sector was costing his fund dearly. Other investors, beguiled by what they believed to be cutting-edge internet businesses, speculated heavily on the future returns of companies that had little more than a website and some intellectual property to show for themselves. The so-called dotcom bubble would reach its zenith on 10 March 2000, when internet companies hit their peak valuations. In the six months up to this point, Woodford's High Income fund lost 13.9 per cent and ranked ninety-fifth out of the ninety-seven funds in its peer group. His loyal band of financial advisers began to lose faith and investors withdrew more than £100 million from the business. Arbib told colleagues at the time that Woodford's reluctance to invest in tech stocks while he was negotiating Perpetual's sale was not just an investment risk, but a business risk. 'There were plenty of companies that looked at the share price and Neil's approach to tech stocks and you could see that they thought we were a bunch of dinosaurs and didn't want to touch us,' remembers Roger Cornick, who was involved in the negotiations.

The severe underperformance of the company's brightest star created pressure within Henley. Arbib was desperate to reverse the poor returns to salvage his lucrative sale to Amvescap and he began to put pressure on his managers to consider taking some bets on tech companies in order to benefit from the sector's surging valuations. Woodford and his fellow managers faced a choice between ceding to the pressure or standing firm. They chose the latter, with the dogmatic Woodford refusing to add a single tech stock to his funds. But his refusal to back down became increasingly uncomfortable the longer his portfolios were punished by the market. The stress gripped Woodford and he immersed himself in his work, spending longer and longer at the office before heading to the gym to let off steam. Bob Yerbury remembers finding Woodford alone in the office late at night, staring at a list of tech stock valuations, muttering to himself, 'I just cannot believe this.' Woodford began to think it was only a matter of time before he lost his job.

On 12 March 2000, two days after the dotcom bubble's peak, the *Mail on Sunday* published the results of a poll by fourteen top financial advisers where all but two said they could no longer recommend Woodford's main fund to their clients, with six saying they would withdraw money from it. Woodford and Perpetual were accused by their former cheerleaders of 'losing their way' and 'having missed the investment boat'. 'Woodford is a good manager, but maybe his pride is getting in the way,' said one of the advisers. 'He is becoming more intransigent.' Hargreaves Lansdown's Mark Dampier was one of only two advisers who did not give up on Woodford.

Yet, not for the last time in his career, Woodford's obstinacy paid off. As the dotcom bubble was pricked and prices in technology, media and telecommunications (TMT) stocks tumbled, Woodford's funds' lack of exposure to tech stocks meant they swiftly overtook rivals. Over the next two months High Income made 15 per cent gains and ranked second among its peer group. 'It was the TMT bubble bursting that really made Neil,' says Yerbury. 'Because we avoided tech stocks, we were accused of being antiquated, but what Neil is really good at is resisting the stampede. That takes a lot of balls.'

Despite the severe pressure on Perpetual's funds throughout the negotiations with Amvescap, Arbib refused to drop his price. He demanded £45 a share for the business he had built up, valuing it at £1.3 billion, or more than 10 per cent of its £11.8 billion of assets. On that basis, it was even more expensive than the already toppy M&G deal. While Charles Brady was still keen on the acquisition, the price proved too steep for his fellow executives at Amvescap, which aborted talks in May. Arbib went back to his corporate broker,

Merrill Lynch, to scout out alternatives. There were many suitors for the strong UK brand, but Arbib's asking price meant conversations did not last long. A merger with fellow manager Foreign & Colonial was considered, but the two sides could not agree terms. Perpetual also attracted bids from US banks Citicorp and JPMorgan, as well as CGNU, the British insurer. JPMorgan had been a serious contender before its own acquisition by Chase Bank meant it was no longer in the running. Neither Citicorp nor CGNU was willing to meet Arbib's £1.3 billion asking price.

Lacking options, Arbib instructed Merrill Lynch to go back to Amvescap, which by this point had more than doubled its share price in a year. The Anglo-American manager was now in a much stronger position, but still winced at the price Arbib was demanding. Eventually Arbib and Brady thrashed out a deal, valuing Perpetual at £1.05 billion. Arbib, who still controlled 40 per cent of Perpetual through various family trusts, walked away from the deal with £130 million in cash and £300 million in Amvescap shares. Within a matter of weeks Amvescap's share price shot up above $50, a level to which it would not get close again for more than two decades.

Arbib had built up the business he had launched from his spare room into one of Europe's biggest and most successful investment companies. The incorrigible gambler was cashing in his chips right at the top of the market.

5

Making Middle England Rich

Aside from a brief tour with the US Navy, Charles Brady had spent his entire life in Atlanta, Georgia. Despite this, the burly business-man had a global vision for the investment industry. His grand plan for Perpetual when he bought it in 2000 was to merge it with Amvescap's other British brand, Invesco, and grow it into the coun-try's biggest investment business, to be known as Invesco Perpetual. Both companies were popular among financial advisers and had managed to build up strong reputations with retail investors. The delicate balancing act for Brady, however, was in bringing the two distinct businesses together, while retaining their own idiosyncra-sies that had made them so successful. Invesco had been built through a series of acquisitions and the power base within the com-pany lay on the commercial side. It was known as a marketing-driven business, with sales executives calling the shots. For them, the key to growing a successful investment company was in designing and launching strong products that could then be promoted heavily to IFAs and investors. While fund managers within the business were respected and well paid, they had little say about the direction the company took. They were integral staff members, but they answered to the commercial bosses. Perpetual, by contrast, was run by the high-powered fund manager barons, who were used to getting their own way. The clash of cultures would not end well.

Brady's first job was to make sure that the star managers – the selling points for both businesses – stayed on. Brady focused his energy on retaining managers with the biggest pulling power: Neil Woodford and Stephen Whittaker from Perpetual and Rory Powe, Invesco's celebrated European stock picker. To buy their loyalty,

Brady offered the three men – plus a handful of other managers from both groups – attractive financial packages with stock options that locked them into the company for at least eighteen months. He also gave guarantees to Woodford and Whittaker that they could continue to run their funds as they always had, unhindered by overbearing bosses. The enticement worked.

The next problem facing Brady was how to bring the two businesses together. Both ran funds that attracted similar clients, but each had their own methods and distinct values. While Perpetual allowed skilful fund managers to flourish by giving them a free rein, Invesco had a stronger focus on processes and a team-based approach, with fund managers confined to strict compliance protocols and risk policies. The group's reputation had been tarnished by a series of scandals in the early 1990s – including being fined £2.3 million over mishandling assets belonging to the Mirror Group pension scheme connected to the £460 million looted by Robert Maxwell – and was wary of being subjected to further regulatory sanctions.

Invesco's fund managers would present their ideas to clients discussing the 'house view', while Perpetual's investors talked of their own beliefs. Despite the conflicting approaches, the Atlanta bosses decided the simplest way forward was to bring the two investment teams together, uprooting Perpetual from its Henley base and moving the business into London's financial district. When news of the plan reached Henley, there was uproar. Much of Perpetual's self-identity was tied up in employees seeing themselves set apart from the rest of the industry. They felt being more than an hour's commute from the centre of the UK's investment sector gave them an entrepreneurial and independent advantage over competitors. Working for the largest employer in town also reinforced their self-confidence. They were big fish in a small pond, and that was the way they liked it.

As the leading managers within Perpetual, and not ones to refuse a fight, Woodford and Whittaker stood up to their new bosses, informing them that unless they and their colleagues were allowed to stay in Henley they would walk away from the business. They were even prepared to give up on big paydays that rewarded them for staying put. The threat worked and Brady backed down. Invesco's and Perpetual's investment teams would, for the time being, be kept separate, with the latter allowed to stay in their bucolic riverside base. 'Neil and Stephen held a shotgun to Charlie's head,' recalls a former executive. 'It fundamentally changed the nature of the UK business.'

For a while the investment teams were divided into two centres of power. The Perpetual managers coalesced around Woodford, whose disdain for authority epitomized the 'Henley way', while Powe was the leading figure on the Invesco side. An unhealthy rivalry developed between the two factions. Despite working for the same company, the teams were based in different offices and saw each other as competitors. But it was not long before the balance of power fell heavily in Woodford's favour. Powe's European Growth fund, Invesco's flagship product, had taken on too much risk. Having been heavily invested in edgy technology companies, it halved in value after the dotcom bubble burst. Woodford's stock, meanwhile, was soaring. He was widely lauded for being the investor who stood firm against the madness of the overhyped internet companies. Investors deserted Powe's fund and his power base collapsed. Within a year of the merger completing, Powe resigned to set up his own hedge fund. The Perpetual managers were victorious.

Woodford's reputation was rising, not only within Invesco Perpetual but also among the investing public. With the dotcom bubble scare behind him, his two main income funds began to roar, and investors noticed. By 2002 a £10,000 investment made in his High Income fund at its launch in February 1988 was worth £80,000, based on dividend payments being reinvested. If that same £10,000 had been invested in a fund that merely tracked the FTSE All-Share index of the 600-odd biggest companies listed in London, it would have been worth less than £50,000. Woodford was helping to make Middle England rich.

Financial advisers were soon speculating about the future of

Perpetual's two leading managers, Woodford and Whittaker. Both were entering the final few months of their lock-in period, after which it would be much easier for rivals to prise them away. Advisers had seen other investment groups such as Newton and Jupiter suffer fund manager desertions after going through corporate upheavals. Conscious that such departures could have a severe knock-on effect on the funds' performance, many advisers stopped recommending their clients invest in Woodford's and Whittaker's products, which by that time managed a combined £6 billion.

Even Woodford's biggest groupie, Mark Dampier, stopped recommending Invesco Perpetual funds to Hargreaves Lansdown's clients over fears about restructures within the business. 'I know that the lock-in for the Perpetual managers finishes next year, and I am a bit concerned that they are all going to leave,' he told trade title *Money Marketing*. 'I do not want to carry on buying funds and find that I have to switch them all in three or four months' time. I get the feeling that it is an unhappy ship at the moment.'

Other Invesco Perpetual managers had already peeled away. Japanese stock specialist Scott McGlashan had left to launch his own business, while Margaret Roddan, the much-respected head of European equities, also departed, with plans to set up a fund that specialized in fine art. Roddan had started out like most of the Perpetual managers, cutting her teeth in the City at well-established investment groups, and moved to Henley in 1992. She had considered leaving the industry a couple of years earlier, but Bob Yerbury, the chief investment officer, convinced her to stay. However, the upheaval of the Amvescap takeover forced her to reconsider her options. With pressure on Amvescap to tie Woodford and Whittaker down to new long-term contracts, the ball lay in the cantankerous managers' court. In negotiations with the Atlanta bosses, Woodford, who hated his work being interfered with, insisted on keeping autonomy when running his fund and that he be given a bumper pay package, threatening to resign if his demands were not met. Once again, the Amvescap bosses yielded, happy to retain their highest-profile British fund manager.

But negotiations with Whittaker proved trickier. Lurking in the background was John Duffield, the Old Harrovian financier who had set up two investment groups that most epitomized star fund manager culture in the UK: Jupiter and New Star. Duffield had had his run-ins with Perpetual in the past, having accused the Henley-based marketing team of running a 'disgraceful and shockingly misleading' advertising campaign that claimed Perpetual had been named fund manager of the year for six years running. But by spring 2002 he was more interested in luring away one of its top managers. In May he convinced Whittaker to leave Henley and join his New Star project. Woodford took over from Whittaker as head of UK equities at Invesco Perpetual and was now the undisputed alpha manager in Henley.

A year later, Invesco's and Perpetual's investment teams were finally merged, and all brought under one roof in Henley – Woodford's domineering influence within the business had crushed any resistance to moving out of London. The impact on the Invesco managers was brutal, with twenty-six of them culled. Some were offered the chance to move to Henley but chose to leave instead. Many Invesco managers lived in and around the Hertfordshire town of Bishop's Stortford and quit when told they needed to replace their relatively easy commutes into London's Square Mile with a tortuous drive around the M25 to Henley. Staff cuts were not limited to fund managers. In the first few years after the Invesco Perpetual merger, headcount fell 40 per cent, from 1,451 to under 900. Under Charles Brady, Amvescap had swallowed several businesses in the run-up to the Perpetual deal and now the company had indigestion. The effect on its share price was severe. Having hit $50 soon after the Perpetual deal was announced, it dropped to just $9.21 within two years.

While disruption to the UK business was distressing for Brady and his fellow Atlanta executives, they were preoccupied with a scandal brewing closer to home. On 2 December 2003 the pugnacious New York State attorney general, Eliot Spitzer, along with the Securities and Exchange Commission (SEC), the US regulator, announced they were bringing civil fraud charges against the US division of Invesco and its chief executive, Raymond Cunningham. Spitzer, who had lofty political ambitions and was dubbed the 'Sheriff of Wall Street' for his tenacity in fighting white-collar crime, accused Invesco and Cunningham of engaging in a practice known as market timing. The investigation also snared several other investment groups.

According to Spitzer, they had allowed certain favoured clients to trade in and out of their funds as much as they wanted, while restricting retail investors to just four trades a year, as required by the funds' rules. Investment groups typically tried to stymie the amount of trading that clients carried out in their funds to keep administrative costs down and limit disruption to the funds' managers. But Spitzer said Invesco and Cunningham had allowed a handful of hedge funds to buy and sell freely – in some cases dozens of times a year. Hedge funds were able to use the investment funds as trading tools and benefit from short-term moves in the market, while Invesco welcomed the cash they invested as it boosted the business's fee income. Though the practice was not illegal, Spitzer argued Invesco had not treated all its customers equally, which forced fund managers to hold higher levels of cash to meet sudden redemption requests and sell at inconvenient times. The result was that retail investors had suffered millions of dollars of losses. 'Top managers knew market timing was harming buy-and-hold investors, but they condoned and facilitated it because it was a lucrative source of management fee revenues,' Spitzer claimed when announcing the charges. Amvescap's share price tumbled on the news.

Initially Amvescap's executives hit back against the charges, claiming they were unmerited and saying market timing was not illegal. They said Invesco's bosses had tried to stop it when it appeared harmful to the funds. But after several weeks of bad headlines, which prompted investors to pull their money out of Invesco's funds, Amvescap admitted its failings in preventing the abusive trading and tried to cut a deal with Spitzer and the SEC. Amvescap eventually settled for $450 million, while several Invesco bosses were barred from the industry and paid fines totalling $340,000 for their part in the scandal. The next day, Charles Brady announced he was stepping down as chief executive of the group he had co-founded, though he would stay on as chairman. It was an ignominious end to Brady's thirteen-year rule of the business. His global ambitions for the company ultimately left it too widely stretched.

In Henley, things were looking up for Neil Woodford. Bob Yerbury, his long-time ally, had been promoted to chief executive and chief investment officer of the UK operation. Despite his promotion, Yerbury still treated his star stock picker with kid gloves, giving him the freedom to manage his funds with minimal interference. Yerbury was a well-liked father figure to the investment team, but not a disciplinarian. If the fund managers were producing the goods, they could carry on as they wished. Woodford had rediscovered his Midas touch and his funds were among the best performers over a ten-year period. He now controlled more than £6 billion – a third of the group's UK assets – and had established himself as one of Britain's best-known investors.

Business was good in Henley. Invesco Perpetual's funds – led by Woodford's Income and High Income products, as well as fixed income funds run by the bond double act of Paul Causer and Paul Reed – were the most popular in Britain, with strong performance records to match. As financial advisers continued to recommend them to clients, Invesco Perpetual's sales teams and fund managers received bumper bonuses. Oxfordshire's luxury car dealerships did brisk trade as the company's staff bought Porsches, McLarens and Audis. But Yerbury restricted employees from bringing their sports cars to the office, fearing it would cause resentment among the less well-paid staff working in junior and administrative roles. The ban did not stay in place for long, however, and soon a small fleet of Ferraris, Lamborghinis and Maseratis was turning up at the Henley offices every morning.

Given the contrasting fortunes between the UK and US

operations, Woodford, Yerbury and several of their colleagues considered mounting a management buyout of the business and cutting themselves loose from their American owners. In 2005 Amvescap brought in a new chief executive – Martin Flanagan, a forty-five-year-old Chicagoan who had been poached from rival Franklin Templeton. Six months younger than Woodford, Flanagan was a rising star in the US investment industry and had big plans for the business. Hoping to take advantage of the disruption to the US operation, Yerbury and Woodford made their case to Flanagan for spinning off the UK division. When Flanagan rejected their suggestion, they turned their attention to negotiating better pay deals for themselves. With the US business in decline, Yerbury and Woodford knew it could ill afford to lose its two leading figures in the UK. On top of their already lucrative bonuses, they demanded Flanagan ensure their allegiance with long-term incentive packages. Flanagan, who had experience of dealing with big-name fund managers from his time at Franklin Templeton, relented.

As head of UK equities, Woodford built a team of hungry young investment managers around him – all eager to learn at the feet of the master stock picker. Mark Barnett had the closest investment approach to Woodford's. He had joined Perpetual in 1996 from Mercury Asset Management, and ran funds that were similar to Woodford's, but a fraction of the size. The two men shared the same outlook when it came to valuing companies. Martin Walker had joined the UK equities team just before the Amvescap takeover and benefited when other more senior managers left, picking up the reins to their funds. Bob Yerbury once said that, at 6ft 3in and with a natural self-confidence, Walker was the only person on the team capable of standing up to Woodford. The youngest of the group was Stephen Anness, who joined as a trainee analyst and quickly rose to become a portfolio manager. Woodford took Anness under his wing, treating him as his protégé. Another colleague in the circle was Nick Hamilton, an Australian who, as product director, linked the fund managers with the sales staff. The team formed a tight-knit group, which was based on working on the same long desk in the open-plan office. 'There was no ego in the team – it was a very real environment,' recalls one former colleague. Team lunches were not lavish affairs – they would venture to the pub down the road or to Villa Marina, the nearby Italian restaurant. 'That was part of the magic.'

The group socialized outside work, spending weekend afternoons on long countryside cycle rides followed by meals at one or other of the members' houses with their partners. Woodford was not close to his parents or brother and soon began to see his colleagues as a surrogate family. The team would take holidays together, often centred around testing themselves physically. On one occasion Woodford embarked on a gruelling 800-mile cycle ride around Spain in a week, while another trip was based on swimming around Greek islands for five days. The Woodfords loved to entertain. After living in a series of homes, they finally settled on a seven-bedroom luxury property a short riverside walk from Invesco Perpetual's Henley office. When they moved in, they discovered more than fifty rabbits had made a home in its five acres of gardens. After a cull, they renamed the property Warren House, which would host their frequent soirées. 'Then it's like a mini-holiday camp,' Jo Woodford once told the *Sunday Times*, 'with people in the pool, people in the Jacuzzi and a games room, which we have changed into a gym. Whoever comes here always says: "Wow, what a lovely house!" It's set in a bowl surrounded by woodland – when you drive up you don't see it immediately. It has a big "wow" factor.'

Each Christmas, Woodford would take his team out for a boozy meal, where members would take it in turns to nominate someone in the company deserving of a 'golden card' or a 'silver bullet'. Golden cards were reserved for colleagues who had performed well or been particularly helpful over the previous year, while those who had been especially troublesome – typically over-officious compliance officers – were dealt a silver bullet. Woodford often reserved his silver bullets for interfering sales staff, whom he loathed. When Invesco and Perpetual merged, several of Invesco's sales directors, who were used to having the upper hand when it came to dealing with the investment staff, were given a rude awakening in their dealings with Woodford. He was keen to show who was boss and regularly dressed them down in public, putting on an aggressive show in the open-plan Henley offices to confirm that he would not be dictated to by lowly commercial managers.

Having become one of the richest men in the affluent Henley area, Woodford poured his money into status symbols befitting his increasing wealth. He bought Ferraris, Porsches and huge properties, including the Grade II listed Fingest House, a seven-bedroom manor house a short drive from Henley in the picturesque Hambleden Valley. The property, which had once been owned by Formula 1 tycoon Flavio Briatore, boasted a wine cellar, walled garden, tennis court, croquet lawn and an outdoor swimming pool with a pavilion changing room. Its ten acres of land also included a two-bedroom cottage. Woodford and Jo moved in and hired a team of domestic staff. But after twenty years together, the relationship did not last. In 2007 Woodford left Jo for his secretary, Madelaine White, with the pair moving into the gamekeeper's cottage while Jo stayed living in the manor house just feet away.

With his domestic life in disarray, Woodford doubled down on his work. For several years leading up to the 2008 financial crisis, Woodford had feared an oncoming recession and steered clear of sectors he felt would be the worst affected. This primarily meant banks, owing to their exposure to the rising levels of debt-fuelled consumption in the economy. Banks had been among Woodford's funds' biggest holdings in the late 1990s, but he gradually sold his stakes in the UK's largest lenders in the early 2000s. This was quite a departure for an income-fund manager as banks accounted for a large portion of the FTSE 100's total dividend payments. In fact, in 2008 the UK's biggest dividend payers were HSBC, Barclays and Lloyds TSB. But when the banking crisis hit, where the likes of Royal Bank of Scotland and Lloyds had to be bailed out by the UK taxpayer, not only did their share prices crash, but they stopped paying dividends. Swathes of the UK's best-known fund managers were blindsided by the crisis – especially those heavily exposed to financial stocks. Woodford's funds were dented but were by no means the worst performers. During the teeth of the crisis in the days following Lehman Brothers' collapse, Woodford's High Income fund was battered, losing 9 per cent in September 2008 and 6.2 per cent in October. But the losses were significantly less than the wider market, with the FTSE All-Share down 13.2 per cent in September and 11.9 per cent in October. Within a year Woodford had made up his fund's losses. Like their manager, his investors survived the crash bruised but not broken.

While Woodford admitted to little knowledge of the complex financial instruments sold by US banks that ignited the firestorm, he attributed his avoidance of banks to his gut instinct and concern over the high levels of consumer debt. He was eulogized in the financial press for preparing his portfolios to skirt the companies hit hardest by the crisis, just as he had done during the dotcom crash. A mythology grew around the star stock picker, casting him as an investing soothsayer who could spot danger in the markets when others could not.

Fresh from battling the tumultuous financial markets, Woodford was soon engaged in another scrap with an equally menacing foe. Jeremy Paxman, the bellicose *Newsnight* presenter, famous for his relentless grilling of politicians, was a near neighbour in the rustic Hambleden Valley. Woodford put in a planning application for a large equestrian centre on farmland near his home in the village of Skirmett. He had developed a passion for riding from Madelaine, and like his old boss Martyn Arbib, this extended to buying horses. The plans proposed demolishing old agricultural buildings and replacing them with stabling for twenty-eight horses, a riding area and several ancillary buildings.

Yet as soon as the plans were published on the local council's website, residents – corralled by Paxman – began a fierce campaign to fight them off. In a letter to the council, Paxman complained that the development was 'enormous, unsightly, inappropriate and environmentally unfriendly'. Former England rugby international and BBC presenter Nigel Starmer-Smith, whose garden backed onto the site, also objected to the plans, while another local resident complained: 'It has not even the architectural pretensions of Auschwitz. It's like a prison camp.' The objectors were successful, and Woodford was forced to scrap his plans. For Woodford, it was the beginning of the end of his time living in the Henley area. Having recently embarked on his new relationship with Madelaine, it was time for a fresh break in his domestic life.

One of Woodford's colleagues at the time was Andrea Leadsom, who would go on to become a Conservative MP and challenge Theresa May as the future prime minister. She also later served as business secretary. In her pitch to lead the country, Leadsom boasted about her prominent role at Invesco Perpetual, which she described as 'senior investment officer and head of corporate governance'. The job title was grandiose and gave the impression she had managed money and policed the companies that Invesco Perpetual invested in. Along with other claims, about being a banker and the youngest ever director at Barclays, her CV implied she was a leading figure in the UK's financial services sector. Indeed, when endorsing her during the leadership campaign, fellow Tory MP Bernard Jenkin praised her senior position at 'a large investment firm where she was responsible for managing hundreds of people and billions of pounds'. But in reality, Leadsom's role at Invesco Perpetual was much more mundane, as she later admitted.

Between 1999 and 2009 she worked in the Henley office, serving as an assistant to Bob Yerbury, carrying out administrative and operational tasks. In the latter years, it was on a part-time basis as she juggled her commitments as a councillor in Oxfordshire, while also mounting a bid to become the MP for South Northamptonshire in the 2010 general election. Despite Jenkin's claims, Leadsom did not in fact manage anybody and had no say over the investment portfolios. She had a desk outside Yerbury's office, alongside his secretary, and generally dealt with the jobs Yerbury did not want to do himself. Colleagues remember her attending the company's monthly investment committee meetings, always the first to arrive and fetching Yerbury's coffee. Sporting a chunky pearl bead necklace, she conscientiously took notes throughout, but never contributed to the discussion.

Confrontation was not Yerbury's style, so one of the main jobs he delegated to Leadsom was carrying out the periodic contract negotiations with fund managers. As a result, some within the business gave her the unofficial job title of 'head of pay and rations'. In this role, she designed the pay structure for the company's top earners, including Woodford. The pay awards were incredibly generous, with lucrative bonuses that made most of the senior fund managers multi-millionaires. As the star attraction, Woodford's pay was especially plenteous. Leadsom tailored the package to offer incentives based on sales of Woodford's funds. The more money that flowed in, the more he personally made. This was an unusual arrangement for fund managers, whose bonuses were typically tied to investment performance. This meant that their interests were aligned with those of their customers. Woodford had performance-based bonuses too, but the sales incentives were generally shunned by other investment managers because there was a risk that if funds grew too big, the manager would have trouble running them effectively. Consequently, Woodford was heavily motivated to ensure his already giant funds continued to attract ever bigger piles of cash from investors. It was a pay structure that would ultimately sow the seeds for Woodford's departure from the business.

Another member of staff who was also heavily incentivized to keep Woodford's funds ballooning was Craig Newman, head of retail sales. With an impish face and ginger hair, Newman was ten years younger than Woodford. There were two sides to Newman's personality – the aggressive and abrasive manager who bullied and publicly shamed staff, and the loyal, obedient subordinate manager trusted to get the job done. Deeply ambitious and obsessed with money, Newman had successfully exploited both character traits to wheedle his way up the corporate ladder. Born in Pembury, Kent, the son of a bricklayer, he grew up just outside Tonbridge, attending the local secondary school and playing for East Peckham &

Paddock Wood rugby club into his twenties. Newman began his career straight after leaving school, starting out at Cornhill Insurance before working in local branches of Bank of Ireland. In his mid-twenties, he joined Invesco's London-based sales department, and was soon running its customer services team, overseeing the call centre and complaints-handling staff. In order to improve his communication skills when dealing with clients, Newman hired a linguistics coach, who became a mentor to him over the years.

Newman's big break came in 2000, when Invesco merged with Perpetual and he landed the job as head of retail sales. He was suddenly in charge of a forty-strong team, most of whom spent the majority of their time on the road, meeting IFAs and pitching the company's funds. Newman was deeply unpopular with his team, who found him excessively interfering and disposed to making explosive outbursts down the phone. Initially, Newman's bosses could see little wrong in the way he ran his staff. He was firm but fair, in their view. He ran a tight ship and got results. The funds he was responsible for grew to £8 billion, which represented a sizeable chunk of the UK operation's assets. But he gradually fell out of favour owing to his erratic behaviour and the increasing amount of time he spent out of the office pursuing his personal projects, including expensive property developments. After nearly a decade in the same role, Newman realized his chances of progressing his career within the business were limited. He needed a lucrative escape plan.

Newman decided to ingratiate himself with Woodford – the closer he could get to the star manager's orbit, the more protected and powerful he could become within the business. Knowing about the fund manager's need to blow off steam through exercise, Newman joined Woodford's gym in Henley and even enlisted the same personal trainer. Until this point, Woodford had treated Newman with the contempt he had shown for most sales staff, but through pumping iron they began to strike up a bond. Soon the pair, who also shared a love of expensive fast cars, were racing each other in Ferraris at weekends.

Invesco Perpetual had overtaken Fidelity as the UK's biggest manager of retail investments. Fidelity's own superstar manager, Anthony Bolton, had retired after an ill-fated attempt to start a China fund, and Woodford replaced him as the UK's best-loved investor. Invesco Perpetual's funds held tens of billions of pounds of Britain's savings – and Woodford's Income and High Income funds accounted for a large portion of that pile. The £10,000 investment made in High Income in 1988 was by 2011 worth more than £175,000, compared to £80,000 if it had been invested in the index. The business was increasingly seen as a one-man show to the outside world, and the risk that he could one day leave was causing anxiety among Amvescap's executives. 'Neil Woodford is Invesco Perpetual's biggest weakness and its biggest strength,' Mark Dampier of Hargreaves Lansdown told the *FT*.

It was around this time that Woodford began taking a much keener interest in small, science-based companies. Ever since studying agricultural economics at university, he had always been fascinated with biotechnology. Over the years he had invested in the odd small business. These were typically early stage companies that owned the intellectual property to a scientific discovery with commercial potential and needed funding. His first foray into this field had been more than a decade earlier – and its outcome would have scared most investors off for life. But for Woodford, the experience only served to heighten his interest in such businesses.

In 1998 Perpetual had accumulated a 9.5 per cent holding in British Biotech, the UK's leading company dedicated to developing drugs based on the increased knowledge of the links between genetics and disease. It was the first UK biotech company to list and at one point was worth £2 billion. Much of the investment was made through Woodford's funds. On 13 February of that year he received a call from an analyst at Goldman Sachs, who suggested he meet Andrew Millar, the head of clinical trials at British Biotech. A week later Woodford and Margaret Roddan, then head of Perpetual's European investments, travelled to the Five

Horseshoes pub in Maidensgrove, a fifteen-minute drive from Woodford's home, for the clandestine meeting. The fund managers already had concerns about British Biotech's plans to spend heavily on a new building without already having a successful drug in the market. When they turned up, they were shocked to hear what Millar had to say. Over several drinks, the whistle-blower told them about a series of drug trials that were not going to plan, yet the company continued to issue upbeat press releases about their progression. He informed them that two regulators – the European Medicines Evaluation Agency and the US Securities and Exchange Commission – had already voiced their concerns to the company. These centred on two drugs in particular: Zacutex, a treatment for acute pancreatitis, which analysts expected to achieve £205 million of sales a year; and Marimastat, a cancer treatment that was forecast to bring in as much as £875 million a year.

After hearing Millar's startling account, Woodford and Roddan were determined for the truth to come out, even if it meant their investment in British Biotech would plummet. They spoke to other shareholders in the business, as well as its non-executive directors. When the management team found out, they fired Millar. Encouraged by Woodford, Millar leaked the story to the *FT* and *The Times*. Then all hell broke loose. The incident became one of the biggest whistle-blower cases in British corporate history and sent confidence in the nascent UK biotech industry plunging. British Biotech's share price fell off a cliff on the back of the public spat, while its founder and chief executive was forced to stand down. The leaked story destroyed the business and for years UK biotech start-ups struggled to raise finance. Woodford was later called before Parliament's Science and Technology Select Committee to give evidence on the case, along with Bob Yerbury and Roddan. When asked about the unusual role he played in exposing the internal wranglings, Woodford defended his involvement: 'The circumstances were highly irregular, I agree, but the nature of our concerns were also highly irregular.' It would not be the last time Woodford would be called to account for his irregular dealings with unconventional companies.

Having had an early taste of how calamitous investments in companies that were so dependent on successful clinical trials could be, Woodford was undaunted. Over the years, he committed small amounts of capital to science-based start-ups with, he believed, the potential to grow into huge businesses with life-changing discoveries. He was particularly interested in a new breed of British businesses that were set up to funnel investment from the City into academic research with the potential for commercial success, known as university spin-off groups. He became an early investor in Imperial Innovations, which had evolved from the technology transfer office at Imperial College London. The business floated in 2006, by which time it had already launched fifty-eight spin-off companies and had ninety-six licensing agreements. Each of the start-ups required a continuous flow of capital to keep them going, but few were ever likely to make a profit. Like sharks needing constantly to swim, the businesses were reliant on a steady stream of financing, otherwise they would die. What could possibly go wrong?

Woodford later invested in IP Group, a similar university spin-off business, which had its origins at Oxford University, but over the years established relationships with research-focused universities around the world. It too had a large portfolio of scientific discoveries that needed financial support. Woodford viewed such investments similarly to how venture capitalists assess their portfolios – they provide funding to scores of start-ups but would need only one or two to explode in value for all the investment to pay off handsomely. As the manager of two of the UK's largest investment funds, controlling tens of billions of pounds, Woodford saw committing the odd few million here and there to small businesses with strong potential as gambles worth taking. It also boosted his ego, knowing that he had the power to make or break these businesses and had a direct influence on whether important scientific breakthroughs came to the market.

Not all Woodford's science investments were through IP Group and Imperial Innovations, which went on to merge. Word soon spread round the corporate broker network that Woodford had an interest in biotech companies and that he would be willing to invest where few others would. He was also in the rare position of sitting on huge piles of ready-to-go capital, with his bosses allowing him to invest where he liked. Specialists from City brokerages Numis, Peel Hunt and Cenkos found a receptive audience when making trips to Henley. Woodford had bought into the compelling idea that the UK had one of the best higher-education sectors in the world, with an enviable concentration of top research universities. Historically these institutions had developed the science behind ground-breaking discoveries – including computer memory at Manchester, MRI scanners at Nottingham and LCD screens at Hull – but had lacked the inclination and ability to cash in on their commercial success. Woodford believed there was an important role for investment managers to provide long-term capital to help these ventures get off the ground, not only to develop important scientific discoveries but also for the benefit of the British economy. He continued to dedicate most of his funds to large, dividend-paying UK companies, but a small and under-the-radar section – typically less than 5 per cent of the portfolio – was invested in tiddly companies with the potential to be hugely profitable.

Another factor that set Woodford apart from other investors was his appetite for buying stakes in private or unquoted companies, of which most managers of retail funds steered clear. These businesses were not listed on a stock exchange, meaning their shares could not be bought or sold in the public markets. While many of these companies were young and exciting, there was very little information about them in the public domain and stakes in the businesses were much harder to sell. Under European rules, funds that allow individual investors to buy and sell shares daily – so-called open-ended funds – could hold a maximum of 10 per cent of their assets in unquoted companies. This was to ensure that in times of market stress, when investors demanded their savings back in droves, fund managers would be able to sell the listed stakes quickly, rather than having to shift unquoted holdings. If anything,

Woodford actively sought out unlisted companies, believing that their best years of growth could be achieved while still private. He was willing to hold on to such companies, and continue to fund their development, until they eventually floated. He believed if they listed too early and without having established themselves, any short-term setbacks could be punished by the market. 'Other investors have disqualified themselves from the sector because they don't have the right investment horizon or the right attitude to risk,' Woodford told the former *FT* editor Geoffrey Owen. 'My industry has a lot to answer for. Our job is to take savings and invest in businesses that need capital. But there are too many intermediaries, pension consultants and so on, getting in the way. Fund managers are obsessed by quarterly performance, they are poorly equipped to do their proper job.'

Woodford increasingly saw himself as the saviour of the sector – the sole major investor willing to support a British industry that had the potential to revolutionize healthcare and technology. One company he helped save from the brink was e-Therapeutics, an Oxford-based pharmacology company that used powerful computers to develop drugs. In 2007 it listed on AIM, the UK's junior stock market, and began trials for a new brain cancer drug that used synthetic versions of chemicals derived from marijuana plants. But three years later it was suffering from a downturn in the biotech sector and was running out of cash. Woodford came to the rescue with a £17 million cash injection. He eventually owned half the business. Another business he helped resuscitate was ReNeuron, which focused on stem cell research and developed drugs for stroke patients. It had launched in 1997 but struggled to find its feet. In 2013 it was on the lookout for £33 million of refinancing, and Woodford was one of a small group of investors who chipped in. As is inevitable with this type of investing, Woodford also suffered some blow-ups. He had been a long-term investor in Phytopharm, another business aimed at developing drugs from plant derivatives. By 2013 Invesco Perpetual owned more than 50 per cent of the business, but when a clinical trial for a Parkinson's treatment showed no benefits over a placebo, the share price dropped 80 per cent and the business collapsed. Woodford was frequently probed about his unquoted holdings at Invesco Perpetual's monthly investment meetings – but despite some failures, he was allowed to pursue his interest.

While small companies were becoming a sideshow for Woodford, his main preoccupation was with the large British blue-chip businesses that made up the bulk of his portfolios. His meddlesome instinct, honed in the 1990s, only intensified as he grew more powerful. His two main funds were now the biggest in the UK, meaning that he was the largest single shareholder in many of Britain's biggest companies. His influence was in full force in 2012, during the so-called shareholder spring, when British investors fought back against what they saw as excessive pay awards to FTSE 100 chief executives. Woodford was instrumental in a behind-the-scenes campaign to oust AstraZeneca boss David Brennan after he presided over a period of shrinking profits. He was later more visibly disruptive when it was revealed that BAE Systems, the FTSE 100 defence company, was in talks to merge with French aerospace group EADS in a €38 billion mega deal. Invesco Perpetual was BAE's biggest shareholder, with 13 per cent of the business, but Woodford was bitterly opposed to the deal, believing it would fail to deliver enough cost cuts or sufficiently boost returns. He also had concerns about political interference in the new company, having seen the influence the French and German governments had on EADS over the years. BAE had historically been a strong dividend payer, typically with a 5.5 per cent yield, whereas EADS paid out 1.7 per cent.

Woodford summoned BAE's chief executive, Ian King, to Henley for an explanation. The two engaged in several hours of heated discussion, during which Woodford set out his opposition to the deal in no uncertain terms. Woodford then rang round other investors in BAE, convincing them that the merits of the deal did not stack up. Invesco Perpetual later released a lengthy statement to the press, setting out Woodford's 'significant reservations' over the deal, saying he 'did not understand the strategic logic' of it. Two days later, the deal collapsed.

In 2013 Woodford reached a quarter of a century of running money in Henley. He was responsible for £25 billion of savings on behalf of the British public. The £10,000 invested in High Income twenty-five years earlier was now worth £240,000, compared to £100,000 if it simply tracked the FTSE All-Share index. Middle England had been made well and truly rich. Woodford was not only the UK's best-known fund manager – the glitziest of star stock pickers – but also a force to be reckoned with inside the wood-panelled boardrooms of corporate Britain. In addition, he had become the most influential investor in the UK's nascent science start-up sector. Along the way, he picked up an ardent following of financial advisers and hundreds of thousands of investors, who continued to entrust him with their life savings. To the outside world, Woodford was at the top of his game, with his reputation entrenched as the foremost investor of his generation. His career had survived two near-death experiences – the dotcom crash and the financial crisis – and he had come out of both stronger. He possessed the supreme self-confidence of a man who knew he had emerged from the two biggest gambles of his life holding the winning hand. But the good times would not last.

6

The Fucking Americans

At 1,045 acres, the sprawling Cotswolds estate in the rolling Glouces-
tershire countryside was nearly two times the size of London's
Olympic Park. Drystone walls and hedgerows encircled the farmland, while estate railings and wrought-iron gates kept outsiders at
a respectable distance from the manor house. Neil Woodford and
his fiancée Madelaine White bought the property for £13.7 million
in 2013. They then set about acquiring adjacent parcels of land and
landscaping the estate to fit their image of the rural idyll.

Woodford retained his fascination with farming from his time
studying agricultural economics at university. At great expense,
he added copses of fully grown trees and introduced rare breeds
of sheep to the land, while continuing to harvest winter cereals
and oilseed rape. The addition of livestock required more grain
stores and three new barns to be built. He also constructed a biomass boiler, in a single-storey energy centre made of natural
rubble stone with a slate roof, to replace the property's previous
dependence on an oil-fired heating system. The new boiler used
sustainably sourced wood pellets, and to accommodate the regular lorry-loads of fuel deliveries, Woodford rebuilt a driveway
behind a row of trees so it would be obscured from the main
house. In their planning application to the council, the couple
stressed they 'wished to make use of renewable technology to
reduce their dependence on fossil fuels, and their carbon foot-
print'. (Woodford's green conscience did not extend to his driving
habits. He built a new garage to house his Porsche, Ferrari, Audi
and Land Rover.)

The main reason for the move to near the village of Cherington, however, was to indulge in Madelaine's passion for horse riding, a pastime with which Woodford had become equally smitten. While the couple's famous neighbours in Buckinghamshire had fought them over their plans for a huge equestrian centre, the Cotswolds was true horse-riding country. Here they found no resistance to building several stable blocks on their land to house their growing stud of eighteen eventing horses, as well as indoor and outdoor training arenas and a full-size dressage manège. The location pro- vided the fund manager with an entrée to England's equine elite. Zara Tindall, granddaughter of Queen Elizabeth and a former world and European three-day eventing champion, was a neigh- bour. Tindall's farm is set on the 600-acre estate of her mother, Princess Anne, another former European equestrian champion and Olympian. Each August the Queen's daughter's Gatcombe Park estate hosts the Festival of British Eventing – a key fixture in the horse-riding season.

While Woodford was entering new social circles outside work, professionally he was already firmly entrenched within the estab- lishment. His reputation as the UK's leading investor had never been stronger. So much so that he was asked to appear as a star witness in a ground-breaking government review into how effect- ive the equity markets were in promoting long-term decision making. For several years, policymakers, academics and corporate governance experts had grown concerned about the lack of account- ability in financial markets. The rise of institutional investors and intermediaries, combined with the increasing number of foreign investors in UK companies, had widened the gulf between the Brit- ish public, whose pension savings were the backbone of the UK economy, and the bosses of the companies that depended on the capital. In the 1960s, 54 per cent of UK shares were directly held by individual investors, by 2010 this had been whittled down to 11.5 per cent. This created what economists referred to as an agency prob- lem, where those who decided which companies to invest in, and who were trusted to hold them to account – the fund managers – were far removed from the end investors whose money they were controlling. A conflict of interest arose when the two sides had different views about what was the best outcome for the investment.

Related to this was a shift in emphasis in the investment markets from owning shares to trading shares. There was growing concern that if different people in the investment chain – from savers to advisers to fund managers to company executives and other corporate stakeholders – had different incentives, it would create a market that would not promote long-lasting, healthy companies. While pension savers might prefer to invest in companies that grow and provide strong dividends for years into the future, fund managers and company executives who earn bonuses based on short-term performance are likely to think very differently. Investors held shares in British companies for an average of eight years in the 1960s, but this had fallen to just seven and a half months by 2007.

In 2011 Vince Cable, the Liberal Democrat business secretary in the Cameron–Clegg coalition government, asked the economist and *FT* columnist John Kay to investigate whether the equity markets encouraged British companies to innovate and develop their workers' skills – and if they did not, what could be done to fix the flaws. The review sought the opinions of the country's foremost corporate governance experts, including Woodford, who was the sole fund manager on the panel. Woodford's experiences in the dotcom bubble and financial crash had burnished his credentials as the most patient of investors – or highlighted his sheer bloody-mindedness, as others saw it. While giving evidence to Parliament's Business, Innovation and Skills Select Committee as part of the Kay Review, Woodford made an impassioned defence of long-term investing: 'If you believe that at the first disappointing piece of news or the first opportunity you can exit the shares and move on to something else, then you will never think like an owner, and therefore you will not be actively engaged with that business,' he said. 'Ownership is crucial – a sense of ownership on behalf of obviously the asset owners as well as the asset manager.' When it was eventually published in 2012, the Kay Review's 40,000-word report held up Woodford's commitment to long-term, patient sharehold-ing as a beacon.

But while Woodford's stock was riding high in the outside world, tension was brewing within the Henley office. The bosses in Atlanta had grown increasingly concerned about the dependence of the UK business on the strength of the Woodford brand and the size of his funds, which, when combined, managed more than £30 billion out of the UK business's £70 billion of assets. Based on an average annual fee of 0.7 per cent – or £7 for every £1,000 invested in his funds – Woodford's funds pulled in around £210 mil-lion of revenue for the company. Invesco Perpetual was increasingly being seen as a one-man show. For many IFAs and investors, the company was synonymous with Woodford. In order to limit this dependency, Invesco's executives decided to reallocate marketing and promotional budgets away from Woodford's main funds and towards smaller products. This infuriated Woodford, whose bonus structure – as designed by Andrea Leadsom – was heavily skewed towards growing the size of the fund by attracting more capital. Woodford resented the Atlanta bosses' interference, and would refuse to see Martin Flanagan, the company's chief executive, in person on his trips to Henley. 'It was always "the fucking Ameri-cans",' recalls a colleague of Woodford's at the time. As the company's star attraction, Woodford felt he was being undermined. For him, it was a sign of disrespect.

The UK management team had changed and Woodford was finding it harder to get his own way. Bob Yerbury had retired and handed over responsibility as chief investment officer to Nick Mus-toe, recruited from Pictet Asset Management. Woodford was the obvious internal candidate to take over from Yerbury, but he wanted to continue to run his funds, so the idea was quickly dis-missed. Even though Mustoe was Woodford's superior, Woodford sat on the committee that appointed him. Woodford also insisted that he report directly to the UK chief executive rather than to Mustoe. The new CIO had a more hands-on approach to managing his team of autonomous investors than Yerbury had. Mustoe had joined after the financial crisis and wanted to have a much stronger oversight of risk management at the business. The US executives also parachuted in a new chief executive to run the UK operation – Mark Armour, a tough-talking Australian who had been at the business for more than a decade. Woodford believed Armour and Mustoe were under orders from executives in Atlanta to rein in the Henley fund managers, who were not afraid to stand up to their American bosses. At one investment summit at the Austrian ski resort of Kitzbühel, Woodford openly grumbled to the attending financial advisers that he was getting increasingly 'pissed off with the Yanks' in Atlanta. 'You knew in the office when Neil was most fiery,' remembers the former colleague. 'The security doors were magnetically locked. Neil's a strong man – he would refuse to use a security pass. If he was angry, he would just rip the doors open. You would just hear this shuddering. You can imagine the facilities team at Henley, how many magnetic locks they must have replaced.'

Meanwhile, Woodford's gym buddy, Craig Newman, was also feeling emasculated. As the head salesman for Woodford's funds, he too felt a sense of injustice when the decision was made to spend less time and energy on selling the company's biggest and highest-revenue products. He also had a fractious relationship with his boss, Ian Trevers, Invesco Perpetual's head of distribution. Newman would play on Woodford's resentment. He convinced the stock picker that despite his having worked at the business for a quarter of a century and helped turn it into one of Europe's best-known investment houses, the jumped-up desk jockeys running the company saw him as little more than a commodity to exploit or drop as they wished. 'The thing that Craig and Neil had in common was the idea that they should not be accountable to anyone – it's not in their DNA,' says a former colleague.

Woodford's bitterness soon spread to the rest of his UK equities team, whom he increasingly saw as riding on his coat-tails. While once Mark Barnett, Martin Walker and Stephen Anness had been his close fraternity, now they were mere hangers-on. Team lunches at Villa Marina and the nearby pubs had all but stopped, and the geographical distance between Henley and the Cotswolds meant out-of-office-hours socializing had been knocked on the head. Woodford had abandoned long weekend cycle rides with friends for equestrian events with Madelaine. As tensions rose on the UK equities desk, Woodford ordered a glass partition to be built so that he could be cut off from the rest of his team. He also bickered with managers on the European equities team, arguing that Britain was in a much better position than the rest of the continent, which was on the verge of imploding, and that the euro would soon fall apart. Having spent many happy years living and working in Henley, Woodford was cutting himself off from his friends and colleagues. If he could up sticks and move to the Cotswolds, what was stopping him leaving Invesco Perpetual too? 'You had changes there and Neil's aggression towards the business, a belief that there were certain actors working against him,' a former colleague says. 'This paranoia was definitely being fed by Craig Newman.'

Woodford's growing belligerence was not confined to the Henley office. His reputation as the scourge of blue-chip boardrooms was reinforced through a series of high-profile scraps. One that caught the media's attention was with the board of Stobart Group, a conglomerate of disparate businesses that was best known for its line of dark-green-liveried Eddie Stobart articulated lorries. The company had joined the FTSE 250 a few years earlier and opened its doors to a popular Channel 5 reality TV show called *Eddie Stobart: Trucks & Trailers*. Woodford had got to know Stobart's maverick chief executive, Andrew Tinkler, a self-made millionaire who had taken over the group in 2007. While the company was synonymous with the UK's biggest road-haulage operation, it also had a wide range of other businesses, including a large warehouse property portfolio, Widnes port near Liverpool, Southend and Carlisle airports, an engineering services unit and a division that provided biomass for energy generation.

But by 2013 the business was suffering. Its share price had halved in two years and it was forced to issue a profits warning. Woodford lost patience with Tinkler, and so flexed his muscles as the company's biggest shareholder, controlling 36 per cent of the business. He forced chairman Rodney Baker-Bates to step down and replaced him with Avril Palmer-Baunack, Tinkler's deputy chief executive who had joined the business a year earlier. Woodford knew Palmer-Baunack from her days running accident claims handler Helphire, when he convinced her to overhaul the company's board by removing the chairman and two non-executive directors, who included the former Conservative Party leader Michael Howard. Now Woodford wanted Palmer-Baunack to break up Stobart. 'There has been a need for a change in leadership on the board and Avril fits that role perfectly,' Woodford said at the time. With Palmer-Baunack becoming executive chairman, Tinkler now reported to his deputy, an odd set-up that was bound to introduce tension. The appointment also contravened the UK's corporate governance code, which argued chairmen should be independent. While Woodford had been praised by corporate governance experts for his role in the Kay Review on long-term investing just a few months earlier, he was now testing their patience by forcing through an unpopular management structure.

Woodford reserved some of his ire for those politicians he felt were interfering unnecessarily in the industries in which he invested. The then Labour leader Ed Miliband was subjected to Woodford's vitriol when he proposed the introduction of price caps on energy bills, which Woodford believed would deter investment in the sector of the billions that the coalition government had said were needed. Energy prices had become a highly contentious political issue and Woodford waded into the maelstrom. 'Here we have a serious politician, standing up and saying what he said, which I think at a stroke torpedoed any chance that any of that investment will happen between now and the next election,' announced the stock picker, who was the largest investor with £1 billion in Centrica, the owner of British Gas. He was also a big shareholder in SSE, another FTSE 100 energy company. 'If Centrica and SSE cannot make any money supplying electricity to the retail market then they won't supply it. The lights will go off, the economy will shut down,' he added, describing Miliband's proposal as 'economic van-dalism at a time when this country needs all the help it can get. It is insane, not least it is also fundamentally dishonest to suggest to the electorate that electricity and gas prices are where they are because of profiteering by the companies.'

Woodford was no longer just the UK's best-known fund man-ager; he was increasingly seen as one of the most influential figures in British business. His private interventions and public outbursts could split boardrooms and break up companies. He was a big name, not only on the personal finance pages but also within the wider business and national news sections of the country's broad-sheet and mid-market newspapers. As his personal brand grew, an ever-larger army of savers entrusted him with their money. To cap it all off, he was made a Commander of the Order of the British Empire in the Queen's birthday honours list, in recognition of his services to the economy.

Woodford's two main funds, Income and High Income, were each bigger than £10 billion – eclipsing the size of many small countries' economies. They had grown so large that some financial advisers became concerned. Sanlam, a private wealth manage-ment company, recommended its clients sell their holdings in the funds, arguing that their considerable size meant Woodford would struggle to adapt the portfolio quickly enough should the market turn. It warned that Woodford was committed to a rela-tively small number of investments, and due to the funds' size, he had had to take very large positions in these companies, often being the largest investor on the shareholder register and in some cases owning more than a third of the business. The large stakes would be hard to sell off and meant the funds were heavily exposed to the fortunes of a small group of companies. Sanlam noted Woodford's defensive investment style, which meant the fund rarely benefited from strong market rallies but came into its own during downturns. The portfolios' top ten holdings – which included pharmaceuticals AstraZeneca, GlaxoSmithKline and Roche, cigarette makers BAT and Imperial Tobacco, as well as two other FTSE stalwarts: BT and BAE Systems – accounted for more than half of the funds' total assets.

The Sanlam report prompted financial advisers to take a closer look at the Woodford funds they were advising to their clients. They wondered whether Woodford was becoming a victim of his own success. But once again Mark Dampier, Woodford's cheerleader-in-chief, came to his defence. The head of research at Hargreaves Lansdown had already helped convince the fund super-market's clients to squirrel away more than £5 billion of their savings into Woodford's funds. 'While fund size can undoubtedly affect the investment process, I believe Neil Woodford's style allows him to run very large sums of money successfully,' wrote Dampier in his weekly column for the *Independent*. 'As ever, he has clearly articulated his views, so it is up to the individual investor to decide whether they agree or disagree with his stance – and invest accordingly. I retain a substantial amount of my own portfolio with his funds, and I regard this as a core holding. I am happy to ignore the short-term noise and continue to back one of the most successful UK managers of our time.'

Nearly all of Woodford's funds were invested in large blue-chip British companies that could be relied upon to produce steady dividend payments. Woodford trusted these businesses, which he felt were undervalued by other investors and were resilient enough to withstand an economic downturn. But he retained an interest in small unlisted and early stage companies. He held about twenty such investments, which made up just under 5 per cent of the portfolios. He believed these businesses would be high fliers in the next ten to fifteen years. By now Woodford controlled £33 billion across his various funds – including Income and High Income, the listed Edinburgh Investment Trust and an assortment of separate accounts managed on behalf of groups such as St James's Place (SJP). The assets had grown tenfold in a decade. It was Woodford's big bets on large, unfancied household-name companies that received most attention, while his private-equity-style holdings in unquoted companies had sparked little interest. But the unlisted portion was soon worth more than £1 billion – a huge exposure for a fund manager who had made his name and attracted a loyal following on the back of investing in large-cap stocks. The scale of the commitments to unquoted companies had certainly not gone unnoticed by the executives in Atlanta. But it was one investment in particular that spooked them into taking action.

Based in Massachusetts, Xyleco was founded by Marshall Medoff, an eccentric octogenarian who had no formal scientific background but possessed a self-acknowledged messiah complex. In his late fifties he had developed an obsession with environmental issues and given up his business career to dedicate himself to scientific research. For fifteen years, Medoff locked himself away in a garage at a remote storage facility and consumed piles of academic papers. He started churning out ideas of his own and applying for patents. Soon the number of his own patents topped 3,000 and stacked boxes containing the paperwork reached the garage ceiling. Several of his ideas centred on converting biomass – such as spent corn cobs from nearby farms – into useful products. Medoff's claims that he was 'saving the world' by producing plant-based alternatives to plastic attracted praise and derision in equal measure. To help legitimize the business, Medoff recruited a stellar cast of directors, made up of Nobel Prize recipients and former US statesmen, including William Perry, the former US defence secretary, George Shultz, the former US secretary of state, and Steven Chu, the former US energy secretary. Perry and Shultz were both board members of Theranos, the much-hyped blood-testing start-up that would later be exposed as one of the biggest frauds in Silicon Valley.

Something in Medoff's bizarre business plan convinced Woodford to make one of the most extravagant and catastrophic investment decisions of his life. It was the moment he abandoned all the lessons he had learnt from investing in well-researched public companies throughout his twenty-five years of managing money, and decided to double down on a private business that would have sent most mainstream fund managers running.

Woodford handed over £252 million from his funds to the venture, according to leaked Invesco Perpetual sales documents. In return he received a 7.6 per cent stake of the company, which valued it at £3.3 billion – a staggering amount for a business that was little more than Medoff's garage full of patents. While Woodford's commitment to Xyleco was worth less than 1 per cent of his main funds' total assets, the amount was significantly higher than he had previously invested in a single private business. Until that point, the Atlanta bosses had indulged Woodford's interest in early stage science companies as the investments had been in the tens of millions of pounds at most. But Xyleco was of a different order – especially as the commitment placed such a high valuation on a business that was subject to so much scepticism by mainstream scientists. Within a couple of years Invesco was forced to write off the Xyleco investment, wiping out £252 million of investors' money. Was it Medoff's conviction in his delusions of grandeur that convinced Woodford to make such a costly mistake, or was it the fund manager's own desire to feel he was helping change the world for the better – but with other people's money?

When they found out about the size of the Xyleco investment, the Atlanta executives were shocked and decided to clamp down on Woodford's unquoted holdings. They set up an internal committee to assess all private investments and any future commitments. It also controlled the process of valuing unquoted holdings and put limits on the amounts that could be invested in them. Crucially, the committee did not include Woodford and went above his head – which further stoked his rage at the American hierarchy and what he saw as their interference in this tried-and-tested investment process. Woodford also wanted to launch a separate fund focused solely on unquoted companies, but Invesco knocked it back. It became clear that Woodford had a choice: stay in Henley and accept orders from above, or leave and do as he wished.

Newman had also grown exasperated by the Invesco leadership, especially his boss Ian Trevers, and the pair were barely on speaking terms. Newman was finding his personal property projects – buying, developing and trying to flip luxury homes in the Henley area – were taking up more of his time and money. He was frequently out of the office dealing with builders, which further irked Trevers. Newman's personal behaviour was also becoming more erratic.

Newman realized that he would only advance his career and his pay packet by switching to another company, or, better still, setting up a new business. He hatched a plan to take possession of Invesco Perpetual's prized lists of sales contacts and convinced two members of his team to lift them from the company's computer system. The lists – later leaked to the *FT* – included the contact details of scores of the leading pension consultants and financial advisory groups across the country, the most important decision makers when it came to directing savers' money into investment funds. The documents also included contact details for Invesco Perpetual's most important institutional clients – including the Kent County Council and BBC pension funds, as well as SJP – along with details about the fees they paid Invesco for Woodford to manage their money. The information would prove invaluable to any company attempting to take Invesco Perpetual's clients.

But the ruse was discovered. Despite Newman's attempts to distance himself from the swiped documents, Invesco Perpetual's managers knew he was behind it. After the company carried out an investigation, it informed Newman he could resign and leave the business immediately or face disciplinary action, which would tarnish his reputation for future employers. Newman chose the former. He signed a non-disclosure agreement and was frogmarched out of the office to the car park, without having the chance to return to his desk to pick up his personal belongings.

Out of work, and facing mounting bills to keep his property projects going, Newman kick-started a plan he had been working on for some time. Having ingratiated himself with Woodford, Newman hoped to use his close connection to Britain's best-known fund manager to his advantage. 'Craig smelled blood in the water,' says a former colleague. Newman knew how embittered Woodford had grown with his bosses. First, they had tried to divert marketing resources away from his blockbuster funds – with the knock-on effect that his own bonus would reduce – then they sought to clamp down on his passion for investing in early stage science companies. Woodford abhorred being interfered with, and he took the actions by Invesco Perpetual's managers – which he believed stemmed from Martin Flanagan and his fellow American executives – as a personal affront. He was the reason investors had flocked to Invesco Perpetual's UK equity funds in such high numbers – not the pen-pushers in Atlanta. 'Any hint of interference and Neil would become quite hostile,' remembers another former colleague. 'He could be quite emotional – particularly if he felt somebody was looking to meddle with the way he managed his portfolio.'

Woodford also grew irate with the monthly investment meetings with his fellow fund managers, where he would continually be challenged about his unquoted holdings. What gave these mediocre managers the right to question the great Neil Woodford? Knowing the resentment Woodford harboured, Newman convinced the stock picker that the two of them should set up on their own. Woodford's reputation would ensure Invesco Perpetual's clients would switch billions of pounds to the new business, and a fresh start would give Woodford the autonomy he had enjoyed earlier in his career. Woodford agreed to the breakaway. The final straw came when Woodford was summoned for a rare trip to Atlanta to meet Invesco Perpetual's executives. Here the American bosses made it clear to Woodford that, though he may have been a big name in the UK, the funds he ran belonged to the business and he reported to them. Woodford's mind was made up.

When, on 29 April 2013, Woodford told Mark Armour and Nick Mustoe he intended to leave the business, the news struck like a lightning bolt. They knew that despite the company's efforts to diversify the UK business, it was still too highly reliant on Woodford's brand. Income and High Income were among Britain's largest funds, and investors who had stuck with him over the years had been made rich. Invesco Perpetual's bosses knew that as soon as

Woodford's departure was announced, investors would withdraw billions of pounds from their funds. Important contracts with the likes of SJP would also be threatened as they relied on the continuity of the fund management team. Influential fund ratings providers such as Morningstar would probably downgrade the funds and the likes of Hargreaves Lansdown could remove them from their lists of recommended products – prompting yet more withdrawals. In short, losing Woodford would be an unmitigated disaster.

Woodford had a twelve-month notice period in his contract, meaning he could not leave until April 2014, but the Invesco Perpetual executives decided they needed time to prepare for the hurricane that would hit as soon as word got out that he was leaving. Consequently, they kept news of his departure quiet for six months – even from SJP, which demanded to know as soon as possible any information that could potentially disrupt their chosen fund managers. It was a risky move by the Invesco Perpetual bosses, because once their biggest clients found out, they would be livid they had not been told earlier.

Meanwhile, another storm was gathering for Invesco Perpetual. The Financial Conduct Authority (FCA) had opened an investigation into its investment procedures and found a series of rule violations that had resulted in the group's clients losing £5.3 million. The FCA discovered that between May 2008 and November 2012 the company's fund managers had made thirty-three trades that breached rules put in place to limit risk for investors. The trades were across fifteen different funds, which represented more than 70 per cent of the company's assets. 'As a result of these failings, Invesco Perpetual's investors were exposed to greater levels of risk than they had been led to expect,' the regulator wrote in its final report on the matter.

The FCA found that over the four-year period, the company's funds had consistently flouted a rule that limited the amount of exposure portfolios could have to a small number of large holdings. Breaches of this rule had resulted in £1.5 million of losses for investors. Another £3.3 million of losses came from trades that meant funds wielded too much influence over a company it invested in by controlling too many voting shares. The regulator identified several other deficiencies in Invesco Perpetual's processes. The group was chastised for not recording trades on time, which meant funds were at risk of being wrongly priced. Another failing the regulator identified was the company's failure to monitor whether trades had been allocated fairly between funds, which meant some funds were disadvantaged.

The investigation also discovered that certain funds, including those managed by Woodford, had invested in complex derivatives that introduced up to £1 billion of leverage into the portfolios. This was equivalent to 5 per cent of the funds' assets. But investors were not informed that this increased the level of risk in the portfolio, with the potential to magnify losses. 'Neil's view was that keeping within the limits was just something that somebody needed to monitor,' says a former fund manager in the business. 'He probably didn't think it was his job to actually monitor the legal limits on his fund. His view was: "I've got people to tell me when I'm crossing over the line. If they don't tell me, it's not my fault." ' Having been caught on the wrong side of a regulatory probe, would Woodford learn the lessons about taking more responsibility for managing his funds in the best interests of his investors?

The FCA had been in operation for only a matter of months, having risen from the embers of the much-derided Financial Services Authority, and was keen to show its teeth. 'In this case investors of all sizes trusted Invesco Perpetual to manage their money. They signed up for a certain level of risk, but we found Invesco Perpetual's actions were at odds with investors' reasonable expectations,' the regulator said at the time. It imposed a £26.6 million fine on Invesco Perpetual, which the investment group managed to negotiate down to £18.6 million by agreeing to cooperate and pay up early. Despite Woodford's funds being at the centre of the scandal, he avoided any personal retribution from the regulator or Invesco Perpetual, pleading ignorance of the complex instruments he had invested in. The fine was the highest ever levied on a fund manager in the UK and was yet another body blow to Invesco Perpetual, which had been put through the wringer by the US Securities and Exchange Commission just less than a decade earlier during the market timing scandal. But more damaging news was to come.

On 15 October 2013 Invesco finally revealed to the outside world that Woodford was leaving. The announcement that Britain's biggest fund manager was quitting his home for more than quarter of a century was national news, leading the business sections of national newspapers and broadcast business bulletins. The company said Woodford would stay on for another six months but would hand over the management of his flagship Income and High Income funds to Mark Barnett. Woodford oversaw funds with a combined value of £33 billion, while Barnett's managed just £1.5 billion. IFAs and analysts speculated Invesco Perpetual would be hit hard by the news, with several brokerages – including Hargreaves Lansdown, Bestinvest and Chelsea Financial Services – deciding to cease recommending them to clients. Some went further, with Brewin Dolphin and Heartwood Wealth Managers pulling their clients' money from the funds. 'Mr Woodford is the finest fund manager of his generation, in my view, and his funds are held by thousands of private investors. The implications of the announcement are therefore huge,' surmised Hargreaves's Dampier at the time.

Woodford's influence on the market was evident as several of his biggest holdings – BAE Systems, Capita, Drax Group, G4S, Imperial Tobacco, Rentokil Initial, AstraZeneca and GlaxoSmithKline – all suffered hits to their share prices as investors speculated that if clients withdrew their money from Woodford's funds en masse, they would be forced to sell down their stakes in the businesses. Shares in Edinburgh Investment Trust, a small listed vehicle that Woodford also managed, shed 10 per cent. Invesco, which by now was listed on the New York stock exchange, itself was stung by a 5 per cent share price fall, wiping out £800 million of market value.

SJP's powerful investment committee had, as expected, reacted badly to the news. The members immediately placed the mandates they had with Invesco under review, but insisted Woodford continue managing them. They had bought into the manager, not the investment company. They were not the only ones bailing on Invesco Perpetual. Within a matter of weeks investors withdrew more than £2 billion from Woodford's two main funds.

Woodford had arrived in Henley as an unknown and inexperienced fund manager twenty-five years earlier. He would leave as a dominant force in British business. Invesco Perpetual, the company that had nurtured him and helped make him a star, was now staring into the abyss.

7

Breakaway

At first glance, Oakley Capital was an odd place for the leading British fund manager of his generation to end up. The Knightsbridge-based finance boutique managed just £700 million for mostly pension funds and wealthy families. It ploughed their money into arcane products like hedge funds, private-equity and venture-capital vehicles, as well as offering advice on complex financial deals. It was a world away from the £33 billion Neil Woodford had managed at Invesco Perpetual for his loyal following of individual investors, and which he had used to buy huge stakes in the UK's biggest listed companies. But on 19 December 2013 Peter Dubens, Oakley's entrepreneurial co-founder, told a stunned financial press that he had just recruited the UK's leading stock picker. 'I am delighted Neil is joining,' Dubens announced. Oakley, he said, would provide support for Woodford to launch a new, much smaller fund for retail investors after his contract with Invesco Perpetual ended the following April.

Woodford had had a long relationship with Dubens, a floppy-haired financier with a passion for yachts. Indeed, Woodford had been a big investor in the group's listed private-equity vehicle, with Invesco Perpetual holding a 31 per cent stake in the business. After the announcement of Woodford's decision to join Oakley, its shares rose 6 per cent, increasing the value of Invesco Perpetual's stake by £4 million. Dubens had launched Oakley with David Till in 2002, after the pair had built up internet businesses 365 Media Group and Pipex Communications through twenty-six acquisitions, and then sold the companies for more than £470 million in total. Oakley was best known for being the private-equity owner of *Time Out* magazine. Dubens announced that Oakley would help Woodford build a 'transformational' investment business, adding: 'We will fully support the transition and in the meantime we will provide an environment in which Neil can have the autonomy and flexibility to best serve the interests of clients.'

In fact, Oakley was merely a front to get Woodford's new business off the ground. When Invesco Perpetual announced in October that Woodford was leaving, several wealth managers got in touch with the investor, saying they wanted him to continue to manage their clients' money and would switch their business to wherever he landed. But crucially, they wanted a seamless transition so that as soon as Woodford left Invesco Perpetual at the end of April, his next fund would be set up and ready to go. This presented Woodford with a problem – launching a fund company from scratch would usually take between a year and eighteen months, yet Woodford had no intention of joining another company and reporting to more over-officious managers. He craved the freedom he had enjoyed at Invesco Perpetual a decade earlier, before the Atlanta bosses started meddling. Under the terms of his notice period with Invesco Perpetual, he was restricted from any involvement in setting up a venture until his contract finished at the end of April 2014. He therefore secured the assistance of Craig Newman, who had been unemployed since being unceremoniously dumped out of the Henley office.

The pair hit upon the idea of using Oakley as a way of getting the new business up and running. Dubens was open to helping his long-term ally out and the opportunity to be involved in a high-profile start-up appealed to his enterprising spirit. Newman began working for Oakley in November and used it as a shell to hire staff for the new venture. Several former Invesco Perpetual colleagues were interested in joining. Among the first recruits were Nick Hamilton, who had worked with Woodford at Perpetual for ten years before moving back to his native Australia, and Gray Smith, a lawyer at Mishcon de Reya, who had personally represented Woodford during the FCA investigation. Hamilton had been part of Woodford's inner circle during the golden years in Henley and the pair enjoyed a sporting rivalry. Smith was more reserved, though Woodford had been impressed by his ability to take the heat out of the regulator's probe. The four men had several phone calls over the Christmas period and finally agreed on 1 January to get the ball rolling on the new business.

They then sounded out several Invesco Perpetual staff who had worked with Woodford and Newman over the years, including institutional salesman Will Deer, marketing writer Mitchell Fraser-Jones and IT manager Paul Green. They also planned to hire three junior fund managers from the UK team: Saku Saha, a former army intelligence officer who specialized in unlisted companies, as well as brothers Stephen and Paul Lamacraft, a former policeman and accountant respectively (a third brother, Ross, would later join in a sales role). But Woodford was barred from poaching investment staff from Invesco Perpetual until the end of his notice period. Another joiner was Paul Farrow, the former personal finance editor of the *Telegraph*, who would become head of PR and communications. Oakley provided Newman with office space, compliance support and a £1 million loan to get the business off the ground. The boutique also provided a valuable safety net in case Newman, Hamilton and Smith were unable to launch on time. If the business had not received the required regulatory authorization by 1 May, when several Invesco Perpetual clients had said they wanted to move their money, Oakley would be able to provide a temporary home for their assets – and for Woodford to manage them – until the new business was given the green light.

On 6 January 2014 Newman, Hamilton and Smith turned up at the Financial Conduct Authority's offices in Canary Wharf and presented officials with a fifty-seven-slide proposal about their plans for the new business. The leaked PowerPoint presentation stated:

Neil wishes to be part of a new business that is owned privately and that places its sole emphasis on delivering long-term investment management and providing transparency to clients. Neil and a number of the team that are being assembled have worked closely together for a number of years. The team share very similar views on the importance of regulatory compliance, a culture of placing the clients' interest foremost and of transparency as an investment business.

To underline the point, it stressed: 'The business will place a very high emphasis on delivering investment management within a tightly controlled environment.' Given Woodford's recent brush with the regulator, Newman, Hamilton and Smith were at pains to stress how closely the new business would stick to the rules – were they setting themselves up for a fall?

Newman took the lead in the meeting with the regulator, using his well-honed salesman's spiel to talk up the aspects of the business plan written to appeal specifically to it. The venture would have a strong emphasis on compliance and be squarely focused on its customers, he insisted. On more technical and legal issues, he let Hamilton and Smith provide the details. The FCA presentation included information about the legal structure of the new business, which stated it would be owned by its partners, who at launch were to be Woodford, Newman, Smith and Hamilton. The plan set out that the initial equity holders would be Woodford and Newman, but that equity would later be shared among the four founders, with ownership also used as a tool to reward and attract staff, as well as helping retain workers long term.

During the meeting at the FCA's headquarters, Newman waxed lyrical about how the new business would turn the investment industry on its head and correct many of the flaws he saw in the existing way of doing things. This included being fully transparent with investors over the fees they were paying and what they were investing in. Fund managers typically provided investors with a list of only their top ten holdings, fearing that showing details of the full portfolio would allow rivals to steal their investment ideas. But the new business would provide full details of every investment made by the fund managers, including the proportion of the portfolio they made up. This would be a significant departure for Woodford, whose taste for investing in small companies and unquoted start-ups had largely gone under the radar at Invesco Perpetual as the focus was on his huge stakes in well-established businesses. The decision to disclose fully the funds' fee levels was designed to give investors more insight into what they were paying for. The regulator was known to have reservations regarding the lack of information clients received about how much they were being charged in trading and research costs. The new business would also aim to have a direct relationship with its customers, using the website as a communication tool so that investors could ask questions of the management team directly, rather than being filtered through financial advisers.

The trio had big ambitions for the new venture. While it was launching as a vehicle for Woodford to continue managing money, they hoped to create a business that could act as a refuge for other talented fund managers looking to escape inhibiting bosses. The idea was to build a strong compliance and risk base with no overhanging issues from previous companies. This would give investment managers the freedom to do what they did best and run their portfolios how they wished. Newman, Smith and Hamilton told the FCA that the business would launch with a fund investing in UK equities run by Woodford that would be a close match to his main Invesco Perpetual Income and High Income funds, but over the years it would launch global equities funds and a suite of bond and mixed-asset products. They even suggested they might require additional licences in the future to operate edgy alternative funds. They projected that, in the first year, the company could reach £9.75 billion of assets, which would produce £7.5 million of profit. This would rise to £17 billion of assets and £46.7 million of profit within three years. It was phenomenally ambitious, but Woodford's three co-founders were optimistic, given the number of Invesco Perpetual clients who had given them an indication that they would switch their business to the new venture.

The only decision still to be finalized was what to call the new business. There was much discussion between the co-founders about whether to brand it as Woodford or not. Woodford was the biggest name in UK fund management, and the brand resonated strongly with British investors. Each year PR firm Broadgate Mainland conducted a survey of brand awareness among financial advisers. In top spot came Invesco Perpetual, but in second – beating some of the best-known investment companies, including Fidelity, Jupiter, Henderson and Neptune – was Neil Woodford himself. With such a strong name in the industry, it was hard to resist using it for the new business. But the decision to do so would tie its fortunes tightly to its star stock picker, introduce an inescapable level of key-person risk and make it practically impossible to convince other high-profile investors to join the business, as it would be clear who the main attraction was. In the end Newman made the call to go with Woodford Investment Management. The short-term benefits were clear, but longer term would the decision ultimately backfire?

Meanwhile, in Henley, Invesco Perpetual's management team were fretting about the impact Woodford's departure would have on the business. The initial client withdrawals from Woodford's funds when his departure had been announced began to slow. But still the funds were shrinking due to natural attrition as investors who retired and took their money out were not being replaced by new customers. With so many financial advisers no longer recommending their clients invest in the Income and High Income funds, the company realized it needed to arrest the decline. Based on a typical fund fee of 0.7 per cent, every £1 billion invested in one of Woodford's funds produced £7 million of revenue. For Invesco Perpetual, the difference between losing £5 billion of assets and £10 billion would be £35 million a year.

In a bid to bring financial advisers back on side, Invesco Perpetual sent out Mark Barnett, who had taken over the running of Woodford's funds, for a blizzard of media interviews and promotional events to boost his profile. 'I've worked for the team for seventeen years, I've sat next to [Neil] and had privileged access to him, so I'm in a unique position to preserve and build on his track record,' Barnett told trade title *Citywire*. 'I'm very excited by the opportunity and the challenge. It's a big promotion for me and I accept everyone is going to be watching me now but I'm not going to behave differently.'

The initial meeting with the FCA in Canary Wharf had gone extremely well, and Newman, Hamilton and Smith busied themselves trying to get the business going. They now had less than four months to ensure it was ready to receive billions of pounds at the start of May and allow Woodford to trade the portfolio from day one. While many of Newman's former clients at Invesco were excited to move their business to the new venture, they all stressed they wanted the transition to be as seamless as possible. They wanted minimal disruption for their customers. The co-founders were feeling the pressure.

While there was much work involved in setting up computer and trading systems, finding office space and preparing marketing material, the trickiest part of the launch was negotiating the fiendishly complex regulatory application process. All companies managing money on behalf of clients were required to be registered and authorized by the FCA. In order to approve a new business, the regulator wanted evidence that it had sufficient risk and compliance processes in place, and also needed to vet all the main executives. A handful of the new venture's first recruits – including Newman, Hamilton, Smith, Green, Stephen Lamacraft and Mary Reilly, a partner at Deloitte who had been chosen as a non-executive director – were required to apply to the FCA to be approved to carry out so-called controlled functions, such as being a director or chief executive or overseeing compliance. Newman tried to put forward his linguistics coach as a director of the company, but the FCA demurred because he had no knowledge or experience of the investment industry. Woodford was already recognized by the FCA, but his authorization was still tied to his employment at Invesco Perpetual.

In Newman's application, leaked to the *FT*, he was asked pointed questions about his departure from Invesco Perpetual – yet his answers did not match the accounts given by several of his former co-workers. Newman was asked whether he had 'ever been the subject of an investigation into allegations of misconduct or malpractice in connection with any business activity'. He was also asked whether he had been 'refused entry to, dismissed, suspended or requested to resign from any profession, vocation, office or employment, or from any fiduciary office or position of trust, whether or not remunerated'. His answer to both questions was a flat 'no'. The regulator would have expected to be told about the details surrounding his departure from his previous employer – especially as Newman was applying to become chief executive of the new business. It was an early indication that, even though Newman told the regulator all the right things in order to become approved, he was not as fully committed to transparency and playing by the rules as he first appeared.

One of the scores of documents submitted to the FCA on 30 January as part of the application for Woodford Investment Management was a detailed statement on the new business's liquidity policy. This was an attempt to manage one of the biggest risks fund managers faced: ensuring that investment portfolios were designed in a way that enough of their holdings could be sold in an orderly fashion in times of stress. Controlling liquidity was especially important for managers of retail funds that allowed clients to invest and withdraw money each day. If a fund suffered a run and investors demanded the return of a substantial amount of their cash on any given day, the portfolio manager would need to make sure they could sell the fund's assets at the going market value quickly enough to pay back the departing clients and protect the savings of those who remained.

It was a tricky balancing act, especially for managers like Woodford, who liked to hold a portion of their funds in small but very hard to sell companies. This challenge was not lost on the founders of the business when they submitted their application to the FCA.

'Liquidity risk management is essential to the long term success of Woodford Investment Management,' the liquidity policy read. 'The firm will ensure that it maintains on its balance sheet and/or arranges with reputable third parties adequate liquidity to meet the obligations of the firm including maintenance of regulatory capital, as and when they fall due. The main drivers for profitability at the firm are not dependent on taking significant liquidity risk.' The intentions seemed noble enough – whether Woodford would stick to them was another matter.

Another crucial part of the application process concerned who would provide the critical though widely overlooked role of authorized corporate director, or ACD. Under UK regulations, each retail investment fund is required to have an ACD, usually in the form of a specialist service provider that takes responsibility for ensuring the fund complies with FCA rules and is run in the best interests of investors. It is a vital role in the investment industry's regulatory framework – but few outside the sector are familiar with it. An ACD's role is to sit as the central cog in the running of the investment fund, linking the portfolio manager to the regulator, custodian, auditor, intermediary and – most importantly – the end investor. The FCA saw the ACD as an extension of its own regulatory arm and relied on the providers to keep the portfolio managers in line with fund rules. The regulator essentially outsourced part of its oversight responsibility to these anonymous service providers.

Among its other responsibilities, the ACD was tasked with producing regulatory documents, maintaining fund administration and overseeing investment and liquidity risk. In a nutshell, the ACD's role was to make sure the fund was legally sound and investors were protected – arguably the most important role in the entire investment industry.

While the vast majority of customers believed that investment managers such as Invesco Perpetual or M&G, whose branding was all over their fund documents, was the recognized fund manager, from a legal perspective it was in fact the ACD, which subcontracted the investment manager to run the portfolio. This was a strange and convoluted set-up that introduced a tricky conflict of interest. From a regulatory perspective, the ACD appointed the investment manager, also known as the sponsor of the fund. But in reality, the sponsor selected the ACD. Fees were agreed between the sponsor and ACD but paid out of the fund. While the sponsor could sack the ACD, subject to their contract, the latter's only recourse was to raise any concern with the regulator or ask the sponsor to find another ACD. As a result, the ACD, which was supposed to police the investment manager and ensure end investors were protected, had an incentive to avoid upsetting its paymaster.

An alternative to this arrangement was for the ACD role to be carried out in-house by the investment manager. But the FCA had reviewed this structure, and, although allowing it to continue, believed it introduced an even bigger conflict of interest as the investment manager would, in effect, be marking its own home-work. In their application to the FCA, Newman, Smith and Hamilton said they intended to set up their own in-house ACD structure, but conceded this would be impossible in the short time available before launch. They therefore proposed using the services of a small but well-respected player in the market named Host Capital. This, they felt, was sure to be approved, but they were taken aback by the regulator's response.

Throughout the process, the FCA's authorization team had responded with only the most rudimentary of follow-up queries and seemed intent on helping Newman, Smith and Hamilton push through the application in record time. The regulator's officials told the trio that the last thing they wanted was Woodford's army of devoted followers to withdraw their investments from his Invesco Perpetual funds and have their cash uninvested for a period while they waited for the new venture to launch. As with the tetchy wealth advisers and IFAs, the FCA wanted as smooth a transition as possible. But on one point in particular the regulators put their foot down. They insisted that Host was too small an operation to act for Woodford IM, which would potentially manage tens of billions of pounds within just a few years. Instead, the FCA insisted the new business use the largest player in the market, Capita Asset Services.

The pressure to choose Capita was odd, not least because Woodford was one of the biggest shareholders in the provider's parent company, the British outsourcing group dubbed 'Crapita' by *Private Eye* for its frequent cock-ups. Apparently, the regulator saw no problems with this glaring conflict of interest, which would mean Capita's ACD team would be tasked with holding to account an investor they knew to be one of their company's biggest and most powerful shareholders. But what was especially surprising about the selection was the fact that the regulator knew Capita's ACD business all too well, having investigated its involvement in two of Britain's worst fund management scandals.

Just days before the application for Woodford IM was sent to the FCA, the regulator announced that up to 20,000 investors who had been trapped in funds known as Arch Cru since 2009 were in line for a £31.5 million redress payment. Capita had been the ACD on the funds, in which retail investors ultimately lost millions of pounds in savings. Capita had suspended the funds owing to a lack of liquidity. Many savers had been convinced to invest up to £400 million with Arch Cru by their financial advisers, believing they were investing in low-risk products. But the portfolios were actually an exotic cocktail of holdings, including investments in student accommodation, fine wine, forestry and Greek shipping. The Arch Cru affair brought regulatory censure for Capita and the business was required to contribute to a £54 million compensation scheme for the funds' investors, which allowed the ACD to escape a £4 million fine.

The Arch Cru debacle coincided with another fund scandal involving Capita. The ACD business had previously worked on a group of funds known as Connaught Income, which collapsed in the wake of the financial crisis, causing £118 million of losses for investors. After a long-running probe, the FCA would eventually find Capita had not carried out adequate due diligence on the funds and did not properly oversee them. The regulator reprimanded

Capita for failing to communicate the problems at Connaught with investors in a fair way that was not misleading. Capita was ordered to pay up to £66 million in compensation to the funds' investors, in addition to £18.5 million to settle a lawsuit brought by the funds' liquidators. In foisting their preferred ACD on Woodford's new business, the regulator told Newman, Smith and Hamilton that it hoped Capita would learn from its involvement in investment implosions and would be primed to prevent further missteps. The logic was naive at best.

Though he could not participate in the regulatory application, Woodford was keeping himself busy. When Invesco Perpetual had finally announced in October that Woodford was leaving the business, the powerful investment committee at SJP, which had entrusted £3.7 billion with the stock picker, were furious. They had a firm policy of insisting they were kept abreast of all personal matters connected to the fund managers they enlisted. This included their employment status, whether they were involved in any internal disputes with their employers, or whether they were seriously ill, off work for more than three weeks, or had other issues that could affect their day job, such as going through a divorce. Such disclosures were rare for employers to pass on to their clients, but SJP was the UK's biggest wealth manager, marshalling tens of billions of pounds for wealthy Britons. It had the heft to be so demanding. SJP's investment committee felt their main responsibility was to protect their own clients' savings and made choices of funds based on the individuals running them. If the manager's performance could suffer for any reason, or if he or she was likely to be replaced, SJP wanted to know as soon as possible.

When the investment committee discovered Invesco Perpetual had kept Woodford's departure from them for six months, they insisted he continue to manage their clients' savings, which were run in an account separate to Woodford's main funds. Fearing SJP would pull contracts worth £8 billion of assets across the group, Invesco Perpetual's bosses relented and allowed Woodford to manage the portfolio until his last day at the company – though he did so mostly from his Cotswold estate rather than venturing into the Henley office. Were it not for SJP's demands, Woo dford would have been put on gardening leave for his final few months at Invesco Perpetual.

With its headquarters in the historic market town of Cirencester, known as the capital of the Cotswolds, SJP's main hub was just a twenty-minute drive from Woodford's country pile. Indeed, David Lamb, managing director of investments at SJP who was soon to become chairman of the investment committee, was a near neighbour. SJP's executives began secret talks with Woodford about what he was putting together for his next venture and whether it would be robust enough to manage SJP's clients' money. Woodford convinced them that the new business would be up to scratch, and SJP's investment committee decided to replace Invesco Perpetual with Woodford IM as manager of the entire £3.7 billion fund when it opened its doors on 1 May. As with the other wealth managers and IFAs who had told Newman they wanted to transfer their business to the new venture, SJP stressed it needed a smooth transition. The stakes were raised for receiving regulatory approval in time.

But SJP's offer had several strings attached. Its terms of business were much more stringent than typically demanded by intermediaries, but the Woodford IM co-founders knew that launching the new company on day one with £3.7 billion of funds on its books would be an incredible start and would set the venture on a sure footing. As it did with all fund managers, SJP regularly monitored Woodford's investment style. It had commissioned investment consultancy Stamford Associates to carry out a series of assessments of how Woodford ran his portfolios. The main findings from these reports were that, while Woodford was the industry leader in picking large undervalued companies and sticking with them, his ability to choose small and unlisted companies was patchy, to say the least. Blow-ups like Xyleco and Phytopharm weighed heavily on SJP's confidence in Woodford as an investor in his increasingly favoured field of science-based start-ups. So SJP had insisted that the money he managed for its clients at Invesco Perpetual be solely invested in listed companies – none of its clients' savings would be used to prop up unstable private businesses. Woodford had taken it as a personal affront each time SJP criticized his record on investing in small companies over the years, but the balance of power lay firmly with the wealth manager. Besides, the empirical evidence of Woodford's failings when it came to backing unlisted companies spoke for itself. Unsurprisingly, SJP made the same demands for the business it would give to Woodford's new venture.

According to a leaked document setting out the terms of business between SJP and Woodford IM, known in the industry as an investment management agreement, SJP expected to know what investments the fund managers made personally. It also stated that SJP could end the relationship immediately if it chose to, while Woodford IM would have to give the wealth manager six months' notice if it decided to terminate the contract. The odds were heavily stacked in SJP's favour. The agreement also confirmed the amount SJP would pay Woodford IM: a flat fee of 0.3 per cent, less than half what the fund manager expected to receive from other intermediaries. It also ensured SJP creamed off a fat 1.5 per cent fee from its own clients for investing in the fund – in addition to the other fees it charged them – despite doing little more than picking and monitoring the investment manager. Even so, the agreement with SJP guaranteed £10.5 million of annual revenue for Woodford IM from launch, a deal the co-founders could not turn down.

SJP was not the only Invesco Perpetual client the breakaway business was trying to poach. A cache of leaked sales documents shows the extent of the efforts by Woodford IM's commercial team to sign up Britain's best-known financial advisers and wealth managers. Woodford IM was the most talked about investment launch for decades, with many of Woodford's loyal followers keen to invest in his new fund from the outset. Intermediaries across the country were eager to cash in on the hype surrounding the launch by switching clients into the new funds and taking their cut of the fee. It meant Will Deer and Simon Dale, the new company's heads of institutional and retail sales, found a receptive audience when they went to pitch for business. Dale had worked for Newman at Invesco Perpetual and left at the same time as his boss.

The lists of client prospects that Deer worked his way through included contact details of the main representatives at the biggest pension consultancies – the gatekeepers to the lucrative retirement market – along with two dozen pension schemes that were clients of Invesco Perpetual. These clients had collectively invested £2.5 billion in Woodford's Invesco Perpetual funds and the new sales team estimated they would lead to more than £15 million a year of fee income if they could be convinced to switch.

During meetings with large pension advisers such as Towers Watson and Mercer, representatives from the consultancies said they felt Woodford had never much cared for institutional investors as he rarely met their advisers while at Invesco Perpetual. But they said they wanted to carry out a detailed assessment of the new business as their clients were keen to commit capital. A meeting with one of the other leading consultants, Hymans Robertson, was very encouraging, not least because four of its own clients – the pension funds of Kent County Council, waste company Pennon and energy group Southern Electric, as well as the shipbuilding industry pension scheme – had long invested in Woodford's Invesco Perpetual funds and were all keen to switch to the new business.

Deer also had positive meetings with a host of pension funds directly, including Kent and insurer Hiscox. The BBC pension fund had invested in Woodford's Invesco Perpetual funds since 2006 but withdrew £416 million as soon as news broke of the fund manager's departure. Despite an initially frosty call with Deer, the BBC's pensions manager warmed to the idea of moving the money to Woodford's new business. From council workers, refuse collectors and electricians to shipbuilders and actuaries, workers up and down the country and from all walks of life were soon to be united in having their pension savings handed over to Woodford's new business.

The sales team's broader list of IFA targets was split into regional groups: western England and Wales, eastern England, northern England and Scotland, and London. Each group had around a hundred of the leading financial advisory companies in the area, along with details of the amount of assets they controlled and who their main sales representative was. The targets also included more than sixty life insurers, which provided personal and workplace pensions to millions of UK savers. An increasingly important set of clients that Woodford's sales team hoped to enlist were the platforms, or fund supermarkets, which allowed individual investors to invest in funds themselves. This sector was dominated by a handful of big names – including Hargreaves Lansdown, Fidelity, Skandia and Standard Life – but there were more than twenty providers in the market, each holding between £500 million and £54 billion of investors' funds. These businesses provided a direct sales channel to the millions of investors who chose their own funds or used IFAs to help them plan for their retirement. Getting them on side would be crucial to the long-term survival of Woodford's new business. Luckily for Woodford's sales team, the fund platforms were desperate to offer his new products.

Usually when sales staff turn up at the offices of prospective clients, the emphasis is on them to impress. But when Woodford's reps turned up at the offices of the country's biggest fund supermarkets, they were given the red-carpet treatment. Deer's meeting with Fidelity went particularly well. The business was one of the UK's best-known investment managers, but it had a very popular distribution arm called FundsNetwork, which sold funds from across the market to retail clients. It had 250,000 customers with more than £40 billion of assets on its platform and had diverted a lot of cash into Woodford's Invesco Perpetual funds over the years. Fidelity's head of personal investing offered Deer a huge marketing campaign to convince investors in Woodford's former Invesco Perpetual funds to switch to his new products. The proposal included emails to its entire network of customers, with those in Invesco Perpetual's funds specifically targeted. Fidelity also offered adverts in the financial press – with the tagline 'Buy Woodford with this year's ISA allowance' – as well as online ads and videos with Woodford on its website, along with promotional features in its client newsletter. Woodford would also be asked to present at its annual investor conference, where 400 rich clients would be present. It was an astounding offer for such a well-established company to make to what was essentially a start-up. Fidelity was clearly desperate to sign Woodford up.

Other key constituents were the wealth managers and other investment groups that offered funds of funds: vehicles whereby they created their own products that invested in a range of underlying funds. One surprising client that was keen to sign up was the Abu Dhabi Investment Authority, one of the world's biggest sovereign wealth funds. It had first got in touch with Deer a couple of years earlier about investing in Woodford's Invesco Perpetual funds, but ended up investing £200 million into the new business instead.

In most cases, Deer and Dale knew within minutes of arriving that selling the Woodford funds was a foregone conclusion. The Woodford stardust was exceptionally potent. But even though the sales meetings were straightforward affairs, Deer and Dale were often asked awkward questions by their hosts, who, despite their enthusiasm to be part of the new venture, had reservations around Woodford's departure from Invesco Perpetual. They wanted to know whether he had been too difficult to manage and if he had fallen out with his bosses. They raised concerns about how much the new business was tied to Woodford himself, whether the naming of the business seemed egotistical and if there was too much risk tied to one individual. They asked for reassurances about how involved Woodford would be in managing the money and how long his commitment was to the business. Usually, their concerns were assuaged, and they happily signed up to the new exciting launch.

Now all that was needed was regulatory approval. Once Newman accepted that he would have to use Capita as the new group's ACD, the FCA gave the launch its thumbs-up, granting authorization in late April, just in time for Woodford to join and manage the departing Invesco Perpetual clients' money from 1 May. The much-hoped-for seamless transition became a reality.

Despite forging an alliance between Woodford, a fund manager it had been investigating over fund-rule breaches just months earlier, and Capita, an ACD it had previously censured for failing to control wayward fund managers, the FCA gave its blessing to the union in record time. It was a marriage that would have devastating consequences for the European investment industry just a few years later.

8

Oracle of Oxford

It was Britain's most eagerly anticipated investment launch. In the weeks running up to Neil Woodford's departure from Invesco Perpetual at the end of April 2014, financial advisers and armchair investors devoured every morsel of information about his new venture – and the financial press duly delivered. The frenzy was fed by a spate of tit-for-tat mudslinging by those hit hardest by the defection.

Woodford bounded through the offices of the City PR agency Broadgate Mainland wearing a bold blue suit and checked shirt. It was his first day of work for his new boutique and Woodford felt invigorated. The fund manager was refreshed and tanned, having spent the previous two months holed up at his Cotswold estate, enjoying the country air. Broadgate had been retained to support Woodford's head of corporate communications, former *Telegraph* personal finance editor Paul Farrow, on dealing with the press. Woodford's very first engagement at his new venture was back-to-back interviews with the *FT* and the *Telegraph* for splashy profile pieces that would run in that weekend's personal finance pages.

Declining the opportunity to be briefed by his press handlers, Woodford waltzed straight into the interviews. Leaning back in his chair with his hands clasped behind his head, his Jaeger-LeCoultre watch catching the light, Woodford was ready to take on the world. The stock picker conceded to the *FT*'s David Oakley that it had been a frustrating twelve months, but refused to be drawn on his troubles with his former employer. Instead, in his bullish manner, Woodford spoke of how much energy he had and how enthusiastic he was about starting his new business. This was his great second act, not just a postscript to his celebrated career at Invesco Perpetual. He compared himself to his idol, Warren Buffett, who was still managing money well into his eighties. 'I think I have the best years ahead of me and I plan to keep going as long as I can,' Woodford bragged.

Before leaving Broadgate's offices, Woodford was asked to take part in an impromptu photoshoot. When Woodford IM's commercial team had been putting together the marketing material for the new business, they had struggled to find professional photos of the star manager. Invesco Perpetual refused to provide any. Remembering an interview he had carried out with Woodford a decade earlier from his *Telegraph* days, Farrow tracked down the freelance photographer who had taken the accompanying shots. When he eventually got through, the photographer was hunkered down on a treacherous assignment in Iraq, but he duly sent over the images he had on file. Farrow paid a couple of hundred pounds for the head shots, which would be plastered all over the new business's promotional material. At the Broadgate offices, Woodford was asked to pose in front of a vast display of paparazzi photographers with long lenses and flashing lights. The image captured the intense media interest in his business from that day on.

In the three-way public spat occasioned by Woodford's departure, St James's Place had struck first. The wealth manager's investment committee were livid with Invesco Perpetual's executives for the six-month delay in telling them that Woodford had handed in his notice. On 3 April SJP announced it was pulling the £3.7 billion Woodford had managed at Invesco Perpetual and moving it to his new business when it launched. The switch was widely anticipated, but SJP's move had a sting in its tail. Not only would the wealth manager remove the money that Woodford had managed, it would also fire the Henley investment group from all the funds it oversaw for the wealth manager, taking a total of £8 billion of business. The sacking was a body blow for Invesco Perpetual and the reverberations were felt 4,000 miles away in Atlanta as the parent company's share price dropped. The scale of SJP's revenge was unparalleled, and one of the largest mandate changes the UK retail investment market had ever seen. The switched assets represented nearly a fifth of the total money SJP looked after for its clients. Of its 400,000 well-to-do customers, half would be moved from Invesco Perpetual to Woodford Investment Management. 'This round of appointments and fund changes is the most significant and high profile in our twenty-three-year history,' Chris Ralph, SJP's chief investment officer, said in announcing the move.

Smarting from the huge loss of business, Invesco Perpetual's bosses hit back at their departing star investor a few weeks later. They had been busy negotiating down the £26.6 million fine the FCA planned to impose for the litany of fund-rule breaches it had committed and, as part of the agreement it had reached with the regulator, Invesco Perpetual was allowed to pick the date on which the sanction would be revealed. In a bid to inflict maximum damage on Woodford's new venture, the bosses in Henley decided the announcement should be made on 29 April, the day before Woodford was due to leave the business. The statement from the FCA gave no details about which Invesco Perpetual funds were involved, but the company's PR team briefed journalists that Woodford's Income and High Income funds were at the centre of the investigation. The timing of the announcement caused some SJP customers to question why their wealth manager was entrusting their savings with an investor whose funds had just been involved in the biggest fine in British retail investment. How could they be sure there would not be further trouble at Woodford's new business?

If Invesco Perpetual's executives felt they could derail the launch of Woodford IM with the timing of the FCA announcement, they had underestimated the level of adulation British investors had for the fund manager. Woodford's sales team began sounding out clients for his first retail product, the Equity Income fund, which was designed to follow an almost identical strategy to his Invesco Perpetual funds. Within days, money was pouring in. John Chatfeild-Roberts, the thoughtful chief investment officer of Jupiter, also ran the asset manager's multi-manager funds, which allocated money to a mix of underlying investment funds. He had been a fan of Woodford's since the mid-1990s and had passed plenty of investors' money his way over the years. He was one of the first to sign up to the new venture, pledging £500 million of Jupiter's clients' savings. Another old contact of Woodford's, Hargreaves Lansdown, was also among the first to back the new business. The group pledged £400 million from its in-house funds. In announcing the commitment, Lee Gardhouse, head of Hargreaves's multi-manager funds, gushed that Woodford was 'perhaps the best manager of his generation', adding:

> Over the long term I can think of no manager to whom I would rather entrust my money. [Woodford's] fund represents a rare opportunity to invest with a manager with an exemplary track record, in a new environment where he has 'skin in the game' – in other words, he has every incentive to perform.

While the multi-manager contracts were very well received, Craig Newman's sales team knew that, long term, the best way of drawing in Woodford's devotees was to woo financial advisory groups and get promoted on the fund supermarkets, with their armies of DIY investor customers. Simon Dale, Woodford's head of retail sales, was charged with putting together a gruelling roadshow of meetings and presentations, contacting hundreds of IFA businesses across the country. The three-week tour took in eight venues in seven different cities, including the Caledonian Hotel in Edinburgh, the Lowry Hotel in Manchester and the Eight Moorgate club in the City of London.

The salesmen found that the hype surrounding Woodford IM's launch meant they were pushing against open doors. The platforms and advisers were desperate to be able to offer their clients the new fund. With £54 billion of client assets, Cofunds – owned by the insurer Legal & General – was the biggest and one of the oldest fund supermarkets. It was the first to secure the new Woodford fund on its platform, agreeing to sell it for 0.75 per cent to its customers. In announcing the agreement, Cofunds' chief executive, David Hobbs, said the deal was of 'paramount importance' owing to the amount of interest in Woodford's new fund from advisers.

But Newman reserved the best deal for the punchy fund supermarket that was on its way to overtaking Cofunds as the country's biggest: Hargreaves Lansdown. Mark Dampier was not the only admirer of Woodford at the Bristol-based group. The Hargreaves marketing team understood that by getting the new Woodford fund on their platform they would be able to win even more customers from rivals. To give themselves a competitive edge, they negotiated a 0.6 per cent fee to be made available exclusively on their platform – cheaper than anywhere else on the market. Other brokers asked for the same discount but were told that it was available only if they could guarantee £500 million of business – and Hargreaves had already committed £400 million from its multi-manager funds. Though not a huge discount compared with what was offered on other platforms, the Hargreaves negotiators recognized the marketing potential of being able to provide the lowest fee on the hottest new fund on the market. After agreeing the fee, Hargreaves's marketing manager told Newman: 'You've done your bit – now leave the rest to us.' And they delivered in spades.

Hargreaves added Woodford's Equity Income fund straight to its much-followed Wealth 150 list of recommended funds. Hargreaves was giving the fund a ringing endorsement to its hundreds of thousands of customers who were making their own choices about where to invest. Trumpeting the deal, Dampier declared: 'Investors have access to a top-flight fund manager at a bargain price.' Hargreaves also published a series of adverts in the financial press with the tagline: 'Best Price Promise: Exclusive deal through Hargreaves Lansdown – reduced annual charge of just 0.6 per cent. You can't buy this fund at the same low price from any other broker.'

In one version of the advert, entitled 'Dare to be great', Peter Hargreaves, the company's blusterous co-founder, gave the fund a personal thumbs-up. 'Today Neil takes a brave step to start his own business,' he extolled. 'As we did over twenty years ago, we are backing his new venture. I will be investing at launch and I suggest investors consider doing the same.' In the same promotion, Dampier gave his endorsement: 'I have no hesitation in adding the fund to our Wealth 150 list of favoured funds, and will be investing my [self-invested personal pension], and my wife will be investing her ISA.'

'Hargreaves just saw this as a bonanza,' recalls someone involved in the discussions between Woodford IM and the broker. 'They were aggressive in their marketing because they knew they could attract new clients who were sitting on other platforms, using Neil Woodford as the lever.'

On 19 June, Equity Income launched with £1.6 billion already in the account, an extraordinary start and a record haul for a new British fund. Combined with the £3.7 billion from SJP, the new business had more than £5 billion under management within weeks of opening its doors. That meant it was already one of the top two dozen investment groups in the UK. To celebrate, Woodford IM held a party for two dozen financial journalists. The venue of Langan's Brasserie in Mayfair was well chosen, renowned as it was for hosting ritzy celebrity bashes over the years. Opened in 1976 as a partnership between Irish restaurateur Peter Langan, actor Michael Caine and Michelin-starred chef Richard Shepherd, the eatery had been a favourite haunt for the likes of Elizabeth Taylor, Mick Jagger, Elton John, Madonna, Muhammad Ali, Jack Nicholson and Rod Stewart. David Hockney had designed the menus. What better venue to host a party on behalf of the investment industry's glitziest rock star? During the wine-fuelled dinner in the upstairs function room, Woodford held court, fielding questions with off-the-cuff insights into the markets and his views on the biggest UK companies. At one point, he said he wanted to create a legacy with the new business that rivalled that of the legendary nineteenth-century financier John Pierpont Morgan, whose JPMorgan empire is still a dominant force in global banking.

In self-congratulatory mood, the Woodford IM team organized a party of their own. The twenty staff members flocked to the Crazy Bear in the Oxfordshire village of Stadhampton. The luxury boutique hotel provided the perfect setting to celebrate what on any measure had been an exceptional launch. Garish chandeliers hung between wooden beams, while a stuffed black bear looked on from the side of the bar. Outside, palm trees splayed over a lily-pad-strewn pond, as subtle lighting bathed the scene in a golden hue. Over the course of the evening, staff knocked back bottles of champagne and beer, while the night was finished off with several rounds of shots. 'Things got really out of control – people were absolutely hammered,' says one attendee. After several months of intense work getting the company approved by the regulator and bringing in billions of pounds of new business, the giddy sense of achievement was palpable.

While the launch party venues were lavish, the choice of location for Woodford IM's headquarters was anything but. The new business was based in a three-storey glass building in a sterile business park on the outskirts of Oxford. It overlooked a Premier Inn budget hotel and a David Lloyd gym. The site had previously been part of the huge Morris Motors factory and on the other side of the nearby Oxford ring road was the main assembly plant for Mini cars. The location was chosen partly to provide Woodford with a shorter commute to work from his Cotswolds estate and partly as a way of being close to the scientific start-up scene around Oxford University. In order to get the offices up and running on time, Newman had busied himself painting the interior, while the uncle of Stephen and Paul Lamacraft – the investment analysts poached from Invesco Perpetual – was drafted in to help build the staff kitchen.

The open-plan office housed several rows of desks, and at the far end was a pair of glass offices – one in each corner – for Woodford and Newman. Woodford's glass box was the archetypal fund manager's lair: a desk with three screens – two for his Bloomberg terminal, one for emails – a phone, a stack of research reports and a copy of that morning's *FT*, always well thumbed. Newman's office, meanwhile, looked more like it belonged to a television detective, with scribbled diagrams and sticky notes covering the partition walls. The other two founders, Nick Hamilton and Gray Smith, had smaller offices in the middle, where there were also desks for Woodford's and Newman's personal assistants. The out-of-town business park had a distinct lack of amenities – the sole pub was a downmarket Beefeater adjacent to the Premier Inn – so a barista-run coffee bar was set up in the reception area, which became the social gathering spot. Taking pride of place on the wall were eight framed sheets of A4 paper containing handwrit-ten notes and dotted with orange highlighter pen. This was the draft of Woodford's first investment portfolio. Meeting rooms were furnished with plush velvet armchairs, leather sofas and pineapple-shaped lamps, with contemporary art hanging on the walls. Dark-wood parquet flooring and low-slung lights gave the office a modern feel.

Woodford's daily routine began just after 5 a.m., when he would wake and shower before choosing which of his commuter cars – Porsche Cayenne, Audi R6 Avant, Range Rover or vintage Audi Quattro – he would use that day. After a forty-minute drive to the office and quick briefing from his head of trading, he would immerse himself in his portfolio before a day of meetings and intense monitoring of the information flowing across his three wide screens. He would typically stay in the office until 7 p.m. before driving home.

Newman had clearly been boning up on the latest management-theory publications while unemployed, not least the ones coming out of Silicon Valley. He wanted to create a relaxed working envir-onment with no dress code and no annual leave allocation – meaning staff were trusted to take what holiday time they needed without restrictions. Newman would wear jeans, trainers and a shirt in the office – adding a jacket for business meetings – while Woodford opted for his trademark jeans and a black tight-fitting sweatshirt. Newman embraced the jargon of tech entrepreneurs, describing the business as 'agile' and 'breaking down the barriers' to build a flatter hierarchical structure. Teams were tasked with working on 'projects'. To check their progress, rather than having regular meetings, staff would gather for twenty-minute 'scrumming' sessions of brisk updates.

Newman wanted to put technology at the heart of the company. From the beginning, the business used a new instant messaging system called Slack, which had been running for only a few months but would go on to be adopted by companies globally. It was used as the company's internal communication tool, allowing staff to be connected throughout the day, no matter their location. Despite being an instinctive technophobe, Woodford soon adapted to the new set-up and would often check in on Slack after 11 p.m., even on weekends. The use of technology allowed staff to work from home, which most – including Woodford – did from time to time. When Woodford was out of the office, he would phone in trades or email instructions to the trading desk, allowing him to manage his portfolio even when taking brisk Friday-morning horse rides. Over time, the business began developing a phone app that would make the process more efficient and without the need for traders to retype instructions into a Bloomberg terminal.

Digital technology was extended to all parts of office life. When guests arrived, they were required to sign in on an iPad, while every order made by staff – from lunchtime sandwiches to stock trades – was carried out through a system that created an audit trail. IT contractors developed a proprietary dashboard system that everyone in the company had access to, which allowed all parts of the business to keep up with what everyone else was doing. It had been designed with a traffic-light system so that any time risk increased in the investment portfolios or some part of the business came close to a compliance breach, staff would be alerted. 'Everybody in the office worked to support Neil. That was the point of the dashboard – it meant everyone was focused on helping Neil do his job and we all felt involved,' says one former employee.

Data from the dashboard were prominently displayed on large

blue screens at one end of the floor. It was all part of Newman's 'violent transparency' policy, which extended to communicating with IFAs and investors through the company's website, using blog posts and videos. The strategy was partly aimed at addressing widespread consumer dissatisfaction over investment groups with-holding information about how much clients were paying and what exactly they were investing in. The policy was initially well received by investors and the media, but, over time, the business would be less forthcoming about some of its more questionable practices.

The decision to list all holdings in investment portfolios was one aspect of the transparency drive. 'We strongly believe that all of our investors have the right to know where their money is invested, from the biggest holding in the fund to the smallest,' Newman said at the time. A few weeks after Equity Income's launch, Woodford IM published the complete list of its holdings – along with their weighting – on its website. It was a bold, unprecedented move for the new business, one that Newman hoped other fund managers would follow. On the day the details were made public, the com-pany's website was overwhelmed by the amount of interest and crashed. At one point, it received 155 requests a second from eager investors. That level of openness was hugely popular with invest-ors, but would it also prove to be an Achilles heel for the new business?

That first portfolio intentionally bore an uncanny resemblance to Woodford's former Invesco Perpetual funds. Woodford and New-man wanted to entice as many Invesco Perpetual customers to the new business as possible, so designed the fund to be a near replica. The top ten holdings were dominated by the blue-chip companies Woodford had become synonymous with: pharmaceuticals Astra-Zeneca, GlaxoSmithKline and Roche, cigarette makers British American Tobacco, Imperial Tobacco and Reynolds American, FTSE 100 stalwarts BT and Rolls-Royce, as well as two other busi-nesses that had long histories with Woodford: Imperial Innovations, the university spin-off group, and the outsourcer Capita. A quarter of the fund was invested in large, safe, dividend-paying healthcare stocks. This was the foundation upon which Woodford built a defensive, income-generating portfolio. To the outside world, Woodford was picking up exactly where he left off at Invesco Perpetual – investors who went with him were expecting a similar ride to his twenty-six years of market-trouncing returns in Henley. But there were signs Woodford was starting to change his approach.

The ten biggest holdings represented nearly half of the fund's assets, yet there were more than fifty other companies in the portfolio, many of which were titchy and unknown to all but the most connected corporate brokers. These were fledgling businesses that Woodford had invested in over the years, mostly centred on health-care and pharmaceuticals. At Invesco Perpetual they had been hidden from view as the company published only Woodford's top ten holdings, and while Woodford's interest in small businesses was occasionally mentioned by clued-up IFAs, the full extent of his commitment to such business was unknown until the full portfolio was published.

The largest twenty-five companies in the fund had an average market cap of £45 billion, while the other public companies – typically listed on the UK's junior AIM stock market – averaged just £1.5 billion. Among the smaller businesses was ReNeuron, the stem cell research company valued at just £58 million. Wood-ford's investment in the business made up 0.5 per cent of the Equity Income portfolio. Another tiny company, Oxford-based e-Therapeutics, had a market value of £79 million and also made up 0.5 per cent of the fund. There were also six unlisted companies, mainly at the smaller end of the portfolio, but Woodford told invest-ors in a video posted on the group's new website that he was on the lookout for more.

Equity Income had launched with a record haul of investor cash, but that was only the start. With the fund being heavily promoted by Hargreaves Lansdown and available on every notable platform, financial advisers flocked to it. The new business was also receiving unrelenting media coverage, prompting investors to pour in their life savings. For the first year, £250 million gushed in each month. Newman lavished bonuses totalling more than £1 million on his handful of sales staff. Will Deer and Simon Dale, the two team managers, were each given £350,000, while more junior members received £184,000 apiece.

Newman and Woodford also treated themselves. Woodford bought himself a Ferrari and, as an added perk, the carmaker let him visit its private test track in Maranello, northern Italy, to try out the model. Newman joined him on the jolly. The pair were pursuing a rock-star lifestyle their clients in Middle England could only dream about. The trip prompted some resentment from others on the team, however – particularly those who had missed out on the bonuses. 'It was a two- or three-day boys' trip at what was a pretty busy time,' recalls one former colleague. 'It was another "fuck you" moment to the rest of us.'

Woodford had carefully picked his initial portfolio, balancing the big Steady-Eddie stocks that would provide dependable dividends with a sprinkling of up-and-coming companies that had the potential for future growth. But as cash flooded in, Woodford was forced to find new ways of putting it to work. After more than quarter of a century of investing in reliable but unexciting blue-chip companies, he was getting bored of the same old businesses. He had not set up the new venture just to carry on as he had done for most of his career. He wanted a new challenge and to test himself on racier start-ups. He had finally cast off the shackles of working in Henley, with Invesco's interfering American bosses breathing down his neck. His name was now above the door, and if he wanted to plough more money into start-ups, he did not expect anyone to block him. If he backed the right ones, they would grow exponentially and he would not only produce blistering investment returns but also be eulogized for unearthing and funding the companies of the future. Having reached his mid-fifties, Woodford was thinking about his legacy. He already had a CBE – could a knighthood be in the offing?

When word got around the City that Woodford, whose great

fascination with science start-ups was widely known, was sitting on a growing pot of money, Oxford Business Park became the top destination for specialist brokers. Those who have known Woodford the longest describe a man who, behind the bluster and the bullying tactics he used to great effect on corporate boards and executives, is at heart very naive and trusting. 'He's easily manipulated,' remembers a former colleague. 'I felt sorry for Neil, because he was so easily taken in.' His keenness to invest in miracle cures and technology that could benefit humankind often made him too easily swayed by the weird and wonderful business plans put in front of him. His desire to play the munificent benefactor overrode his natural instincts to question where he was placing his investors' money.

Woodford's old contacts at brokerages such as Numis, Peel Hunt and Cenkos began making regular trips to the new company's offices, offering an eclectic mix of start-ups in need of funding. Seeing himself as the great saviour of British bioscience, and with a growing war chest to deploy, Woodford sprayed the cash around liberally. 'There was practically a queue of people around the block,' recalls one early employee of the business:

> Neil was very good on public company selections, when you're looking at documents that all have rules and regulations around them. But he applied the same thinking to private companies, where they would say, 'Next year, we're going to get this drug authorized and we'll make billions,' and he'd say, 'I'm in for that.' So, there was no due diligence done. Neil literally wanted to invest in everything that came in.

One of those involved in raising money for start-ups was Paul Pindar, the veteran chief executive of Capita, who had recently left the outsourcer. Having previously worked in private equity, Pindar was trying to establish a portfolio of chairmanships to see himself towards a lucrative retirement. He knew Woodford well, from the fund manager's long history as a big investor in Capita.

Pindar became a regular at Oxford Business Park, introducing new businesses to Woodford for him to invest in. One of the first was Purplebricks, a new online estate agency that tried to upend the property market by charging vendors a fixed fee of just £599 to help them sell their house. Pindar, who had already made a personal investment in the business, convinced Woodford to hand over £7 million from Equity Income for a 30 per cent stake in the company. Pindar would go on to join the Purplebricks board and become chairman. Another start-up he introduced Woodford to was online mattress maker Eve Sleep, of which Pindar was also made chairman. Both companies were hot internet ventures that attempted to disrupt traditional industries – exactly the sort of business Woodford had steered clear of during the dotcom boom. They both got off to a flying start, but within a couple of years of going public they struggled badly.

Woodford's largesse when it came to doling out money to up-and-coming businesses began to create tension within the new office. While Woodford chose the investments, it was the job of his three investment analysts – Stephen and Paul Lamacraft plus Saku Saha – to carry out rigorous assessments of the companies and put them through their paces. Saha concentrated on private businesses. Once due diligence had been carried out, any private investments needed to be signed off by Gray Smith, the company's head of legal and compliance. Smith became increasingly concerned by the volume of requests for unquoted investments coming through. He also had misgivings about how thoroughly the analysts were vetting them. This led to heated discussions between Smith and Woodford, who hated having his investment methods tampered with.

Tension came to a head over one company in particular. Evofem was a US bioscience business that made products for women's sexual and reproductive health. Woodford had invested heavily in Evofem while at Invesco Perpetual and wanted to do so again. His former colleagues in Henley, who were less enamoured with the business, were only too happy to sell him the stake, but it would cost Woodford $250 million. Smith baulked at the price and asked to see what due diligence had been carried out. Dissatisfied by what the analysts presented, Smith went on to ask where the notes were from trips made to Evofem's San Diego headquarters – but was shocked to discover no one had been to see the premises in person despite promising to commit $250 million of investors' money to the business.

A row ensued between Woodford and his investment team, who believed the lawyer was needlessly meddling, and Smith, who dug his heels in. Eventually they reached a compromise whereby Smith and Saha would travel to San Diego to assess the operation. When they got there, an Evofem executive told them over beers that he had met Woodford twice in London, where he had told the fund manager about his business, and Woodford seemed keen to invest. But while the executive was waiting for a follow-up round of in-depth questions, the money from Invesco Perpetual came flowing through without any due diligence process taking place. It was the easiest money he had ever raised. Smith's exasperation hit new heights.

Unquoted holdings aside, Equity Income got off to a strong start in a tricky market, returning 3.3 per cent in its first four months. That made it the best performer among the eighty-eight funds in its peer group, which on average lost 2.7 per cent over the same period. But in a sign of things to come, the fund missed its target on its very first quarterly dividend payment, shelling out 0.8p per share compared to the 1p it had promised investors. While not a complete disaster, it was a worrying omen for Woodford, who had built a reputation on consistently providing investors with a regular stream of healthy dividends over twenty-five-years. Yet few investors seemed to care as the fund continued to bloat, swelling to £3 billion.

It was around this time that Woodford's loyal disciple Mark Dampier of Hargreaves Lansdown made his first pilgrimage to Oxford Business Park. In his *Independent* column, Dampier gushingly reported back on his meeting with Woodford and his analysts, where they discussed the 'number of exciting opportunities' they had uncovered at the small and unquoted end of the market:

> [I]t is clear Mr Woodford is confident in the exciting, young companies in which he has invested. Given time, capital and patience, these businesses could grow into global players of the future. In my view, this is an extremely attractive proposition when combined with companies already paying a healthy yield with good visibility of earnings. I consider this to be a core UK equity income fund for investors who can truly think long term.

Woodford continued to load up on start-ups, and by this point the number of private businesses in his portfolio had moved into double figures. Combined, they made up just over 5 per cent of the portfolio. Most were early stage healthcare companies, such as Emba and Viamet, along with the odd few businesses like semiconductor maker Spin Memory and rural broadband provider Gigaclear. Another, Propelair, designed water-saving toilet systems. It raised £2.6 million, with £2 million coming from Woodford.

Responding to Dampier's glowing dispatch from Oxford Business Park, Woodford wrote a comment piece to be prominently displayed on the Hargreaves Lansdown website, where he extolled the virtues of investing in start-ups. 'This part of the market is unloved and undervalued and, consequently, I believe it represents an area of huge untapped potential,' he wrote. 'The risks are higher than in the more mainstream investment universe, but when adjusted for these additional risks, the potential rewards look extremely attractive.'

Woodford told colleagues he intended to raise the unquoted portion to between 7 per cent and 10 per cent of the portfolio. But this was met with resistance from Gray Smith and Nick Hamilton, two of the founding partners, who were increasingly coming into confrontation with Woodford and his sidekick Newman. Smith and Hamilton were anxious about what they saw as a deeply flawed due diligence process within Woodford's investment team. The analysts relied on forecasts provided by the companies that were trying to attract capital. They then put the data into a standard template, which was sent to Duff & Phelps, a consultancy that provided independent valuations for Woodford. Duff & Phelps would send back a series of potential values for the company based on the data received, and Woodford's investment team would then pick the middle of the range.

Smith and Hamilton argued that the analysts were accepting the numbers provided by the companies in blind faith without scrutinizing them sufficiently. They called for a limit on unquoted holdings in the fund that was much lower than the 10 per cent defined by European investment rules, commonly known as the trash ratio. But Newman and Woodford pushed back vehemently. For Woodford, this felt like history repeating itself after Invesco Perpetual's bosses had tried to restrict his investments in unquoted companies. It touched a nerve. Meanwhile, Newman's aggressive bullying tactics, known so well to his former sales staff in Henley, reared their head once again. Smith and Hamilton were in his crosshairs.

'This is not a fucking control environment. This is about giving Neil the freedom he did not have at Invesco,' Newman yelled at them during one explosive encounter. In long, tense meetings between the four founders, viewed by staff through the internal glass walls, Newman would pace around gesticulating and shouting obscenities. While these arguments blazed, Woodford would simmer in silence, turning the bezel on his chunky watch.

Despite their agreement from the outset – and the plan outlined to the regulator as part of the business application – Smith and Hamilton had never been given equity in the business, which was carved up between Newman and Woodford. Newman had needed the cover of Smith's legal experience and Hamilton's operational background to get the application signed off by the regulator. Without them, he would never have been allowed to set up an investment business, given his lack of senior management experience or regulatory knowhow. Smith and Hamilton had served their purpose in giving the new business a veneer of respectability to the FCA and clients, but now the company had started with a roaring success, they were surplus to requirements. Newman saw them merely as costly expenses that could be stripped out. With relations between the four founders at their lowest, Newman set about trying to find ways of ousting them from the business.

Smith and Hamilton already had serious concerns about the way the business was being run and the long-term threat to it of Woodford's obsession with investing in start-ups. When they grasped the extent to which Newman wanted them gone – and realizing they would never be made equity partners – they decided to leave of their own accord. Both resigned in December 2014 – just over six months after the company's heady inauguration. The FCA's ears pricked up at such high-profile departures so soon after the launch of the business. It requested the pair come in to explain why they were leaving and provide a full run-down of the state of the company from the inside, which they did. But despite their accounts, the regulator did nothing. This was the first of many red flags the regulator failed to act on.

With Smith and Hamilton out of the picture, Woodford found little resistance to investing in small businesses that he believed had the power to change the world. With fewer restraints in place, his choices grew more eccentric. He was seduced by silver-tongued brokers offering start-ups with remedies to incurable diseases or solutions to environmental catastrophes. The epitome of his hare-brained investments was Industrial Heat, a North Carolina venture based on ideas at the fringes of mainstream science. The company had been launched in 2012 by Thomas Darden, a businessman who had previously worked in brickmaking and cleaning up contaminated industrial sites. He had been approached by researchers into cold fusion, a theory of producing near limitless nuclear energy at low temperatures. The concept had been debunked in the 1980s and was widely ridiculed by scientists. Darden later admitted that he had initially seen cold fusion as 'pathological science', where believers saw what they wanted to see. But over time he became a convert.

Darden struck a deal with a controversial Italian entrepreneur named Andrea Rossi, who claimed to have invented a cold fusion reactor, which he called Energy Catalyzer or E-Cat. It was the agreement for Industrial Heat to license and commercialize Rossi's invention that convinced Woodford and his analysts to back Darden's company. This was even though Rossi's claims for E-Cat had never been independently verified. The business had already attracted investment from the actor Brad Pitt, and would later sign up Laurene Powell Jobs, the widow of Apple founder Steve Jobs, as another financial backer. But unlike these celebrity investors, who committed just a few million dollars each, Woodford was convinced enough to hand over £54 million of his clients' savings. Woodford would eventually own a quarter of the business. If ever there was a sign that Woodford was developing a hero complex, it was his investment in Industrial Heat.

After the investment was made, a PhD physics student who had an interest in working as a researcher in the investment industry set up a meeting with Saku Saha, the analyst responsible for assessing unquoted companies Woodford wanted to plough money into. The get-together was arranged through a mutual acquaintance as a way of providing the student with an insight into what life was like working for an asset management company. After a broad chat about the demands of the role, the student began asking about the fund's science-based holdings. When he heard about the large investment in Industrial Heat in a field of physics he viewed as bunkum, he was taken aback. He delicately tried to explain his distrust of cold fusion, but Saha dismissed his concerns out of hand. Woodford's chief analyst of private companies – who had no formal science qualifications – would not be told about the credibility of the companies he had signed off on by a mere PhD student.

With Woodford's growing thirst for backing early stage science companies showing no signs of being quenched, the business set about plans to launch a dedicated vehicle for his more outlandish investments. From the very beginning, the four Woodford IM founders had discussed setting up a fund that would allow

Woodford to indulge in his passion. Indeed, the leaked documents submitted to the FCA show that the founders had at one time contemplated launching a fund for private holdings from the outset, but these plans had been put on ice owing to the complexity of setting up more than one vehicle at a time. Launching Equity Income and preparing to manage multi-billion-pound mandates for the likes of SJP were prioritized as they brought in revenue from the start.

But, given that EU rules restricted funds aimed at retail investors to holding only 10 per cent of the portfolio in unquoted shares, a different structure was required. The plan was to launch an investment trust, which would be listed on the stock market and run as a separate company with its own board of directors. These products had been a mainstay of the British market since 1868, and the earliest funds were the world's first collective investment schemes. Investors committed capital from the outset and were given listed shares in the trust, which they could buy and sell freely on the stock exchange. The legal structure allowed Woodford to invest in as many unlisted companies as he wished, as there were not the same pressures on selling assets if investors fled, known as liquidity risk. Another advantage of the investment trust structure was that it allowed Woodford to borrow money, known as leverage, to help juice returns. This was not possible in more mainstream retail funds. 'The only reason to [launch the trust] was to satisfy Neil's desire. It's his guilty pleasure to do these unquoteds, to be the big man,' says someone close to the business. 'This is Neil believing a story, getting his big, strong fists, and going, "Right, I am doing this to you. I've got a massive chequebook. £250 million, done. Make it happen." It's just ego. It's a terrible male weakness as we get older.'

The new fund, known as Woodford Patient Capital Trust, was planned to float in April 2015 and expected to raise £200 million in its initial public offering. In another attempt to disrupt the fund management industry, Woodford and Newman decided that, unlike most funds, the trust would not charge investors based on a percentage of the fund's assets. Instead, it would charge a performance fee, but only if it returned more than 10 per cent a year. They hoped that if the companies were as successful as Woodford expected, the fund would explode in value over time and the pair would later reap the rewards. The fund was designed to invest in between fifty and a hundred stocks, with three-quarters being early stage companies, some of which Woodford already invested in through Equity Income. The rest would be large, mature companies that would provide enough dividend income to meet the fund's running costs. 'I've been investing in early stage businesses for the best part of twenty years and unquoted businesses for ten years, and I've learned a hell of a lot. What became very clear is that we have an amazing untapped opportunity here,' Woodford told the *FT* when announcing the new fund. 'Britain has a record of great innovation and invention, but we haven't been good at turning this into commercial success for the economy.'

Woodford's orbit proved so strong that by the time of the IPO, the investment trust attracted £864 million in commitments, which was scaled down to £800 million. It was Britain's biggest ever investment trust launch – yet another record for the superstar stock picker. Because of the huge overdemand for the fund, within days of its flotation its stock market value exceeded the value of its underlying holdings by 15 per cent – a rare premium for investment trusts, which typically trade at a discount.

The trust required a board of independent directors to monitor the fund and ensure it was being run by the portfolio manager in its investors' best interests. For those roles, Woodford picked a coterie of his closest contacts, whose businesses he had backed heavily. Susan Searle was chosen as chair. The silver-haired technology enthusiast had known Woodford for years, having co-founded a university spin-off group with connections to Oxford, Cambridge and Imperial College London that the fund manager had invested in. She was also on the board of several other companies in which Woodford held stakes. The other board members were Steven Harris, chief executive of Circassia Pharmaceuticals, Scott Brown, chief executive of battery producers Nexeon, and Louise Makin, chief executive of BTG Management Services – all companies Woodford backed. The set-up was rife with potential conflicts of interest. The board was supposed to be independent and responsible for holding Woodford to account, but he held sway over them by being one of the biggest shareholders in their businesses. Could they be trusted to keep him in line when their companies depended on him for financial support?

In June 2015 Equity Income celebrated its first anniversary. Since its launch it had walloped the market with a 19.6 per cent return including dividends, compared to a 13.3 per cent return for Woodford's former Income fund at Invesco Perpetual and 6.5 per cent for the FTSE All-Share index. To mark the occasion, Woodford gave an interview to the BBC, which dubbed him 'Britain's very own Warren Buffett' and 'the man who can't stop making money'. During the interview, Woodford was asked which personal qualities he believed made a good fund manager. 'I would suggest that a healthy balance between arrogance and humility is helpful,' he replied, displaying one more than the other. Bloomberg would later dub Woodford the 'Oracle of Oxford', mirroring Buffett's own nickname of the 'Oracle of Omaha'.

Though the top-line performance figures were undoubtedly impressive, under the bonnet something strange was going on in the portfolio. Several of Woodford's long-term favourite blue-chip stocks, which had proved so reliable over the years, were suffering. Rolls-Royce, one of the fund's ten biggest holdings, took a tumble after reporting less than impressive results, while Babcock, the engineering group, had been hit by a market sell-off after it warned it would be especially vulnerable if Scotland voted for independence in the 2014 referendum. Meanwhile, the portfolio appeared to be enjoying a small-cap bounce, as a handful of previously unknown businesses shot up in value, pulling the performance of the overall fund with them. Small companies accounted for 15 per cent of the portfolio, but 40 per cent of the outperformance.

Among the big winners was Prothena, an Irish biotechnology company that aimed to develop treatments for rare diseases, which returned 249 per cent in one year, contributing 2.3 percentage points of outperformance to the portfolio. Another business that underwent a spectacular growth spurt was Allied Minds, an intellectual property business with links to top US universities and the defence industry. The company floated on the London stock exchange at the same time that Equity Income launched, and Woodford was one of the first to invest. Over the course of its first year its value soared more than 200 per cent. Several other former private companies that Woodford invested in had breakneck starts on the stock market, including RM2, which made high-tech shipping pallets, and Xeros, a company dedicated to reducing water usage in the textiles industry.

But the biggest contributor to Equity Income's outperformance in the first year was a piddling private business called Stratified Medical, which would later be rebranded as Benevolent AI. Stratified Medical trained powerful computers to sift through data from medical trials to identify discoveries that would treat conditions such as Alzheimer's disease. Woodford initially invested £40 million in the business on a valuation of £190 million. Later, he joined a handful of US investors in a subsequent round that raised just £6.7 million, but which gave the company a valuation of £1.2 billion, more than six times its perceived worth just a few months earlier. The mark-up meant that Stratified Medical, a business with just twenty-three staff and turnover of £1.2 million, made a bigger contribution to the outperformance of Equity Income in its first year than a host of global corporations, including AstraZeneca, GlaxoSmithKline and BT. Either Woodford had a sixth sense for picking companies of the future, or the hundreds of thousands of armchair investors who had entrusted him with their life savings were in for a very rude awakening.

9

Liquidity Trap

In autumn 2016 more than two dozen founders and chief executives of small British businesses received a curious invitation with an intriguing sign-off: 'We very much hope you can attend but please be aware that this event is highly confidential and by invitation only.' The email came from Neil Woodford, the rock-star fund manager with whom the recipients were very well acquainted. Nearly all ran science-based businesses that depended on Woodford's largesse to survive. For many, he was their largest shareholder. He was inviting them to Saïd Business School, part of Oxford University, for an afternoon's discussion with two of Britain's most powerful public officials – Sir Jeremy Heywood, the cabinet secretary who ran the civil service, and Gareth Davies, director general of business and science at the Department for Business, Energy and Industrial Strategy. Among the attendees at the top-secret event were the chief executives of Oxford Nanopore, IP Group and Imperial Innovations, as well as Sir John Bell, Regius professor of medicine at Oxford University and an adviser to former prime minister David Cameron.

Woodford had been courting Heywood for several years and had arranged the gathering as a way of showing off what he believed to be the best of Britain's young tech companies. He wanted to convince the influential mandarins to push for more political support for start-ups. 'We want Jeremy to get a sense of the quality and depth of British science being developed at our universities, to better understand the challenges early stage businesses face on the road to scaled success, and finally to learn how the government could do more to help grow and develop Britain's knowledge economy,' the invitation read.

The event was a great success. Just two weeks later, on 21 November, prime minister Theresa May announced the launch of a Treasury-led review to identify how best the government could help fledgling companies raise money. In a sign of the influence Woodford had over the review, not only was he named on the contributing panel, but also the title of the review was lifted from his recently launched investment trust: Patient Capital. Two days later, during his autumn statement, chancellor Philip Hammond announced a £400 million investment in British venture capital funds as part of an effort to tackle the 'long-standing problem of our fastest growing technology firms being snapped up by bigger companies, rather than growing to scale'. The speech could have been written by Woodford himself. The transformation of Woodford from blue-chip investing guru to champion of start-ups was complete. He was now both a force to be reckoned with in FTSE 100 boardrooms and also helping mould government policy to support a new British economy of research-led businesses. Woodford's legacy was taking shape.

In its short life, Woodford Investment Management had become one of the dominant names in the UK's investment industry. By the end of 2015, Equity Income had swollen to £8.2 billion, making it one of Britain's biggest funds, despite having been in existence for only just over eighteen months. The close relationship with Hargreaves Lansdown – and its ferocious marketing machine – had been crucial to that growth, with close to 40 per cent of assets in the fund coming from the broker's clients.

But the twelve months since Nick Hamilton and Gray Smith had left the business had not been plain sailing. Craig Newman struggled to appoint a long-term successor to fill Hamilton's joint role as head of both compliance and risk. The functions were split, with the new risk manager lasting barely nine months, while the head of compliance was replaced after a couple of years. A succession of contractors was used to carry out compliance roles on different projects as the business grew. The result was a lack of a strong personality internally to hold Woodford and Newman to account. Was that by accident or design?

In late 2015 the group also suffered its first significant rupture from an investment in a small business. Woodford had committed $180 million for a 28 per cent stake in a US biotech company called Northwest Biotherapeutics. He invested in the Maryland-based business, which specialized in cancer treatments, through both Equity Income and Patient Capital. Little was known about the business in the UK, but a rudimentary Google search would have shown a string of stories from US news outlets raising concerns about its business practices. In October 2015 an anonymous research report appeared online that alleged inappropriate financial dealing between companies owned by Northwest's chief executive, Linda Powers. She denied the allegations, but it was not enough to prevent a spectacular market sell-off. In the months that followed, the share price came crashing down more than 90 per cent, wiping out most of Woodford's investment in the business. For the first time, financial advisers began to question whether the due diligence carried out by Woodford's team was up to scratch.

The failure of the Northwest investment and a handful of other early stage companies caused Patient Capital to lose 11.8 per cent in its first year, meaning Woodford IM was not paid for running the fund as it had not achieved its 10 per cent target return. The board had considered issuing new shares in the trust, but after the tough first year and sensing it would be difficult to raise further capital, they shelved the plans. The trust's share price shrank to a discount to its net asset value, meaning investors were sceptical about the quality of the underlying holdings.

Woodford was soon hit by the implosion of another of his prized companies. Circassia, an Oxford-based business that was one of the leading lights of the UK's bioscience scene, had listed a few weeks before Woodford launched his new business in 2014. Valued at £581 million, it was the biggest float of a British biotech company for decades. The business specialized in asthma and anti-allergy treatments and was backed by Imperial Innovations, one of Woodford's favoured university spin-off groups. Woodford did not need much convincing to buy a 21 per cent stake in Circassia, and for two years it seemed like a respectable bet on a company with huge potential. But all that changed in June 2016 when the business was forced to announce to the stock market that tests of a cat-allergy drug it had been developing – and which analysts expected to be the company's first big commercial success – proved just as effective as the placebo. Within hours, Circassia's share price plunged more than two-thirds and Woodford's investors were yet again nursing heavy paper losses. But Woodford brushed off the failures and continued to invest in risky start-ups, hoping to pick one or two that would take off and overshadow the rest.

Despite such setbacks, Woodford remained Britain's best-known and most-followed fund manager. His legion of devotees included some unexpected recruits. One such fan was Lacey Banghard, a glamour model best known for appearing topless on Page 3 of the *Sun* and as a contestant on *Celebrity Big Brother*. She entered a *Sun* share-tipping contest, choosing a portfolio of 'sin stocks' that was heavily influenced by Woodford's own choices, including British American Tobacco, Imperial Tobacco and Diageo, the maker of Guinness. On hearing that over a twelve-month period her picks had outperformed Woodford's own fund, Banghard told the *Sun*: 'Neil should give me a call. We should go for lunch. I might be able to give him some advice.' In his reply via *The Times*'s City gossip column, Woodford skirted the offer of lunch, but added: 'She's more than free to send in her new business plans for us to review.'

The issue dominating the national debate at the time was the run-up to the British referendum on whether to leave the EU. Woodford was careful not to voice his own opinion on the matter, but being a staunch supporter of British business – and having fought interference from foreign players in the companies he invested in – he believed there were opportunities for the UK in branching out alone. Just as in the dotcom bubble and the run-up to the financial crisis, Woodford again found himself at odds with the mainstream business thinking on the issue of the day. Bosses of the largest British businesses queued up to warn of the disastrous consequences of leaving the bloc. It was the contrarian position in which Woodford felt most at home. He commissioned think-tank Capital Economics to write a research report looking into the economic consequences of leaving the EU, which he published in the months leading up to the vote. In it, the consultants argued that, while there was a chance that Brexit could have a slight negative impact on growth and jobs, it was more probable that the outcome would be modestly positive.

Just hours after Britain's historic vote to leave the EU in June 2016, Woodford wrote to his investors, seeking to calm their nerves. 'My job is to peer through this short-term uncertainty and focus on the long-term fundamentals of the economy and the businesses in which we invest,' he reassured in a blog on the company's website. 'In the longer term, it is my view that the trajectory of the UK economy and, more importantly, the world economy, will not be influenced significantly by today's outcome.' Over the following months, Woodford became increasingly bullish about Brexit, believing that the naysayers would be proved wrong and that companies undervalued by the market would surge once details of the divorce were finalized. He would talk about vast pools of foreign money waiting to flood UK businesses as soon as certainty returned.

With their company enjoying a warm reception from the media, Newman and Woodford made several changes to how it was run. They wanted to show how they were ripping up the old ways of doing business. First, they announced that clients would no longer be charged for the research Woodford's investment team used. For several years, consumer rights campaigners had complained that fund managers paid for pricey analyst notes out of the money in the funds, meaning investment returns for the end investor were diminished. Across the industry, billions of pounds' worth of investment bank research was being deducted from the returns passed on to clients. Campaigners argued fund managers were not incentivized to be selective about what research they used as they were not the ones paying for it. There was little transparency over the amount of money each fund spent on research, so investors had no idea how much it affected their returns. The industry was also rife with opaque deals where brokers provided research for free in return for fund managers using their trading services. Newman announced to the press that his company would shoulder the costs of research. The move was welcomed by consumer advocates, who called on other fund managers to follow the lead.

Newman and Woodford's next announcement appeared even more radical. To the consternation of fund managers across the City, they revealed they were scrapping bonuses completely within their business. Lucrative financial rewards were regarded as sacrosanct within the investment industry, with incentive schemes making up the largest part of the pay packet for many of those who worked in it. The general consensus was that, without bonuses, it was impossible to motivate and keep hold of staff. But instead Newman and Woodford decided to raise staff salaries and remove their discretionary pay, in a move that was cost neutral for the business. When explaining the move to *The Times*, Newman said: 'While bonuses are an established feature of the financial sector, Neil and I wanted to take the opportunity to do something different that supports the firm's culture and ethos of challenging the status quo.' A pay consultant quoted in the same article expressed her shock at the decision. 'I've never come across anything like this,' she said. 'It's very unusual. Banks and fund managers have been working to make their incentive systems work better, but I don't know of anyone scrapping them altogether.'

Woodford took his crusade against excessive executive pay a step further. He joined forces with Paul Myners, the former City minister and one-time chairman of Marks & Spencer, in pressing the government to introduce a series of reforms to curb big pay deals. They included mandatory disclosure of the pay ratio between chief executives and their median workers, and an annual binding shareholder vote on executive pay. They also called for committees to be set up comprising a company's five biggest shareholders plus an employee to ratify pay policy and packages. The proposals won the backing of the High Pay Centre, a research group that lobbies against excessive rewards.

But behind the scenes, staff at Oxford Business Park had other ideas about why bonuses were discarded. They believed that Newman expected the company to continue to grow exponentially, scooping up billions of pounds each year. He did not want to share the spoils with the rest of the employees, and so set staff pay at a fixed level so that when the business grew, he and Woodford could reap all the increased profits for themselves. 'Craig's entirely money motivated – he wanted to milk that business for all it was worth,' says one former employee. Woodford and Newman continued to own the entire company between them, having scrapped their original idea of offering equity in the business as an incentive to attract and retain staff. Not that the company's senior workers were too upset about the change in pay structure. Even though they had their bonuses removed, they were still paid well, especially as they did not have to commute in and out of London every day. They had little incentive to move elsewhere.

That year's accounts for the business revealed Woodford's and Newman's true feelings towards lavish pay deals. The company turned £35.5 million of profit in its second year, of which Woodford and Newman siphoned a third off into their personal bank accounts. Woodford drew the lion's share, taking home £7.2 million, while Newman picked up £3.9 million. The rest of the thirty or so full-time staff members took home £5.2 million between them, averaging just over £170,000 each. Curbing excessive pay was an issue for other companies to worry about – not, it appeared, for those sitting in the corner offices at Woodford Investment Management.

Woodford's and Newman's bountiful payouts inversely correlated with their clients' experience of investing in their funds. For the 2016 calendar year, Equity Income – which by then was close to £10 billion in size – returned just 3.2 per cent, compared to 16.8 per cent for the FTSE All-Share index. It was the first period in which the fund underperformed the market and one of the few dud years in Woodford's CV to that point. For the first time since Woodford set the business up, his army of followers would have been better off placing their savings in a simple tracker fund that merely mimicked the index for a fraction of the fee, rather than entrusting their money with the lionized fund manager. Patient Capital also trailed the market, and Woodford was on track to mark another year of failing to meet his performance targets.

Equity Income's underperformance reflected the way Woodford managed the portfolio. He increasingly favoured early stage healthcare ventures, selling off his holdings in large stable companies to buy more unquoted and small listed businesses. By the end of 2016, 40 per cent of his portfolio was in healthcare, though such companies made up less than 10 per cent of the FTSE All-Share index. He had avoided investing in mining and oil companies, whose stocks soared throughout the year. The proportion of unlisted and listed speculative stocks in the portfolio had doubled to 35 per cent since the fund launched, while the share of conservative holdings halved to 25 per cent. The fund looked less like a basket of undervalued profitable companies, as Woodford's earlier Invesco Perpetual funds had, and more like a concentrated bet on risky healthcare businesses. Yet despite the poor performance, investors continued to direct their savings to Oxford. Woodford IM was the sixth best-selling UK fund manager in 2016.

Woodford's big commitment to unlisted businesses soon caught the eye of the regulator. The FCA carried out a series of workshops with twenty investment groups in late 2016 and early 2017, trying to get a better understanding of how fund managers treated hard-to-value assets. During a meeting with representatives from Woodford IM in November, the regulator became alarmed at the valuation process taking place within the business. 'At that time Woodford Investment Management was also the valuer of the fund, so it was acting in several roles,' the regulator's chief executive, Andrew Bailey, later told the UK Parliament's Treasury Select Committee. Although Duff & Phelps, the company employed to advise on valuations, was an external one, it was relying on information given to it by Woodford's investment analysts and reported directly to the investment company, which paid its fee. This created yet more conflicts of interest. When the FCA found out, it informed Capita, the fund's authorized corporate director. 'We cannot have that. You have to appoint an independent valuer,' as Bailey later told it. 'We are not comfortable with this.' The FCA required the valuation process to be carried out by Capita as a third party, with the assistance of Duff & Phelps, to take away the responsibility from Woodford's own analysts. The watchdog was bewildered that Capita had failed to spot and rectify this clear conflict of interest without being told to do so.

The regulator's intervention was yet another example of interfering busybodies meddling with the way Woodford wanted to run his business and his investment portfolio, as he saw it. He vented his spleen a few weeks later while appearing as a star witness at the House of Lords Science and Technology Select Committee. He was asked about what held back investment in early stage British companies. He groused:

> The problem that we have had in the past is that the regulator has a great focus on liquidity in retail funds and on the valuation of hard-to-value securities. If a company is not quoted and its share price is not established in a market, it is hard, although not impossible, to arrive at an acceptable value that you can carry in a fund that retail investors are investing in . . . It is really about approach and the tone of voice used by the regulator when it engages with the companies that are investing, as I am, in such businesses. If the tone of voice were to change, I think there would be less disincentive to invest in these things.

Woodford's patience with the FCA was wearing thin. Perhaps next time he did not need to be as open with the regulator about his dealings with unquoted companies.

A month later, Woodford IM launched a new equity fund that was aimed at savers close to retirement. Income Focus was designed to be less risky than Equity Income and would not invest in unquoted holdings. But it still held lots of the same public companies Woodford favoured, including many small, recently listed businesses. It was set up to provide a steady stream of dividend payments to investors, which Equity Income had struggled to do. When the new fund opened for business in April 2017, it had attracted £553 million. That made it one of the biggest launches in UK history – but less than a third of the haul raised by Equity Income when it came to the market. The older sibling had recently tipped over the £10 billion mark. The new money flooding in helped Woodford IM's assets surge to just shy of £18 billion in June 2017, an astounding achievement for a business just three years old. It was more than half the money Woodford managed when he left Invesco Perpetual. Woodford and Newman treated themselves to £12.7 million in dividends for six months' work, with Woodford taking £8.3 million and Newman £4.4 million. Sources close to the company say the pair took out around £25 million in total for the full twelve months.

With his business booming, and the prospect of many more years of bumper dividends to come, Woodford began to think about the future. He was nearing sixty and had accumulated enough personal wealth for several generations to thrive. Two decades earlier, Martyn Arbib had faced a similar decision and chose to cash in on Perpetual, but Woodford had other ideas. He still had the energy to keep going for many years and was enjoying the freedom to invest in edgy start-ups. SJP had also started thinking about what the business would look like if Woodford left. David Lamb, the head of SJP's investment committee who lived in the next village over from Woodford, met up with the fund manager for dinner and a few pints in a local pub. Lamb wanted to know about Woodford's long-term plan for the business and whether he had identified anyone who would eventually take it on. Had he considered selling it or bringing in up-and-coming managers to take over? But Lamb was taken aback when Woodford told him that, when he did eventually finish, he would close the business and return all money to his clients. It was an exit strategy more common among hedge-fund and private-equity managers than retail investment groups. It showed Woodford was already planning for his glorious exit from the world of investing. Unfortunately for Woodford, his ultimate legacy would be far from celebrated.

June 2017 proved to be the business's peak. In the months that followed, Woodford's portfolio was torched from all angles as several of his cherished companies self-combusted. It was a summer from hell for Woodford and his hundreds of thousands of loyal followers. How did such a glittering career unravel so quickly?

First AstraZeneca, Equity Income's largest holding, suffered a 16 per cent drop in its share price after it reported a lung-cancer drug with huge potential had failed a crucial clinical trial. It was the pharmaceutical giant's largest ever one-day fall. The plunge wiped £128 million from Woodford's flagship fund. More bad news followed as another big Woodford holding, roadside rescuer the AA, sacked its executive chairman for misconduct after a drunken brawl, sending its shares lower. Next, the US Food and Drug Administration announced it would cut the amount of nicotine in cigarettes, which caused a 10 per cent drop in the share price of Imperial Tobacco, the second biggest holding in Equity Income.

Then came turmoil at Provident Financial, the doorstep lender in which Woodford owned a 19 per cent stake. When the stock market opened on 22 August, the Bradford-based business delivered a quadruple whammy. It announced a second profits warning in three months, said it was suspending its dividends, disclosed it was under investigation by the FCA and revealed its chief executive had resigned. Within minutes its share price nosedived 66 per cent. It was one of the biggest one-day falls of any company in the history of the FTSE 100. The Provvy, as it was known, had been the fourth biggest holding in Equity Income, making up 4 per cent of the fund, and was also held in Woodford's other funds. Worse, Woodford later admitted he increased his holding in the lender after its initial profit warning earlier in the year, having expected the share price to recover. Later that same day, Allied Minds, the US intellectual property business that focused on university and military research, revealed its half-year profits were worse than expected, sending the already depressed shares even lower.

Other companies Woodford invested in also had a tumultuous time – including outsourcer Capita and Touchstone Innovations, the university spin-off group formerly known as Imperial Innovations – with several losing more than a third of their value. Meanwhile, several small companies in which Woodford held big stakes were pulverized. Pharmaceutical group 4D Pharma lost more than half its market value over twelve months, while the pallet maker RM2, Sphere Medical, a Cambridge-based biotech business, and Halo-Source, a clean water company, all fell by more than three-quarters.

By the end of the summer, Equity Income was the worst performing UK equity income fund for the previous twelve months and the only one to have made a loss over that period. It was a stark reversal of fortunes for a fund that for most of its short existence had led the pack. Those brutal few months proved to be a pivotal point in the fortunes of Woodford Investment Management, as well as for its superstar stock picker.

The horrendous performance of some of Woodford's biggest holdings began to cause the fund manager sleepless nights. Despite his advocacy of the long-term outlook, he soon became concerned when things went wrong and the businesses he backed imploded. In a candid interview with trade title *Citywire*, Woodford revealed that, for all his bluster, he had a soft underbelly:

> I still am affected by the day-to-day slings and arrows of the market and the criticism that comes with [it]. I'm not immune to it. Of course it frustrates me. Often because it is ill-informed and it is so short term . . . If you have been in this game as long as I have, to some extent it's water off a duck's back. But I sort of worry a bit more about some of the young companies we've invested in . . . That's where it can do real damage if it's not well thought through

and well-founded criticism. So, I'm not immune to it, it does sort of hurt, I have to say, it hurts.

Woodford began to see the parlous state of his funds as a repeat of the trickiest point of his career up to that point – the late stages of the dotcom bubble. Just as he had survived that period without changing course, he believed he could ride out the storm again with his reputation intact. Having beaten the market for most of the past twenty-five years, Woodford had reached peak hubris. He believed the hype that he possessed a Midas touch. Yet not all his followers were as convinced. Investors began submitting pointed questions to Woodford IM's website, which were grouped in a section called the Awkward Corner, including 'Do you have a big enough team?' and 'Has Neil Woodford lost it?' In a video response, the fund manager was defiant, his cool blue eyes staring directly into the camera lens:

> I don't think I've lost it. I've been criticized before in my career; in fact, those very same words were used about me in late 1999 and early 2000 as a result of the underperformance I was experiencing at that time . . . But this is a long game, I've always believed that, and I'm not going to cut and run, and run away from the strategy and the investment discipline and the investment principles that I've followed for all of my investment life.

Yet the steely display failed to calm nervy clients. For the first time since the business launched, investors started to take their money out. The first big defector was John Chatfeild-Roberts, the former chief investment officer at fund manager Jupiter, who oversaw the group's multi-manager funds, picking other managers to run assets on Jupiter's behalf. He had been investing in Woodford's funds for more than twenty years. At one point, Jupiter's multi-asset funds supplied £1 billion to Woodford IM, but Chatfeild-Roberts had gradually lost faith. The horrendous summer of 2017 had been the final straw, and he withdrew the final £300 million he had allocated to Woodford's funds in September. At the time, Chatfeild-Roberts kept the reasons for selling out of Woodford's funds to himself, but later conceded it was due to his concerns over Woodford's exposure to unquoted companies. 'We had lost confidence with what was happening with the fund,' Chatfeild-Roberts later said. 'When we had started there were six unquoted in the fund and by the time we'd sold there were forty-five.' He added that Jupiter initially had not been forthcoming about the reasons for the withdrawal because he had not wanted to spark a panic among other investors, thereby creating a run on the fund.

As if the terrible performance and client desertions were not bad enough, Woodford was also having to balance the demands of the scores of cash-hungry small companies he had invested in. The nature of their businesses meant they needed several years of continuous funding before they could hope to turn a meaningful profit. But, as Woodford frequently moaned, few UK investors were willing to back them. Two other investors were also big backers of small British tech businesses: Mark Barnett, Woodford's one-time understudy at Invesco Perpetual, and the hedge fund Lansdowne Partners, run by Peter Davies, the best man at former chancellor George Osborne's wedding. Few others dared make the commitment. The three investors were often among the biggest shareholders in the same companies. They collectively owned more than half of IP Group and three-quarters of Touchstone, the two university spin-off companies. Woodford, Barnett and Lansdowne also owned big stakes in many of the businesses launched by IP Group and Touchstone. Woodford realized that he would soon be unable to continue to fund the development of the start-ups he had invested in. Barnett and Lansdowne were also showing signs of fatigue. To make sure the early stage businesses did not wither away – and with them their investments – the three fund managers knew that the pool of investors willing to back the UK's start-ups needed to expand.

Alan Aubrey, the chief executive of IP Group, struck upon an idea to solve all their problems. He proposed IP Group taking over

Touchstone to create a powerhouse of UK academic research that could market itself to investors around the world. That would reduce the burden on Woodford, Barnett and Lansdowne. Aubrey proposed the idea to the three investors, who saw the rationale, with Woodford and Barnett particularly keen. But when IP Group put the idea to Touchstone's bosses, they rejected the idea, preferring to stay independent. The offer was also on the low side, without the typical premium a takeover bid would require. Yet IP Group already had the backing of Touchstone's biggest investors, who were on both sides of the deal, so was able to force through a hostile takeover. It was a glimmer of hope for Woodford, but one that proved to be no more than a false dawn.

Towards the end of 2017, Woodford IM's annus horribilis, Woodford agreed to a rare press interview, with the *FT*'s personal finance editor, Claer Barrett, and investment reporter, Kate Beioley. As the conversation turned to the fund manager's crumbling investment portfolio, Woodford admitted he doubted his own judgement daily. 'It's an incredibly uncomfortable place to be, where I am now. It is the most uncomfortable position I have been in during my career,' he admitted. 'But I believe I'm absolutely right. I don't know when I'm going to be proved right, but I'm utterly convinced that I am right, as I have been right before.'

Investors had withdrawn £1.3 billion throughout the year, with redemptions ramping up during the autumn following the abysmal summer. A fair amount of the outflow was the result of Jupiter's desertion, but other institutional investors also turned their backs on Woodford, including the insurer Aviva. In a bid to halt the exodus, Newman ordered his tech team to develop a system whereby the company could deal with retail investors directly, rather than going through intermediaries such as other investment groups or the financial advisory networks and fund supermarkets. From the launch of the business, Newman envisaged having a direct relationship with investors in the fund, building the website to communicate with them through videos and blogs. Now he wanted to take full commercial advantage of those closer bonds by selling directly to them. By controlling the relationship with end investors, there would be less risk that the go-betweens could suddenly lose faith in Woodford's investment abilities and pull hundreds of millions of pounds in one swoop. Crucially, direct sales also cut out the fees paid to brokers, meaning bigger profits for Woodford and Newman. The cost of the project was significant, but Newman expected it would lead to fatter returns further down the line.

Newman was clearly feeling the pressure. His expletive-strewn outbursts were occurring increasingly often. Sales staff on the road who reported that their contacts were wavering received blistering attacks over the phone, while representatives from Hargreaves Lansdown and Capita who raised questions about the way the company was operating would be treated in the same way. 'In business, you don't really have stand-up shouting matches. But that was how Craig communicated half the time,' recalls an ex-employee. Junior staff felt vulnerable, while some women in the office were uncomfortable with the sexist language and obscene jokes that some of the senior managers came out with. One member of the investment team used to say, 'If trading was easy, birds would do it,' while Newman once told a colleague that he had hired one female worker 'because she had the best tits of anyone who'd applied'. On one occasion a manager was found to have pornography on his work computer. According to two former employees, the junior member of staff who reported the incident was sacked. In many offices, such behaviour would not be tolerated, but Woodford and Newman ran the business how they wished, with dissenters pushed out.

As tension grew at work, Woodford let off steam on horseback, competing in eventing meetings at weekends. These entailed mastering the three main equestrian disciplines of dressage, show-jumping and riding cross-country – an undertaking that caused Woodford several injuries when he fell from his first horse, Ennis Lad. He later upgraded to Willows Spunky, an expensive Irish gelding standing at 16.2 hands. Throughout the summer months, Woodford competed in several amateur events, travelling to

Worcester, Wiltshire and Warwickshire to take part. By now Woodford also had two young children to occupy his time away from the office. He loathed going away on holiday, and so would spend most of his downtime at his vast Cotswolds estate. There he would take walks in the surrounding countryside or retreat to his private office to devour economic papers and books on military history, especially about the two world wars. He had retained his youthful love of Led Zeppelin, and of Jimmy Page, the group's guitarist, in particular. When his family did convince him to take a break, he would most often be found in the £6.4 million holiday home he had bought outright in 2017 in the Devon resort of Salcombe. The six-bedroom property overlooked the bay and was described by the *Daily Mail* as a 'Bond villain's lair', complete with slate floors and wooden balconies. But even there, Woodford could not switch off from work, checking in on his portfolio throughout the day and into the evening.

As more clients asked for their money back, Woodford was forced to shed the easier-to-sell holdings within his fund, which typically were the largest listed companies with the most frequently traded stocks. This meant that the harder-to-sell unquoted portion gradually became a larger slice of the overall pie. The compliance team knew that if it went over 10 per cent of the portfolio, the regulator would weigh down on the business.

The traffic-light system on Woodford's risk dashboard showed amber if the unquoted portion of a fund rose above 7.5 per cent and a red light if it went above 8.5 per cent. As 2017 drew to a close, the signal was flashing red and Woodford's Equity Income portfolio was dangerously close to breaching the trash ratio limit on unquoted holdings. The company devised three approaches to dealing with the problem – with two more creative than the other. The most obvious escape route was simply to sell the unquoted stakes at whatever price could be achieved. But Woodford resisted giving up on companies he believed could grow huge in the next few years. He had ploughed hundreds of millions of pounds into the businesses and did not want to sell them cheap. He was showing clear symptoms of what behavioural economists describe as the disposition effect, where investors act irrationally and hold on to tumbling stocks for far too long as they fear realizing the losses. He also did not want to sell the more attractive small companies because they were the best performers in the fund, so losing them would mean more short-term pain.

The next option Woodford's team came up with was to try to get some of the unlisted companies to commit themselves to going public. The third option was to move the tricky-to-sell assets into other funds run by Woodford. As Income Focus was restricted from investing in private companies, it left only Patient Capital to receive stakes, plus a small fund called Omnis Income and Growth that Woodford ran for the Openwork financial adviser group. Woodford began shifting stakes in unquoted companies from Equity Income to the investment trust and Omnis fund in return for cash injections into the main vehicle. This enabled him to reduce the unquoted proportion of Equity Income, while also giving him capital to pay back fleeing investors.

In the largest such transaction, Woodford switched £48.8 million of his stake in Benevolent AI, a fast-growing drug developer, to Patient Capital. There were several other transfers around this time, including unquoted businesses such as Genomics and Mission Therapeutics. The moves were within the rules, but unorthodox. Despite Newman's commitment to 'violent transparency', the deals were not made public. Had investors been aware of them at the time, they would undoubtedly have questioned whether the transactions were in the overall best interests of Woodford's clients. They would have also been concerned about what pressures had forced the manager into carrying out such unconventional manoeuvres.

As Woodford's investment and compliance staff furiously assessed the Equity Income portfolio to decide what to do with each unquoted holding, the stock picker was offered a lifeline by one of his long-time associates. Fourteen years earlier, while at Invesco Perpetual, Woodford had backed multi-millionaire property mogul Anton Bilton when he floated a business that invested in Russian property. Bilton's latest venture, Sabina Estates, developed luxury homes in Ibiza. Once again, Woodford invested in the business. Woodford had committed to invest further in Sabina, but were he to do so he was in danger of tipping Equity Income over the 10 per cent limit on unquoted holdings. Realizing the additional capital injection was in jeopardy, Sabina's managers came up with a solution. The business would float on the Guernsey stock exchange, meaning it would no longer be classed as unquoted. For the trick to work, Capita – which had since been sold to an Australian business and rebranded as Link – was required to class Guernsey's bourse as an 'eligible market' from a regulatory perspective.

There were several question marks hanging over the Guernsey exchange, not least that of its size, which was considerably smaller than the major markets across Europe. An earlier iteration of the Guernsey market, known as the Channel Islands Stock Exchange, had been the home for the scandal-hit Arch Cru fund more than a decade earlier. The exchange had been fined £190,000 for its role in the fund's collapse. Those responsible for the exchange – including the co-founder of Hargreaves Lansdown, Stephen Lansdown, a Guernsey resident – had tried to rejuvenate its brand, restructuring it and naming it the International Stock Exchange.

Link signed off on the Sabina proposal, and the property developer was no longer seen as an unquoted holding by the FCA rules. The move enabled Woodford to continue to invest in the business without breaching regulations. Sabina was a very small holding in Equity Income, so it did not move the needle by much, but was a transaction that revealed a very useful loophole. Could this be Woodford's get-out-of-jail-free card?

The new year had an eerie feeling of familiarity for Woodford. Within the first few weeks of 2018, Purplebricks, the online estate agency in which Woodford owned a 30 per cent stake, sank in value after an analyst's report revealed just half of its customers managed to sell their home within ten months, compared to the 88 per cent the chief executive had claimed. The AA was also stung as a profit downgrade and dividend cut caused its shares to shed 30 per cent of their value in one day. Despite the Sabina move, Equity Income had begun the year with 9.5 per cent of its holdings in unquoted shares, which grew to 9.7 per cent a month later. Once again, Woodford's dashboard was flashing red. Of the 122 companies Equity Income invested in, thirty-nine were unlisted. In another departure from Newman's 'violent transparency' approach, the business tried to shield investors from the problems growing within its funds. It stopped publishing details of the proportion of the fund that was unquoted.

In February the fund breached the 10 per cent limit for the first time, which brought it to the attention of the FCA. Under the regulator's rules the breach was classed as passive, as it was not a result of a new trade but due to market moves. Yet it still needed to be rectified. Woodford rejigged the portfolio, but within weeks the fund had breached the limit again. Recognizing the dire straits the fund manager was in, the FCA began to have monthly discussions with Link and Northern Trust, the depositary, to discuss the liquidity within Woodford's flagship fund. As part of these discussions, Link introduced a new way of analysing the portfolio to see how it would cope if it continued to be hit by a stream of redemption requests. It assessed each holding based on how quickly it could be sold in normal market conditions. In its first analysis of the fund on this basis, Link believed just 21 per cent of the portfolio could be sold within a week without having to discount, while 25 per cent would take more than a year to shift. Most retail funds rarely had much more than 3 per cent of their assets in such illiquid holdings – if they had any at all.

With the regulator circling, Woodford was under more pressure to fix the liquidity crisis escalating in his flagship fund. After breaching the unquoted limit twice in two months, the fund manager needed to take more drastic action to keep the wolf from the door. Fund rules stipulated that if private companies announced they intended to float within the following twelve months they could be classed as quoted holdings. Accordingly, Woodford tried to convince his largest private companies to make a commitment that they would go public. He managed to persuade Benevolent AI, his largest unquoted holding, and Proton Partners, a cancer treatment company, to cancel the shares he owned in the businesses and reissue them with a pledge to float within twelve months. While neither business was any easier to trade than it had been before the share reissues, the sleight of hand allowed them to be excluded from the dangerously high portion of unquoted holdings.

But even bending the rules was not enough. Woodford still needed to dump unquoted holdings from his portfolio, starting with the easiest to sell. One of the first he sold was a 25 per cent stake in rural broadband provider Gigaclear, which he offloaded to M&G for £69 million. Another was an 8 per cent stake in A. J. Bell, a fast-rising fund supermarket that was starting to give Hargreaves Lansdown a run for its money. Woodford had a close relationship with Andy Bell, the group's founder, and had first invested in the business in 2007, having bought out Bell's business partner. Now the company was gearing up to go public with a market valuation of £500 million. It meant there were plenty of buyers for Woodford's stake in it, which he sold for £40 million, partly to his former apprentice Mark Barnett at Invesco Perpetual and partly to Bell himself. The deal provided short-term relief for Woodford in helping him keep below the 10 per cent unquoted cap, but over the coming months he would rue the sale as he watched A. J. Bell's market cap triple soon after it listed. It proved to be the one that got away and made Woodford even more resistant to selling off any more start-ups.

More bad news was to follow in late March, when Woodford's flagship fund was ejected from the Investment Association's UK Equity Income sector for failing to produce enough dividends for investors. Over the previous three years, the fund had mustered a yield of just 3.5 per cent, compared to 3.6 per cent for the FTSE All-Share index. It was a humiliating blow for Woodford. For close to three decades he had built his reputation on investing in undervalued companies that consistently provided a steady income for his fan base, many of whom relied on his investment decisions to fund their retirement. At the point at which his ability to pick undervalued stocks was being seriously questioned, he was no longer able to fall back on his record for selecting dividend generators.

It was not only Equity Income that was suffering; Patient Capital continued to underperform the market badly. The listed trust had invested heavily in Prothena, the Irish biotech company focused on finding treatments for rare diseases. In April Prothena announced that clinical trials for a drug it had been developing had failed. The company's share price crashed by two-thirds, causing an 11 per cent fall in the shares of Patient Capital. 'Prothena was really big,' says a former employee of Woodford IM. 'After that we expected a fatal run on the business – but it didn't happen. We were lucky to see out 2018. From that point on we were on borrowed time.'

Yet the increasingly precarious state of affairs did not prevent Woodford and Newman skimming off a further £36.5 million for themselves, despite the company making only £33.7 million of profit for the financial year. Woodford took home £23.7 million, leaving £12.8 million for Newman. But even that was not enough. Newman also raided Woodford IM's coffers for a £3 million interest-free loan. By now Woodford had accepted that even if the business did survive, it would be controlling a fraction of the £18 billion it once managed. That did not stop the two co-founders taking as much out of it as they could while there was still money left to withdraw. After all, the cash cow might run out of milk before too long.

Newman's pickings were going towards multi-million-pound property projects. He had paid £3.4 million for a seven-bedroom mansion in the ornate arts-and-crafts style just outside Henley. Set in fifteen acres of land that included bluebell woods and the remains of a Roman villa, the house had been designed by an architect who trained alongside the famed Sir Edwin Lutyens. Over the years, Newman spent a small fortune adding an orangery, tennis courts, a gatehouse and a barn, and expanding the garage to accommodate four cars. He also built a six-bedroom red-brick property just outside the Berkshire village of Wargrave.

Woodford and Newman were not the only ones taking money out of the business. Investors continued to withdraw from the funds in droves, with Equity Income falling close to half its peak. The big fund distributors that had been so crucial to the early success of Woodford IM also started giving up on the business. Online stockbroker Charles Stanley Direct took Equity Income off its list of recommended funds, while A. J. Bell – the company that was for so long backed by Woodford – did the same a few months later.

In late 2018, as Woodford battled to save his business, he received an unwanted distraction in the form of a summons to the High Court. He was still a big investor in hodgepodge conglomerate Stobart Group, owning just under 20 per cent of the business. The company's maverick former chief executive, Andrew Tinkler, had become involved in yet another boardroom tussle, this time trying to dislodge chairman Iain Ferguson and replace him with the Dubai-based retail billionaire Philip Day. Tinkler convinced Woodford, as one of the largest shareholders in the business, to support his move. But it backfired when Mark Barnett, another big investor in the group, backed Ferguson, who survived a shareholder vote by a narrow margin. The company then fired Tinkler. After much recrimination, Stobart took Tinkler to court, alleging he had conspired with Woodford to buy a large stake in the company's aviation business and sell it shortly after for double what they paid. Taking the witness stand, Woodford said he was 'shocked' at the 'completely false' accusations. When Judge Russen QC eventually ruled against Tinkler, he described Woodford's version of events as 'patchy', adding: 'My general impression of Mr Woodford, supported by the contemporaneous evidence, is that from the outset he was too wedded to seeing matters from Mr Tinkler's perspective. The result was that he failed to get the balanced understanding of matters that he claimed to have.'

As Equity Income shrank, Woodford desperately sold whatever he could in the portfolio to keep it from exceeding the 10 per cent cap on unquoted stocks. He was also feeling pressure from Link over the liquidity profile of the portfolio. But even as the noose tightened, he could not help himself from making the situation worse by supporting dramatic mark-ups in value of a handful of his unquoted holdings. In one, at Benevolent AI, he contributed to a $115 million fundraising round that increased the company's value from £1.2 billion to £1.5 billion. In September, Woodford's Patient Capital Trust marked up the value of Industrial Heat, the cold fusion business, by a staggering 357 per cent, suggesting an overall valuation of $918 million for the company, based on dubious scientific theory. The mark-up meant the company grew to almost 10 per cent of Patient Capital overnight.

The uplift also caused the company to grow to 4 per cent of Equity Income. The flagship fund was becoming dominated by large stakes in small and volatile companies as Woodford was forced to sell holdings in reliable blue-chip businesses in order to pay off fleeing investors. The fund's top ten holdings – once a roll call of the UK's most dependable large companies – now comprised a jumble of struggling businesses and obscure science start-ups that were yet to turn profitable. Selling such companies was near impossible without accepting bargain-basement prices. Woodford had set himself a classic liquidity trap, with no escape in sight.

On 18 December 2018, Woodford travelled to Exeter University to receive an honorary degree from his alma mater. Days later, it was the Woodford IM staff Christmas party. The two dozen full-time workers gathered at a countryside retreat. It was a sombre affair – a world away from the heady night at the Crazy Bear four years earlier. Most had joined the company hoping it would grow to become one of the biggest players in the global investment market. They now realized it would be lucky to survive another year. Almost everyone assembled had a personal stake in the business as Equity Income was the default pension fund offered to employees.

They knew all too well how savers across the country had seen their retirement pots decimated during the previous two years under Woodford's stewardship. The crestfallen fund manager gave a downbeat speech, apologizing for the pressure staff were under and vowing to turn things round. Those present noticed his wavering voice and a tear in his eye. The pendulum had swung from arrogance to humility.

Self-Combustion

For weeks, Neil Woodford's press advisers had prepared him for the interview. They had coached him on the tactics he should stick to – be clear about his valuation-driven investment approach and demonstrate empathy and humility. It was vital he follow the script. Unlike most of the media interviews he had done in his career, this was not an opportunity to brag about his investment successes. It was a make-or-break moment for Woodford Investment Management. The business was in a tailspin, but if he managed to come across as composed and in control, it might help boost confidence in his funds and revive the company.

So went the plan, but after a testy two hours of probing questions from Peter Smith, the *FT*'s asset management editor, in a glass-walled meeting room in the company's Oxford Business Park headquarters, the irascible stock picker finally cracked. 'I don't run my life, my professional life, my personal life based on how I think that you people are going to interpret my actions,' Woodford ranted. 'I have a moral compass. I have a moral compass in everything I do; for the way I invest, the discipline that I embrace, the fact that I am prepared to go through the most miserable two and a half years of my life professionally by enduring this sort of shit because I stick to the discipline that I stick to.' Smith, a seasoned Australian journalist with a pugnacious interviewing style, pressed Woodford on the alarming rate at which his flagship fund was shrinking. By this point, it had suffered investor redemptions for twenty-one straight months. 'On that trajectory, how long can it go on?' Smith demanded to know. 'Well, you can do the sums,' Woodford snapped back sarcastically. 'Presumably, we'll be out of business in two and a half years.' It was a hasty prediction, born of irritation, that proved hopelessly optimistic.

Later, after Woodford calmed a little and the interview drew to a close, he reflected: 'The reason you're here is because, over a thirty-odd-year period, I actually did have reasonably good performance. I've had a shit two years. I don't expect to have a shit next two years. In fact, I expect to have a spectacular next two years, actually. Maybe we'll have another meeting here and you'll be scratching your head, wondering "how the hell did that happen?"'

The interview took place in March 2019, at a point when Woodford's business appeared especially precarious. The new year had begun well enough. Hargreaves Lansdown, the fund supermarket, announced it was slashing the number of funds it recommended. The so-called best-buy list was overwhelmingly influential in convincing Hargreaves's army of DIY investing customers where to park their savings. Hargreaves was Woodford's most important client, with its customers still accounting for 30 per cent of assets in Woodford's bellwether Equity Income fund and 62 per cent in the smaller Income Focus fund. Woodford IM received around £50 million in fees from Hargreaves clients over the previous three years. Incredibly, despite Woodford's shocking performance for more than eighteen months, the two funds survived the best-buy list cull and Hargreaves was still happy to recommend them to its clients. Equity Income investors were down 17 per cent in 2018 alone. As part of the negotiations to stay on the list, Woodford and Newman agreed they would reduce their fee to 0.5 per cent, where investors on rival platforms were still being charged 0.75 per cent. Hargreaves also continued to send clients' money Woodford's way through its £8.5 billion multi-manager fund range.

Mark Dampier, Woodford's ever-loyal supporter, led the team that compiled the best-buy list. Yet even he sounded like he was starting to doubt the great investor. 'Neil has gone through at least two poorer periods over his time,' he said when discussing the slimmed-down list. 'We're patient investors. The easy thing would be to take it off the list and I think that's what a lot of people do.

We've met Neil a lot over the last eighteen months. We agonize over things like Woodford all the time. I can't sleep at night sometimes.'

Dampier and his colleagues at Hargreaves had in fact held serious reservations about Woodford's investment performance for some time. As far back as November 2017 they had noticed that the level of small and unquoted holdings in the Equity Income fund had grown significantly. They met Woodford that month to stress how uncomfortable they were with the level of hard-to-sell assets in his funds and urged him to address it. Woodford promised Dampier and his team that he would make no new investments in unquoted businesses from that point on. The Hargreaves executives, including Lee Gardhouse, head of Hargreaves's multi-manager funds, also made clear to Woodford that he should stay well under the 10 per cent threshold of unquoted holdings. If he ever breached them, they said, he should inform Hargreaves as soon as possible. Yet on the two occasions in March and April 2018 when he did crash through that ceiling, he kept it from them. When they asked him outright on several occasions whether the fund had come close to breaching the limit, he denied it had.

From January 2018 onwards, Dampier, Gardhouse and their colleagues insisted on having monthly updates from Woodford specifically on the unquoted stocks in the portfolio. Each time, the Hargreaves managers wanted Woodford to reassure them that he was doing all he could to reduce his exposure. The discussions would frequently get quite heated, with the Hargreaves contingent growing exasperated that Woodford would not sell off his precious unlisted holdings. He would tell them that he had offers for some of the stakes but he felt he could get much better prices in the future. They would respond that he did not have the luxury of time and should get rid as soon as he could. 'It's fair to say, "What the fuck are you doing about this?" was said on more than one occasion,' says someone involved in the discussions.

Despite their concerns – which they did not make public – Dampier and his fellow researchers at Hargreaves continued to recommend that clients invest in Woodford's funds. In some respects, they were caught in a bind. Because they had promoted Woodford's business so strongly since its launch, and spent so much of their marketing resources on convincing their own clients to invest with the manager, the funds were now deeply dependent on the relationship continuing. Hargreaves Lansdown and Woodford IM had become unhealthily intertwined. Out of Hargreaves's 1.1 million customers, close to a third had money in Equity Income, with more than 130,000 investing directly. Tens of thousands had flocked to the fund supermarket from rivals on the promise of being able to access Woodford's funds at the cheapest rate offered anywhere in the market. Since the fund's launch, Hargreaves had received nearly £40 million of fees from clients who invested in Equity Income. It was no wonder Dampier was having sleepless nights. He was losing faith in Woodford's investment prowess, but if he were to cut the products from Hargreaves's best-buy list, investors would flee and he would be the one to spark a run on Woodford's funds, so bringing down the curtain on his idol's career, and quite possibly his own.

Though Woodford could still count on protection from Hargreaves, more bad news soon followed. In February 2019, Equity Income was added to the ignominious Spot the Dog list of the worst-performing UK funds. The list, compiled by financial planner Bestinvest, was widely covered by the personal finance press and exposed funds that had been losing money for three years. It showed that £100 invested in Equity Income three years earlier was now worth just £87. It was the first time Woodford's own funds had made the list, with Equity Income in second place, just behind his former Invesco Perpetual fund run by Mark Barnett. The fund Woodford ran for SJP also made the list. It was yet another humiliation for Woodford, and investors responded to the bad headlines by pulling out more cash.

Equity Income, meanwhile, continued to suffer from a pile-up of crashing companies. On one day in mid-February, Purplebricks, lost a quarter of its market value after cutting sales forecasts and announcing both its UK and US chief executives were leaving. The fall caused Woodford a £32 million paper loss. Another business Woodford had long backed, energy broking group Utilitywise, revealed it did not have enough funds to meet its liabilities and appointed administrators. Woodford was the largest shareholder in Utilitywise, which had been named company of the year on London's junior AIM market just five years earlier.

Despite having sold a couple of his easier-to-shift private companies, Woodford's Equity Income portfolio was still butting up against the 10 per cent cap on unquoted holdings. This time the fund manager, who was loath to sell any more businesses, came up with an altogether more creative way of staying within the rules. Though legal, his latest ploy was highly unconventional and not without controversy. He devised a plan to sell stakes worth £73 million in five unquoted companies from Equity Income to Patient Capital in exchange for a stake in the investment trust. The plan worked because the trust was a listed company and a constituent of the FTSE 250, so Woodford was essentially converting his private holdings into a stake in a listed business. It meant Equity Income's unquoted holdings fell below 8 per cent and relieved some of the growing pressure on the fund.

The complex shares-for-assets swap stretched the rules and introduced yet more conflicts of interest as Woodford was on both sides of the deal. He had designed it to give himself breathing space, but whether it was in the best interests of the Equity Income investors or the shareholders of Patient Capital was another matter. The stakes in the five companies – Atom Bank, Carrick Therapeutics, Cell Medica, RateSetter and Spin Memory – were exchanged for new shares in Patient Capital equivalent to 9.9 per cent of the trust, just below the 10 per cent threshold that would have required shareholder approval. Because the shares were newly issued, Equity Income investors lost out on more than £10 million compared to if the shares had been bought on the secondary market. It also meant Woodford's Equity Income fund was now the largest shareholder in the investment trust he managed – yet another governance red flag.

Woodford plotted the move for a while. He had to spend a great deal of time convincing Susan Searle and her fellow members of the Patient Capital board, as well as Duff & Phelps, the valuer, and Link, the authorized corporate director on both funds. But despite being involved in discussions over the contentious plan for months – and being required to provide the FCA with regular updates about the fund's liquidity – Link did not inform the regulator until 28 February, the day of the transaction.

Woodford claimed he was choosing to hold on to his unquoted companies because of his unflinching belief in their potential to grow. But his huge stakes in small businesses – and even in listed companies – made it nearly impossible to sell them without accepting fire-sale prices. For many of the early stage companies he had invested in, Woodford had committed more money in later funding rounds, gradually building up bigger and bigger holdings in the businesses. Woodford was the largest shareholder in tens of the businesses he backed, with stakes of more than 20 per cent common. Indeed, several of Equity Income's top ten holdings by that point were in businesses in which Woodford had between 20 and 30 per cent ownership: Provident Financial, Theravance Biopharma, NewRiver Reit and Autolus. He could not get rid of them even if he wanted to. It was another knot Woodford had tied himself up in.

In early March, Woodford finally bowed to pressure from Hargreaves and his other concerned clients and said he would remove all the unquoted holdings in Equity Income over time. The tetchy interview with the *FT* took place days later. The resulting news article, on the front page of the paper on the 15th, centred on Woodford's comments that he was on course to be 'out of business in about two-and-a-half years', as well as his attack on critics, who, he said, were leading investors into 'appallingly bad decisions' to quit his funds. The outburst – rare in the normally staid world of investment management – was picked up by the rest of the national press. But in the *FT*'s accompanying feature, Woodford was adamant that his portfolio was under short-term strain that would be relieved after the vexing question of Brexit was resolved. At which point, he argued, investment from overseas would pour into the UK, and specifically the companies he held, which would provide a huge boost to his funds. Yet again Mark Dampier fought his corner – though less forcefully than he might have done for most of his career. 'You have to get Brexit out of the way,' he told the *FT*. 'We are going to see a change in the marketplace but the question is whether he will still be around.'

Pressure was building on Woodford. It had been just under a year since he had convinced two of his biggest unquoted companies to reissue shares and announce their intention to float. This legal – though controversial – tactic had allowed Equity Income to scrape just below the regulatory cap on unlisted holdings. But as the deadline approached, neither Proton Partners nor Benevolent AI had gone public. The pair accounted for more than 5 per cent of Equity Income, so if they did not list by the agreed date, they would tip the portfolio well over the limit. At the last minute, a year to the day after agreeing to do so, Proton Partners finally announced it was listing on the little-known NEX exchange for small and medium companies. The exchange was so far under the radar that, while giving testimony in the Stobart–Tinkler case at the High Court a few months earlier, Woodford had claimed: 'I don't even know what NEX is.' Across his funds, Woodford owned 45 per cent of Proton Partners. In agreeing to list, and sensing Woodford's desperation, Proton Partners' managers demanded Woodford invest a further £80 million into the business at times of their choosing. It was an expensive bill for Woodford, but allowed him to survive another day.

Then came Benevolent AI – Woodford's largest unquoted holding, whose value had shot up just a few months earlier when the fund manager contributed to a $115 million fundraising round. It accounted for more than 4 per cent of Equity Income. As with Proton Partners, Benevolent AI's managers showed little enthusiasm for going public. As the 22 March deadline got closer, there were still no plans to list even on the most junior of markets. Since

Woodford had convinced Benevolent AI to commit to listing, the company had brought in a new chief executive, Joanna Shields, a former government adviser and one-time head of Europe for Facebook. She was steadfastly against going public. Woodford needed to conjure another trick. This time he opted for an even more contentious scheme – one that he had already used to great effect on three previous occasions. Remembering the ease with which he had listed his Sabina Estates holding on the Guernsey stock exchange a year earlier, Woodford had repeated the ruse with two other companies – Ombu Group, a tech business, and Industrial Heat, the US company based on theories at the fringe of mainstream physics. Over the previous year his stakes in these businesses, rather then the businesses themselves, had been listed on the Guernsey exchange – a move that Link, the authorized corporate director, had signed off as kosher. Sabina, Ombu and Industrial Heat were relatively small businesses, and these moves had been made without being acknowledged publicly by Woodford IM – again flouting the company's much publicized commitment to full transparency. Benevolent AI, on the other hand, was of a different order. It was one of the UK's few so-called unicorns – private start-ups valued at more than $1 billion. It also made up a huge part of Woodford's funds. Woodford used the same Channel Islands administrator to act as a sponsor in each of the listings, a little-known company called Belasko, which means 'little raven' in Basque. Belasko's shareholders included the property tycoon Anton Bilton and his business partner Glyn Hirsch, who were chairman and a non-executive director of Sabina respectively. The pair also ran Raven Property Group, another Woodford holding, which invested in Russian warehouses.

It was another last-minute deal that saw Woodford's stake in the business transfer to the Guernsey stock exchange on 21 March. While Link had again been heavily involved in the negotiations, and was in monthly discussions with the Financial Conduct Authority over Woodford's liquidity management, it did not inform the regulator. Andrew Bailey, chief executive of the FCA, would later concede Link was not required to inform the FCA of the transfer, but that this was a flaw in the rules. Was Link really acting in investors' best interests?

The stakes of the four businesses listed in Guernsey were valued at £425 million, which accounted for 9 per cent of Equity Income. Had they not listed, the unquoted portion of the fund would have smashed through the 10 per cent limit, reaching 16 per cent – which would have caused the regulator to hit the roof. Even though the four businesses were classed as quoted, they were no more liquid than they had been before they listed as it was just Woodford's stakes in the companies that were on the exchange. The shares were not being traded. The financial jiggery-pokery would later be described by Bailey, as allowed by the fund rulebook but 'on the wrong side of the spirit of it'.

It was not only the regulatory restrictions that weighed on Woodford's unquoted holdings. He was also coming under pressure from his biggest clients – in particular Hargreaves Lansdown – over his exposure to such holdings. Woodford promised to remove most of his unlisted companies from Equity Income and proposed more internal switches with the Patient Capital Trust. But he wanted to keep his most promising private ventures – Oxford Nanopore and Immunocore – in the portfolio, believing they were on the path to listing, and that when they did, they would explode in value.

The extent of Woodford's dicey predicament was laid bare a week after Benevolent AI floated, when *Citywire* published a report by the journalist Daniel Grote revealing the Guernsey listings. It was the first time Woodford's investors had been made fully aware of the financial chicanery he was using to keep his funds under control. It was also the first time the FCA knew of the Guernsey dealings, despite its monthly conversations with Link and Northern Trust over Woodford's liquidity position. Alarmed, the regulator grilled Link on its risk management strategy, querying what stress testing it was carrying out and what plans were in place to reduce Equity Income's exposure to unquoted companies.

By this point, the fund's liquidity profile had rapidly deteriorated. The regulator had expected Link to take control of the situation and put pressure on Woodford to make the portfolio easier to trade. Yet just 8 per cent of the fund was now in stocks that could be sold within seven days without having to accept rock-bottom prices. That compared to 21 per cent in June 2018. For the least liquid portion of the fund – those holdings that would take between six months and a year or more to shift without slashing the price – the weighting had increased from 25 per cent to 33 per cent. The situation was becoming drastically worse. The FCA became anxious and demanded Link provide it with daily updates on Woodford's funds. Link told the regulator that, if either the hardest-to-sell portion rose above 35 per cent or the most liquid group fell below 5 per cent, it would act.

The Guernsey stunt had given Woodford some breathing space, but his plans would once again unravel. At 6 p.m. on Thursday, 11 April 2019, the Guernsey stock exchange announced it was suspending the listings in three of the companies Woodford owned: Ombu, Industrial Heat and Benevolent AI. The exchange had concerns over the valuations of the companies, not least due to their huge growth in the time since Woodford set up his own business five years earlier. The Guernsey authorities were also worried that the listings breached FCA rules.

Meanwhile, investors continued to demand their money back. All Woodford could do was keep selling his listed businesses. It was now twenty-two consecutive months of client redemptions. To raise cash, he sold a £42 million stake in listed property business NewRiver Reit to Mark Barnett, and an £86 million stake in peer-to-peer lender P2P Global to wealth manager Quilter. He also sold a £159 million stake in Imperial Tobacco, the cigarette maker that had long been one of his top holdings. As the quoted stocks were sold off, the unquoted holdings grew to an even bigger portion of Equity Income. The tricky balancing act continued. So Woodford went back to his tried-and-tested creative manoeuvres. This time he convinced DNA sequencer Oxford Nanopore and the much smaller Accelerated Digital Ventures, a funding platform, to reissue shares and commit to listing within twelve months. This meant they too could be switched to the quoted portion of the fund.

During the spring of 2019 it had become increasingly clear that Woodford's investment empire was crumbling. His funds were performing woefully, coming bottom of the pack compared with scores of similar products. Despite a strong first eighteen months, Equity Income now heavily trailed the FTSE All-Share index over one, three and five years. An investment made when the fund launched in June 2014 had risen just 10 per cent, compared to a 30 per cent gain for the index. Those who had invested from 2015 onwards were suffering badly. Yet there was still one last payday for Woodford and Newman. In the year to March, they scooped up another £13.8 million from the business, with Woodford pocketing £9 million and Newman £4.8 million. They were intent on squeezing out every last drop.

The terminal trajectory of Woodford's business had not gone unnoticed by the clients he depended on most – many of whom were unnerved by the revelations about the desperate measures the stock picker was taking to rebalance his funds. In early March, Woodford and Newman were summoned to the Middle East to meet the managers of the Abu Dhabi Investment Authority, one of the biggest sovereign wealth funds in the world. The ADIA had been an early backer of Woodford's new business five years earlier, committing £200 million. Woodford ran the money in a vehicle called the West Fund. ADIA was unable to invest in unquoted companies, so the fund was structured in a similar way to the St James's Place mandate, which mirrored Equity Income but with the unlisted and small companies stripped out. The ADIA managers wanted to know what Woodford was going to do about the fund's dire performance and gave him one last chance to turn it round. During the three-day trip Woodford and Newman met other Middle Eastern investors whom they hoped they could convince to buy into the same young British tech companies Woodford had been supporting. Within a month, however, the ADIA managers finally lost their patience with Woodford and pulled the mandate.

Just under 3,400 miles away, in Maidstone, the Kent council officials were coming to a similar conclusion. In the March meeting of the superannuation committee, trustees quizzed Nick Vickers, the council's head of financial services and one of Woodford's most ardent followers, about the fund manager. They had read all about the controversial transfer of assets between Equity Income and Patient Capital, which had taken place without their consent. They had also seen the fund's alarming underperformance over the previous two years and had recently learnt about Woodford's troubles in keeping his investment portfolio within regulatory limits. They instructed Vickers to demand an explanation from the fund manager over the asset swap and said they would consider pulling the mandate in June. Woodford was officially on watch – though both sides knew the relationship was coming to an end.

Another of Woodford's most important clients, SJP, was also keeping the fund manager on a very tight leash. As its mandate did not include unquoted holdings and was run separately from the main funds, the heavy outflows suffered by Woodford IM were not a concern for the wealth manager. But SJP customers who invested in the Woodford-managed fund were still nursing heavy losses – and paying high fees for the pleasure. In early 2019 SJP commissioned Stamford Associates, a consultancy, to carry out a study into Woodford's investment mistakes throughout the previous year. The paper concluded that, while there had been plenty of bad calls, it was not that out of whack with previous times when Woodford's funds underperformed. What made this time worse, however, was that his investment style of seeking value instead of riding market momentum was out of favour.

SJP's investment committee hauled Woodford in to probe him on his decisions and stock selections. Woodford sailed through the interrogation, giving detailed insights into the companies he had invested in and providing strong arguments about why they would eventually come good. But throughout April and May SJP's investment analysts had regular discussions with Woodford, his sales rep Will Deer and Newman. The SJP team were concerned that Woodford was spending too much time managing the unquoted holdings in his other funds and neglecting the SJP mandate.

Even Woodford's biggest cheerleaders at Hargreaves Lansdown had given up on him. In May, Lee Gardhouse, the Hargreaves chief investment officer, sold a fifth of his stake in Equity Income from a Hargreaves multi-manager fund he co-ran. The sale was not disclosed to the fund's investors for another six months. Hargreaves's multi-manager funds had become an important source of business for Woodford, providing more than £500 million of assets for Equity Income. Gardhouse also helped choose the funds that made it onto Hargreaves's best-buy list, since renamed the Wealth 50. Gardhouse's dual role upset rivals, who claimed it was a conflict of interest. They said the fact he had shovelled clients' money from his multi-manager funds into Equity Income made it impossible for him to stop recommending the fund in the best-buy list. In total, 291,520 Hargreaves customers had invested in Equity Income, entrusting £1.6 billion of their savings with Woodford. Most of them had been convinced to do so by the likes of Mark Dampier and Gardhouse. But, without acknowledging it publicly, both had major concerns about Woodford's nous for choosing private companies and his ability to manage his funds out of his self-inflicted liquidity trap. They knew it was only a matter of time before either Woodford's business buckled or Hargreaves would have to abandon him. Either scenario had the potential to be devastating for Hargreaves and the relationship it had built up with its 1.1 million clients. Questions would be asked about why Hargreaves continued to funnel savers' money into Woodford's funds and recommend them while its top investment researchers had serious misgivings about the stock picker.

Yet, on the surface, Dampier was still as fawning as ever. In early May the fund management kingmaker sent a reassuring note to Hargreaves's clients, explaining why he still endorsed Woodford's funds. 'This isn't the first time in his career Neil Woodford's under-performed,' he consoled. 'We've stuck with him during difficult times before, and in the past investors have been rewarded for such patience. Our analysis of Woodford's long-term track record gives us the confidence to retain the Equity Income fund on the Wealth 50, and we think he's still got the skill to deliver excellent long-term performance.' But just days later, on 15 May, Gardhouse cashed in £546,000 of shares in Hargreaves. The next day Dampier sold £600,000 worth of company stock, while his wife offloaded an additional £5 million of shares. When the details of these share sales later emerged, Dampier and Gardhouse would be accused of behaviour close to insider dealing, given their knowledge of the dire state of Woodford's funds and the blowback Hargreaves would receive if they closed. Those who had done most to convince Hargreaves's customers to hand over their retirement pots to Woodford were making sure their personal wealth was protected from the fallout when his fund inevitably collapsed.

After the Guernsey stock exchange suspended the listings of three of Woodford's portfolio companies, citing concerns about whether the moves contravened UK fund rules, it tried to get some clarification from the UK regulator. The first few attempts to set up a meeting went nowhere as calls and emails were directed to the wrong department and the messages got lost in the regulatory machine. Eventually, after an exchange of email messages between the two sides that betrayed a lack of urgency from the FCA, a call was set up for 8 May. By this point, the Guernsey exchange had begun lifting the suspensions on Woodford's holdings, though it did not reveal why it changed its mind. During the twenty-minute conversation, the Guernsey executives apprised their FCA counterparts of their concerns over the valuations of the listed companies. It was a further two weeks before the Guernsey executives sent the FCA a follow-up email providing more details about their apprehension. The emailed exchange over the following weeks centred around setting up a formal agreement to share information between the two parties, rather than on the more pressing issue of Woodford's disintegrating fund.

Meanwhile, Woodford was finding distractions to take his mind off his imploding business. During April and May he travelled round the country at weekends to compete in a succession of amateur equestrian events. On 19 May he took Willows Spunky to Tweseldown Racecourse in Hampshire, the location for the dressage and eventing competitions in the 1948 Olympics. Woodford gave a decent account of himself in dressage, and picked up only four show-jumping penalty points before scoring poorly during the cross-country segment. Out of the thirteen riders in his pool, Woodford finished the day second bottom. It was to be the last competition he would take part in for more than a year. As he dismounted Willows Spunky and dusted himself down after a hard day's eventing, Woodford had little idea that within two weeks his business and reputation would be hanging by a thread.

The following day Woodford suffered the first in a series of body blows that would culminate in his downfall. Morningstar, the influential fund ratings agency, stung the fund manager by downgrading Equity Income from bronze to neutral – its second lowest rank. The research company's ratings were closely followed by retail and institutional investors, with many unable or unwilling to invest in funds once they fell below certain thresholds. A year earlier Morningstar had marked the fund down from silver, its second highest rating. It was now just one level above negative, the ultimate badge of dishonour.

Peter Brunt, an analyst at Morningstar, said the downgrade had been prompted because Equity Income was now one of the least liquid funds in the market:

> Persistent redemptions, underperformance and stock-specific issues, combined with the manager's relentless willingness to push the portfolio to its liquidity limit, have resulted in portfolio positioning that we consider extreme . . . Contrarian investing comes with a degree of risk, and issues can be expected from time to time. However, the nature of some of the stock specific problems and their

respective position sizes, combined with the extreme portfolio positioning, give us cause for concern.

What the ratings provider did not divulge was that it had already cut and run from Woodford. Three months earlier, in the last week of February, Morningstar withdrew £30 million from Equity Income from its own line of multi-manager portfolios.

The downgrade sparked a further flurry of withdrawals as investors were given a stark warning of the parlous state of Equity Income – yet still Hargreaves promoted the fund on its best-buy list. As investors withdrew, Woodford was forced to sell even more of his treasured holdings. Despite his long-term commitment to the university spin-off sector, Woodford sold his entire £55 million stake in Oxford Sciences Innovation, one of Britain's main groups and one of the few private holdings he could shift quickly.

Less than a week later, on 30 May, the FT published its damning front-page story that revealed Equity Income had shrivelled by £560 million in less than four weeks owing to withdrawals and underperformance, and that the regulator was deeply concerned about the startling shrinkage. The fund held just £3.7 billion – down two-thirds from its peak of £10.2 billion two years earlier. Investors withdrew an average of £10 million a day throughout May, which was the twenty-third consecutive month the fund had suffered outflows. More than half the redemptions hit after Morningstar's downgrade. Investment performance had also taken its toll, with the fund losing 8.3 per cent in May alone. Executives across Britain's £9 trillion investment industry were beginning to fret about the wider fallout from the terminal decline of the country's best-known stock picker.

The next day, as Kent's pension trustees were making their fateful decision to cut ties with Woodford, similar discussions were happening at St James's Place. David Lamb, the head of SJP's investment committee, had finally run out of patience with Woodford. He believed the fund manager had lost control of his business and was too distracted with fighting fires among his unquoted holdings. The *FT* story had brutally exposed the mess Woodford had got himself into. Throughout the weekend of 1–2 June, while Woodford's investment team plotted how to cope with losing the Kent mandate, SJP's investment committee came to the conclusion that they too were going to have to fire the stock picker from managing their clients' £3.5 billion. In the five years Woodford had run the money at his new business, SJP's clients had lost hundreds of millions of pounds. The decision to sack him was one they knew would kill his business.

By the morning of Monday, 3 June, SJP's executive board still needed to sign off the decision to fire Woodford, while the FTSE-listed wealth manager also needed to inform the regulator and its shareholders. Meanwhile, Kent's stand-in finance manager was putting in a request to recoup the pension scheme's £263 million investment in the fund. Under Equity Income's rules, as detailed in its prospectus, Link as the authorized corporate director was required to consider offering a so-called in-specie transfer if an investor with a large holding in the fund wished to withdraw. This would see the departing client paid back with a basket of the fund's assets relative to the size of its investment, rather than in cash. In effect, it would be like receiving a mini version of the overall fund. Equity Income's prospectus ordered that Link weigh up this route if the withdrawal was 'substantial in relation to the total size of a fund or in some way detrimental to the fund', but gave the ACD discretion in whether it offered this option. Since the amount of money Kent was looking to recoup was equivalent to 7 per cent of the fund, which by this point had already exhausted its cash reserves, an in-specie transfer should certainly have been discussed. But instead of talking these options through with Kent, Karl Midl, head of Link's ACD business and primarily responsible for servicing Equity Income, decided instead to suspend trading in the fund immediately.

The day had already got off to a bad start for Woodford, who had watched one of his favourite businesses, construction group Kier, suffer a 40 per cent crash in its share price after it issued a profits warning. But when the call came through from Midl that Equity Income was to be suspended, the fund manager was dumbstruck. He had spent the weekend preparing to breathe one last lungful of air into his ailing business, but it had all been in vain.

Fund suspensions are exceptionally rare in the investment world. The basic idea of investors being able to access their money whenever they need to is well established. For investors to be blocked from taking out their money means one of two things: either the fund has been rattled by unexpected geopolitical events, as was seen after the global financial crisis and Britain's vote to leave the EU, or the fund manager has been sloppy. Woodford certainly fell into the latter category. He had failed to stay in control of his fund and prepare it for the time when investors would want their money back. His obstinacy and refusal to change course resulted in 400,000 UK investors suffering huge losses and having their life savings locked up for the best part of two years. It was Europe's biggest investment scandal for more than a decade. How could Woodford – and the investment industry at large – possibly survive this?

11

Built on a Lie

Mark Carney, the debonair governor of the Bank of England, took his seat in the stuffy House of Commons meeting room. He had been summoned to appear before the Treasury Select Committee as part of a routine catch-up on the bank's outlook for inflation. But it was not long before he was asked about the biggest business story of the summer – the plight of Neil Woodford's crumbling investment company and its implications for millions of British savers. At this point the normally unflappable Canadian suddenly went off script. 'This is a big deal. You can see something that could be systemic,' he said in response to a question about whether fund managers with retail customers should invest in hard-to-sell unlisted companies. 'These funds are built on a lie, which is that you can have daily liquidity for assets that fundamentally aren't liquid. And that leads to an expectation of individuals that it's not that different to having money in a bank.'

His comments sent shock waves through the financial press. One of the most powerful figures in global economics was calling attention to a significant flaw in the investment industry – one that put the life savings of millions of British workers in jeopardy. If savers did not fully grasp how the funds they chose worked, how could they possibly make the right decisions? Was the misunderstanding the fault of the savers themselves or the industry at large? The governor seemed to be suggesting the problems the Woodford scandal exposed went much further than a single rogue fund manager. Trust in professional investors was, in fact, built on a false premise.

Ever since Link had alerted Woodford's investors on the afternoon of 3 June that his flagship fund was suspended, the story had dominated the business media. Woodford's name was splashed across the front page of the *FT* in four of the next five editions, while thousands of column inches were dedicated to the stock picker's demise throughout the wider press. Politicians and business leaders queued up to give their views on the topic du jour. One industry veteran who had known Woodford for twenty years told the *FT* when the suspension was announced that it was a 'bonfire of reputation and a terrible moment for investor confidence'.

Within minutes of Link's announcement that Equity Income was suspended, the rot began to spread to Woodford's other funds. Hargreaves Lansdown, which had harboured reservations about Woodford's stock picking for two years despite still promoting his funds, was the first to act. The online brokerage announced it was removing both Equity Income and the smaller Income Focus fund from their much-coveted positions on the Wealth 50 best-buy list. Removing the gated Equity Income fund was an obvious decision as clients could no longer invest in it – but Income Focus was still open for business. Mark Dampier, who oversaw the list, had finally renounced his idol.

That night, the chief executives of the biggest British fund managers met as part of a pre-planned get-together, arranged by the Investment Association lobby group. The only topic of discussion was the Equity Income suspension and the wider repercussions for their industry. It was a gloomy evening. Despite being competitors of Woodford's over the years, the industry bosses indulged in little gloating. No one was in any doubt that the ramifications would be huge and they would all be hit.

When the market reopened the following day, Woodford's reverse Midas touch was in full effect. Hargreaves Lansdown's shares immediately shed 6 per cent, with the fund supermarket falling to the bottom of the FTSE 100 as shareholders fretted about how closely entangled with the fund manager Hargreaves had become. Woodford's listed Patient Capital Trust fell 12 per cent. Of the top five most-viewed stocks on the Hargreaves platform on 4

June, two were Patient Capital and Hargreaves itself. The fund distributor's own customers were even selling its shares. Meanwhile, several businesses in which Woodford was a major shareholder were also clobbered as investors feared he would be forced into a fire sale to pay back deserting investors. Allied Minds and Circassia each dropped more than 10 per cent, while Burford Capital, Eve Sleep, NewRiver Reit, Kier Group and Redde all suffered.

As his portfolio collapsed, Woodford sat in his company's desolate offices, surrounded by contemporary furniture and modern wall art. Staring straight down the camera lens, and wearing his trademark black sweatshirt, Woodford gave a grovelling apology to his investors. 'I'm extremely sorry we've had to take this decision,' he said in a video posted that evening on the company website. 'We understand our investors' frustration. All I can say in response is that this decision was motivated by your interests, our investors. When it is appropriate, we will reopen the fund so you can buy and sell as normal.'

The next day, 5 June, it was the turn of another long-time Woodford patron to jump ship. Having spent the past few days preparing to brief shareholders and the regulator, SJP finally told the fund manager his time was up. Conventionally, the wealth manager's chief investment officer, Chris Ralph, would deliver the bad news to a fired fund manager in person. But he was on a family holiday in Spain, so the responsibility fell to David Lamb, head of the investment committee. Lamb's hasty call to Woodford was a body blow, one the fund manager did not take well. After ending the call abruptly, a wave of resignation overcame him.

In one fell swoop, SJP yanked away 40 per cent of Woodford's business. The favourable terms SJP negotiated five years earlier meant the wealth manager could boot Woodford off the £3.5 billion mandate immediately, without a drawn-out notice period. SJP's investment committee had already lined up two rival portfolio managers to pick up the chunky fund and take it over straight away. SJP had worked with Woodford for more than eighteen years – including his time at Invesco Perpetual – and enjoyed bountiful returns during his best years. The wealth manager's four-paragraph perfunctory statement announcing the end of the relationship therefore seemed a tad callous. SJP's £3.5 billion was kept in a separate pot to the gated Equity Income fund and was not invested in the troublesome small and unlisted companies. Commentators speculated that because the wealth manager was not immediately affected by Woodford's most pressing problems, the decision to sack him at that point was more about saving face and avoiding being tainted by association than about protecting its clients' investments. Those toiling in Oxford Business Park certainly felt betrayed.

On Thursday, Woodford's final big client bailed. Openwork, the advisory network, sacked Woodford as manager of its £330 million Omnis fund, while investors pulled more than £30 million from his Income Focus fund. At the same time, shareholders sold out of his listed Patient Capital investment trust, causing its discount to net asset value to widen to 25 per cent.

Despite not being able to access their savings, Equity Income investors were still being charged £65,000 a day. Consumer rights advocates began demanding that Woodford drop the charges. But he refused, arguing there were still expenses involved in keeping the fund running. Trading costs, in particular, had risen as Woodford sold off what he could to raise much-needed cash. He managed to shift holdings in several of his biggest listed investments, including Kier, Provident Financial and Purplebricks – all at sharp discounts to their share prices just a few months earlier. There were also the fees due to service providers, including Link, Northern Trust, the depositary, and Grant Thornton, the auditor. But that did not stop the clamour. Hargreaves Lansdown took similar flak over the money it was earning from customers stuck in the fund, so announced it would waive platform fees. The fund supermarket, which had vehemently defended Woodford for so many years, called on the stock picker to follow suit.

More bad news was to follow as the Treasury Select Committee announced it would scrutinize the suspension of Woodford's fund.

The well-respected former corporate lawyer who led the committee, Conservative MP Nicky Morgan, added her voice to the tumult. 'The suspension of trading has provided Mr Woodford with some breathing room to fix his fund; he should afford his investors the same space and waive the fund's fees while the fund is suspended,' she ordered.

As tensions heightened, the blame game began. Politicians were beginning to ask why the Financial Conduct Authority, the UK regulator, had allowed Woodford to stretch the fund rules and list unquoted holdings in Guernsey. The watchdog claimed it had previously been unaware of the decision to float the shares offshore. But in an extraordinary public spat, the Guernsey exchange published a statement disputing the FCA's account. 'It is important to note that The International Stock Exchange Authority made several attempts to contact the FCA back in April 2019 but with no initial response, finally securing a call with them on 8 May 2019,' claimed Fiona Le Poidevin, chief executive of the parent group of Guernsey exchange. 'The International Stock Exchange Authority proactively engaged with the FCA in the spirit of regulatory cooperation but subsequently was given no prior warning of the FCA statement or its content.' It was a telling insight into the disjointed nature of the relationship between two close regulatory bodies.

By Friday, attention turned to Dampier, Woodford's long-time standard-bearer. Hargreaves's share price had shed 14 per cent since Equity Income's suspension and was down more than 20 per cent since Dampier and his wife had sold £5.6 million of shares just weeks earlier. The newspapers went to town on his luxury lifestyle, his two multi-million-pound homes, his 25ft yacht and taste for expensive skiing and fishing holidays. Dampier was Britain's best-known financial adviser and had made a career – and personal fortune – recommending Woodford's funds to Hargreaves's 1.1 million DIY investors. Despite losing confidence in the fund manager's ability for more than two years, he continued to give hearty and personal endorsements for Woodford right up until the fund's suspension. Vince Cable, the former Liberal Democrat leader and business secretary, told the *Mail* about his concerns over the share sale. 'This sounds like something which, even if legal, is perilously close to insider dealing. Financial advisers have struggled to rebuild their reputation after previous scandals and this episode reflects badly on the profession as a whole.'

The weekend newspapers carried a torrent of features and commentaries, assessing the reasons for Woodford's undoing and who was to blame for what was fast becoming a huge scandal. The personal finance pages pored over Hargreaves Lansdown's failings. Angry investors demanded to know how much longer they were going to be stuck in the moribund fund and what more it would cost them. They turned their ire on the intermediaries who had convinced them to go with Woodford. It was clear by now that Nicky Morgan's Treasury Select Committee also had the UK's biggest fund supermarket in its sights. In response, Chris Hill, chief executive of Hargreaves, published a statement saying he wished to 'apologize personally to all clients who have been affected by the recent problems' with Equity Income. He said Hargreaves would carry out a review into the controversial decision at the start of the year to keep the fund on its best-buy list.

The situation was spiralling out of control. Woodford felt he needed more advice on how to deal with the barrage of negative press. Through a mutual acquaintance, he set up a meeting with Roland Rudd, the multi-millionaire City spin doctor who ran PR consultancy Finsbury. Rudd, a former *FT* journalist and brother of Conservative MP Amber Rudd, turned up at Oxford Business Park and sat down for a ninety-minute meeting with Woodford. Rudd, who had friends trapped in the fund and felt the scandal was already turning toxic, had been sceptical about the meeting, but he and Woodford hit it off. Then Newman barged into the room. He was angry that the meeting was taking place without him and sat in the corner, brooding. Finally, Newman stood up and demanded to know what Rudd would want in exchange for his firefighting services. Rudd told him that his fees varied, but in one recent case he had charged £400,000. Rudd then insisted that if they were to work together, the fee could not come out of the trapped fund – it would need to be paid for by the business, and ultimately eat into any remaining profits Woodford and Newman hoped to collect. It was at this point that the conversation ended. Newman did not want to hear any more.

Woodford, meanwhile, was frantically trying to sell his holdings to raise the money to repay Kent County Council's pension fund, plus all the other investors who would inevitably demand their money back. When Equity Income suspended a week earlier, it was £3.7 billion in size. Link said it would review its decision to reopen the fund twenty-eight days after gating it. Woodford still hung on to the hope that if he raised enough cash to pay off Kent and a raft of other investors, the fund could reopen within a few months and carry on at around half its size. With Income Focus and Patient Capital, his business would still manage more than £3 billion, which would provide enough juicy dividends for him and Newman to maintain their mansions and fleets of sports cars. But in order to do so he needed to sell what he could in the portfolio without taking too great a hit on the price. The trouble was, he was now Britain's best-known distressed seller. Hedge-fund managers began to circle like vultures, betting against companies they expected him to sell in order to make a quick profit, causing Woodford IM to remove from its website the funds' full lists of holdings, which had been introduced to great fanfare when the business launched five years earlier as part of Newman's 'violent transparency' drive.

On Tuesday, 11 June, Nicky Morgan laid down the gauntlet to Chris Hill. In a letter to the Hargreaves boss, she demanded to know how much money the broker had made from its relationship with Woodford over the years and what discounts the two parties had agreed. She also wanted a timeline of when the decision makers within Hargreaves had first started having doubts about the way Woodford was running his funds. Morgan's select committee had also said it would scrutinize the FCA's role in the debacle, and Andrew Bailey was due to appear before the MPs. The FCA chief executive was under pressure to get a grip of the unfolding drama and so announced the regulator would 'look again' at fund supermarkets like Hargreaves to make sure they were being impartial when deciding which funds were included in their best-buy lists.

While the focus had mostly been on Equity Income, Woodford's two other remaining vehicles were beginning to teeter. Woodford had ensured the loyalty of the Patient Capital board by filling it with long-time allies who were closely connected to companies he invested in. But after he became one of the most notorious figures in British business, even their allegiances were wearing thin. The board drafted in Winterflood Securities to act as broker, at a cost of more than £100,000 a month – to be paid for out of the fund. The board, under the leadership of Susan Searle, held discussions with Winterflood about terminating Woodford's contract and considered which other fund managers could take his place. With the fate of Equity Income far from certain, and Patient Capital hanging by a thread, Woodford faced the prospect of being left with just his junior Income Focus fund. But that too was shrivelling. In the two weeks after Equity Income's suspension, Income Focus contracted by a third, leaving it at just £333 million. Less than two years earlier, Woodford's empire stood at £18 billion – now it looked like it would be drained to a fraction of that.

Three weeks to the day after Kent's pension committee made the fateful decision to fire Woodford, the flock of councillors, local government officials and retirees met up again. It had been a surreal time. Their unanimous choice in the same damp room a few weeks earlier had made the front pages of the British press, and once again the financial matters of the sleepy local authority were of national interest. For most of the committee members, their only experience of being at the centre of a breaking news story was when council decisions over library opening hours exercised readers of the *Kent Messenger*. But Nick Vickers, who had led the council's fight in the Icelandic courts to reclaim its deposits in the country's banks a decade earlier, was all too familiar with negative publicity.

On the agenda for that day's meeting was an update from Woodford and his client relationship manager, Ross Lamacraft. The pair had always planned to attend the meeting – as Woodford had done every six months or so while managing Kent's money. It was the date on which Woodford had long suspected he would be told his investment services were no longer required. He had not expected to be let go three weeks earlier. The last time Woodford had visited the former courthouse in Maidstone was the previous November, to present his cocksure defence of his investment process. This time, the fund manager was far less bullish. Rather than boasting about his stock-picking abilities, now he was explaining what measures he was taking to sell off his portfolio and give Kent's pensioners their savings back.

The suspension of Equity Income perversely provided some relief to Woodford. For the first time in two years, he was not dogged by a consistent stream of investor withdrawals. Rather than spending his time worrying about finding cash to pay back departing clients, he was now able to focus on managing the portfolio. His priority was tackling the large portion of unlisted companies in Equity Income. He had promised to rid the fund of these assets and knew that, if it was to be revived, he would need to make sure he had them under control. The Patient Capital board ordered Link to revalue the trust's unquoted assets. Over the summer, Link wrote down the value of a handful of Woodford's smallest unlisted holdings, as well as Immunocore, one of his favoured businesses. The mark-down cut the biotechnology group's valuation in half. The revaluation further tainted Woodford's record of investing in start-ups and caused additional losses for his funds' investors.

Realizing he needed to speed up the divestment of unquoted companies, Woodford had already begun talks with PJT Park Hill, a boutique investment bank, about selling them in one go. PJT

Partners, the parent group, was run by Paul Taubman, a Wall Street wheeler-dealer who had once been the second-highest-paid chief executive in America. The business specialized in selling privately held assets to hedge funds and private equity managers. Woodford had in fact been in talks with PJT even before Equity Income was suspended and believed he could use his contacts in the City to sell stakes in the biggest unquoted companies over the summer. When Link heard about the discussions with PJT, it intervened and said it should take over the talks; after all, it was the authorized corporate director's role to hire the investment bank. The negotiations centred on a plan codenamed Project Oak, which was to package up the unquoted holdings and sell them either in one block or to several different investors.

Andrew Bailey had long coveted Mark Carney's job as head of the Bank of England. In many ways, he was the natural successor, having previously been deputy governor and with the experience of running a large financial regulator on his CV. Carney was due to step down the following year, leaving Bailey with a free run. But his time at the FCA had been plagued with controversy, not least over its handling of the collapse of mini-bond lender London Capital & Finance, which went into administration owing 11,000 investors a total of £236 million. The scandal caused politicians to doubt Bailey's competency to take on one of the UK economy's most important jobs. Bailey needed to get on top of the Woodford fiasco. He opened a formal FCA investigation into the suspension of the fund and the circumstances leading up to it. The probe would pay particular attention to the role of Woodford IM and Link, the fund's authorized corporate director.

On the morning of 25 June Bailey was called before the Treasury Select Committee, along with Charles Randell, his chairman at the FCA. Many commentators saw it as a public job interview for the role of governor of the Bank of England. The stated intention of the session was to examine the work of the regulator under Bailey's watch, but it centred on the fallout from the Woodford scandal.

From the outset it was clear how much public interest there was in the case as two members of the committee – Conservative MPs Steve Baker and Simon Clarke – had declared that they were not only customers of Hargreaves Lansdown but also trapped investors in Equity Income.

Nicky Morgan began by asking Bailey why it had taken the watchdog so long to identify problems at the Woodford fund. 'The market could see how many days it would take to liquidate the fund. Is that not a marker for the FCA of a need to intervene or to ask questions?' demanded Morgan, who was settling into her role as inquisitor-in-chief. Bailey proceeded to give an overview of the 'somewhat odd structure' that governed European investment funds, where Link's role as the authorized corporate director was so pivotal but little understood. Link had primary responsibility, Bailey insisted.

Next, Morgan moved on to the contentious Guernsey listings, and what role the FCA played in monitoring them. Very little, it turned out. Why had it taken so long for the FCA and the Guernsey stock exchange to discuss the listings – and why was the FCA so slow to respond, even after details of the arrangement were reported in the press. 'Does anyone in the FCA actually read the newspapers and listen to what is going on in the industry?' berated Morgan. Bailey brushed aside the sarcasm, but made it clear what he thought of the 'regulatory arbitrage' Woodford had engaged in when listing the companies offshore, adding that the fund manager had been 'sailing close to the wind' on the quantity of unquoted illiquid assets held in the fund.

Morgan, the trained lawyer, again went on the offensive. 'Should the regulator not have a requirement to ask questions and to watch out for public coverage, press coverage and words in the industry about concerns that are being raised about investments or where consumers are not getting the protection that they think they are entitled to?' she wanted to know. 'Should they not be warned that they are not getting that protection?' Bailey responded that Woodford's fund had exploited existing regulations 'to the full' and the

FCA relied on Link to keep it informed. But Link followed the rules to the letter without considering the reasons why the rules had been written in the first place. It had therefore not let the regulator know what was going on. Had it done so, the fund may have been suspended earlier, Bailey argued. 'That might have saved the people who have invested in it since,' Morgan admonished. 'There are people who put money in right up until suspension in June, who are now finding that they cannot get access to their money.'

Later in the cross-examination Charlie Elphicke, the MP for Dover, whose constituents were locked in Equity Income as members of the Kent pension scheme, asked Bailey about whether Hargreaves's clients were given enough information on the poor state of the fund while the broker continued to recommend it to them. Bailey responded that the FCA had already investigated Hargreaves's best-buy lists on several occasions, both directly and as part of industry-wide probes, and had asked the fund platform to make changes. He said the FCA was carrying out another review of Hargreaves to see if it should have ceased recommending Woodford's fund earlier.

Bailey was also asked pointedly whether the Woodford debacle was a failure of the FCA or of the rules governing the funds – in answer to which he, unsurprisingly, blamed the latter. Just as the interrogation was about to switch topics, Bailey and Morgan found a point on which they could agree: Woodford should drop his management fee while the fund was suspended. 'I totally agree with you that, as a sign to his investors, it would be a good thing to do,' said Bailey. 'He has not actually done that, I am afraid.'

The next day it was the turn of Mark Carney to face the parliamentary grilling. His off-the-cuff comment that funds like Woodford's were built on a lie caused a media storm. There were billions of dollars around the world held in funds that promised investors daily dealing, but invested in hard-to-shift assets, he said. He warned that such funds had the potential to cause serious economic shocks. 'We do have to be very deliberate about the types of measures that need to be taken – something that better aligns the redemption terms with the actual liquidity of the underlying investment is infinitely preferable to the situation we have today,' he said.

While politicians and regulators argued about where the blame should lie, Woodford was busy managing his desperate portfolio. Though he no longer had a torrent of outflows to deal with, the companies he had invested in were still prone to self-immolation. RM2, the maker of pallets using smart technology, announced to the stock market that it was fast running out of cash and had failed to agree a deal for new funding with its lenders. The business had just $3.3 million of cash and was burning through $2.3 million a month. Woodford had previously bailed it out and owned more than 60 per cent of the business after participating in rescue fundraisings. But he was no longer able to dip into his suspended Equity Income fund. RM2's share price crashed by more than 70 per cent when the market opened for business. Woodford was offered another lifeline by his long-term contacts Anton Bilton and Glyn Hirsch, the property developers whose businesses had helped him list his unquoted stakes in Guernsey. The Russian property company they ran, Raven, bought back his 12 per cent share in the group. Woodford had already sold down his stakes in several other listed companies, including Horizon Discovery, BCA Marketplace, NewRiver Reit and Oakley Capital, the hedge fund that had incubated his fledgling business over five years earlier.

On the afternoon of 1 July, twenty-eight days after suspending Equity Income, Link announced that it would not be lifting the trading gate on the fund and the suspension would continue indefinitely. That night, in a heavily edited video posted on the fund manager's website, Woodford appeared in a checked shirt, sitting at his desk and looking as if he had the weight of the world on his shoulders. 'So, we completely understand the frustration of our investors,' he said. 'But what we must do in that period of time is execute the strategy in a way that doesn't disadvantage our unitholders. And that's what we're working night and day on.'

The unfolding crisis was taking its toll on the staff at Woodford IM's headquarters. Not only were they working under the most intense pressure of their careers, but nearly all had their retirement savings tied up in the suspended Equity Income fund. To make matters worse, staff were being told their jobs could go. Woodford and Newman had built the business to have a 'flexible' cost structure – which, in reality, meant employing as few staff on full-time contracts as possible and plugging the gaps with workers on short-term deals. It meant that in leaner times, the temporary workers could be jettisoned with minimal fuss. But the dire straits the company found itself in meant several administrative staff were told their jobs were threatened, while the writing was on the wall for those in roles that seemed no longer necessary, such as sales reps for the big clients that had all bolted.

On 11 July Will Deer, the head of institutional sales, was let go. Deer had been one of the first employees to sign up to Woodford's new business five years earlier, leaving a comfortable role at Invesco Perpetual. Deer had been responsible for bringing on board the largest clients, including SJP, Kent, the Abu Dhabi Investment Authority and Omnis, the adviser group. He was also charged with keeping the relationships going while the tide began to turn for Woodford. Saku Saha, the British army veteran who had joined from Invesco Perpetual, had also left the company. Saha's main responsibility had been to analyse the unquoted companies before Woodford invested in them. As there were no institutional clients on the books and no new unlisted companies being invested in, it was clear that Deer and Saha no longer had roles to play at the business. But their departures were a sign that if the company ever did recover, it would be more focused on retail investors and would avoid investing in the problematic private start-ups that had sowed the seeds for its fall.

Link was also thinking about clearing the decks. From late June, the authorized corporate director began to consider whether it could salvage Equity Income, but without Woodford as manager. Karl Midl, head of Link's ACD business, started scouting around for alternatives. On 2 July Tony Stenning – a former managing director at BlackRock, the world's biggest fund manager – emailed Midl to suggest he contact Nick Hogwood, head of BlackRock's transition management business, which was set up to help shift investment funds from one investment manager to another. Stenning would later become Link's chairman.

Meanwhile, Woodford faced pressure from the board of Patient Capital, his FTSE 250 listed investment trust. For four years the directors – led by Susan Searle – had backed their fund manager to the hilt, but after Equity Income's suspension, and the ensuing downpour of negative coverage they received, the directors belatedly developed a backbone. They not only hired the pricey Winterflood Securities to act as broker to the trust but also parachuted in the financial PR advisers FTI Consulting to deal with media inquiries. They wanted to separate themselves from Woodford and his press handlers.

The board was concerned about a £150 million overdraft facility the trust had with its depositary, Northern Trust, a Chicago-based bank. That had been maxed out at the end of 2018, but after Woodford managed to raise cash by selling some of the fund's assets, the overdraft was down to £126 million. The board announced its intention to reduce the level to £75 million within six months and to nothing within a year. However, what was making that job harder was the funding commitments Woodford had signed up to. When cancer therapy company Proton Partners had listed in February, Woodford had agreed to hand £80 million to the business over the following eighteen months at times of the company's choosing. With Woodford's business now in a tailspin, the Proton Partners managers realized they needed to call in the commitment before the funds were bled dry. As Equity Income was suspended, Woodford was forced to make the payments from Patient Capital. By July, Proton Partners had already called in £35 million. Woodford had also agreed to buy an additional $10 million of shares in the Nasdaq-listed bioscience business Evofem just days after Equity Income's suspension.

Wary of any further commitments Woodford would make, the board clipped his wings. It introduced additional controls that required the fund manager to seek the board's permission to sell assets held by his other funds, invest in new companies or give additional money to companies he had already invested in. They were the types of restrictions Woodford had railed against his entire career. The intense loathing he had of interference in the way he ran his funds – which had led to his ill-fated departure from Invesco Perpetual five years earlier – reared its head again. Who were these directors to dictate to him how he should invest the fund that bore his name? If anything, they should be grateful for the patronage he had bestowed upon their companies over the years. In an act of defiance – which he would later attribute to needing to meet a personal tax bill – Woodford sold £1 million of his personal shares in the trust, which equated to 60 per cent of his holding in it. He had so little regard for the board by that point that he gave them no forewarning and did not notify them for three weeks.

Woodford also continued to sign cheques for companies he had invested in over the years. He had been the first large investor to back Atom Bank, the disruptive digital lender that hoped to challenge the stranglehold of Britain's biggest high-street banks. Mark Mullen, Atom's chief executive, even said that without Woodford's support the mobile-focused challenger would not have survived. So, when in late July Atom needed to attract more funds to meet banking rules on protecting depositors, Woodford was happy to chip in on a £50 million fundraising.

Meanwhile, Hargreaves Lansdown was still in the firing line over its role in promoting Woodford's funds until the suspension. By now its chief executive Chris Hill had defended its backing of Woodford in his response to questions from Nicky Morgan. He said that over Woodford's three-decade career managing money, he had had barren spells, but he always came back stronger. There was a belief among Hargreaves's investment analysts that this time would be the same. His letter to Morgan also laid bare the extent to which Hargreaves's 1.1 million trusting clients had followed its recommendations, with more than a quarter being trapped in Equity Income. He did not provide figures for his clients' investments in Woodford's other two funds.

Hargreaves was criticized for allowing Equity Income and Income Focus to survive the cull on the best-buy list at the beginning of the year, despite their woeful performance. Hargreaves said at the time that they had survived in part because they offered a further discount to the fund supermarket's customers. This was seized upon by Hargreaves's rivals. Richard Wilson, chief executive of Interactive Investor, another online broker, told Morgan that the discount Woodford reserved solely for Hargreaves meant the latter's customers who tried to switch their accounts to other providers were unable to do so. 'Investors who hold the . . . fund have both hands tied behind their back – they can neither exit the fund, nor transfer their assets to platforms which might better suit their needs,' he wrote to the committee chair. 'At what is already a difficult time for these investors, we think this is unacceptable.' He said several Hargreaves customers had tried to move to his business but had been blocked by Link. Hargreaves and Link eventually relented to the calls to allow clients to switch.

Three weeks after dumping £1 million of shares in his own investment trust, Woodford finally got around to telling the board. The once-loyal directors were enraged when they found out on Saturday, 27 July. In hastily arranged conference calls over the weekend involving the board, Winterflood and FTI, a plan was hatched to exact their revenge. At 7 a.m. on the following Monday, the board issued a statement to the stock market announcing Woodford's share sale. It made clear that he had kept the sale from them for three weeks and let them know only the previous Saturday. The board said that, while it was not required to make the dealing public, it had decided it should do so right away. In an accompanying statement, the board acknowledged it had held preliminary discussions with other fund managers about replacing Woodford. The *FT* had previously reported on these discussions, but this was the first time the board had admitted to them. As with the details of Woodford's share sale, the board was not required to make such information public – but it had chosen to do so to signal that its relationship with the fund manager was ruptured beyond repair.

A private investor in the trust told the *FT* that it was 'disgraceful' that Woodford had sold his shares without making it public. 'The market has been kept in the dark,' he said. 'Neil Woodford should be made to stand in front of the Treasury Select Committee to explain himself as soon as possible.' Woodford's share sale was a kick in the teeth to the investors who had stuck by him for so long. At the same time he was recording videos imploring them to hold tight, he was pulling his own cash from the funds and protecting his personal wealth from any more shocks.

The level of hypocrisy went down like a lead balloon at Oxford Business Park, where the threat of redundancy hung in the air. Several contractors had been let go at a moment's notice, asked to clear their desks and leave the office immediately. Morale was low. Those still working knew that, whatever the outcome, Woodford IM would always be a blot on their CV, something they would need to explain away in future job interviews. Staff who had backed their leader throughout – most of whom had left well-paid jobs to join him – and invested their own pensions in his funds were now seeing his true colours. Despite his claims that they were all in it together, and his tearful speech at the Christmas party seven months earlier, Woodford was leaving them high and dry.

Woodford was not the only one looking to cash out. Craig Newman had appointed a high-end property dealer to produce sales brochures for his luxury properties. He sent these to contacts, giving the seven-bedroom arts-and-crafts mansion a £10 million price tag and valuing his Wargrave six-bedroom property at £4.9 million. Newman and Woodford had already extracted £13.8 million from the business personally that year in one final chunky dividend payment, and continued to bill trapped investors £65,000 a day, despite growing calls from regulators, politicians and the media to drop the charges. The cash cow was running dry, but Woodford and Newman were making sure they milked it completly dry.

Woodford certainly felt he was earning his fee. At the end of July, the Guernsey stock exchange announced it was cancelling the listings of Woodford's holdings, including two of his biggest investments, Benevolent AI and Industrial Heat. Guernsey, which had been stung a decade earlier by its association with the bust Arch Cru funds, was looking to avoid being tarred by the latest British investment scandal. The move meant the unquoted portion of Equity Income smashed through the 10 per cent regulatory limit. Close to 20 per cent of the fund was now in unlisted companies. By this point, Link had told Woodford to work towards a notional date of early December to reopen the fund. While Woodford had made progress in offloading some holdings, he knew he needed to get on top of the private portion by December.

Yet the other companies in his portfolio continued to throw up problems. Burford Capital, a business that financed litigation, was attacked in early August by US hedge-fund manager Carson Block, who accused the business of aggressive accounting. Block published an explosive research paper on the business, which sent its share price tumbling 57 per cent in one of the most devastating short-selling attacks the UK had seen. Woodford had been a long-time backer of Burford and took a £119 million paper hit on the fall.

More bad news followed. Link, on the instructions of the Patient Capital board, continued reassessing the valuations on Woodford's private holdings. Many of the companies had received sky-high appraisals from Link over the years, helped by advice given to it by Duff & Phelps, the independent consultants. But Link had replaced D&P with IHS Markit, another third party, which had a different view on the companies. Link and IHS took another look at Industrial Heat, the cold fusion business that had recently been kicked off the Guernsey stock exchange, and decided it was not as promising as it first appeared. Industrial Heat was one of the biggest holdings in Patient Capital, and when Link and IHS cut its valuation by 40 per cent, the trust's net asset value sank 4 per cent, prompting a 13 per cent fall in the share price. The company was also a big holding in Equity Income, with the write-down wiping out more than £40 million for the fund's captive investors. Less than a year earlier Woodford had participated in a funding round that had increased Industrial Heat's value by 357 per cent. The valuation process appeared chaotic and Link's handling of it inept.

Link had attracted a considerable amount of flak for its role in Equity Income's suspension. The FCA was investigating its involvement and interactions with Woodford, while Andrew Bailey had made it plain during his Treasury Select Committee appearance that he felt the business had questions to answer about how much information it fed back to the regulator. The revaluations of Woodford's unquoted companies – which Link was responsible for – were also embarrassing for the business, since it had marked them so high in the first place. Throughout August the FCA began telling Link's fellow authorized corporate directors that they should prepare for an industry probe. The crucial role the niche service providers played in the governance of the UK's investment industry had been laid bare by the implosion of Woodford's funds. It had also exposed the failings and lack of accountability within the regulatory structure.

Woodford and Newman were also becoming increasingly frustrated with Link. For weeks, the Woodford IM compliance team, as well as representatives from Link and PJT, the boutique investment bank, had been discussing Project Oak, the plan to sell the unquoted assets. Woodford believed this was key to making sure that when the fund reopened – which he still hoped would be in December – it would be able to survive without further suspensions. But Link had delayed formally hiring PJT to begin the work of shifting the assets, despite Woodford opening discussions with the investment bank in May. He began to harbour suspicions that Link was drawing out the appointment unnecessarily.

Things continued to go from bad to worse at Patient Capital. Responding to claims that the directors had been too close to Woodford over the years, the trust revamped its board. One of

Woodford's long-standing allies, Steven Harris, who was chief executive of Woodford favourite Circassia Pharmaceuticals, stepped down and was replaced by Jane Tufnell, an experienced investment trust director with little connection to the fund manager. The trust was in a sorry state, with its share price having halved that year. It was on course to crash out of the FTSE 250 index of mid-size British companies. The spate of write-downs had only made matters worse. Benevolent AI, the fund's largest holding, was the latest to suffer a horrific devaluation. A year earlier its value was set at £1.5 billion, but when Temasek, the Singaporean sovereign wealth fund, injected more cash into the business, the investment triggered its value to halve.

The trust also had a weighty overdraft hanging round its neck. While the amount it owed to Northern Trust was slowly coming down, the trust was restricted to borrowing only 20 per cent of its assets. This meant that every time one of its holdings was devalued – or Woodford committed further cash to companies – more of the overdraft needed to be paid back. In return for more flexibility over the loan, Woodford was forced to allow Northern Trust a final say over any further investments he made from Patient Capital.

By early October the private devaluations and public company wipe-outs had taken their toll on Equity Income. An *FT* analysis put the losses for trapped investors at 20 per cent of their holdings from the time the fund was frozen four months earlier. During that period, the FTSE All-Share had been flat. Hundreds of thousands of investors in the fund could do little but watch in horror as their life savings disintegrated before their eyes. Since the suspension, they had paid more than £8 million in fees. Meanwhile, investors in Woodford's still open Income Focus fund had lost 16 per cent over the same period.

Despite the woeful performance, Link's administrators told Newman they were encouraged with the progress Woodford was making in rejigging the portfolio in preparation for opening Equity Income's gates in early December. Woodford had been selling what unquoted and small companies he could and reinvesting the proceeds into FTSE 100 and 250 companies – the types of businesses he built his reputation on investing in. But for two weeks, Link went silent. Newman's calls and emails to the authorized corporate director went unanswered. Again, Woodford and Newman got the impression that something was going on in the background.

Then, out of the blue, on Friday, 11 October, Karl Midl emailed Newman to invite him and Woodford to Link's London offices for a meeting the following Monday afternoon. Midl said plans for Equity Income had reached a crucial stage and he wanted to provide them with an update on Project Oak. He also wanted Newman and Woodford to let him know how the portfolio adjustment was going so that he could keep the FCA up to speed. Attendees should be kept to a minimum, Midl said, so just Newman and Woodford were invited from Woodford IM. The meeting was set for 4 p.m.

Over the weekend, Woodford, Newman and the compliance staff put together a presentation to show Link how far the investment team had gone in making the portfolio more liquid. The proportion of the fund in the hardest-to-shift assets had dropped from 34 per cent to 23 per cent, while the most liquid assets now comprised 43 per cent, up from 12 per cent when the fund was suspended. Woodford hoped PJT would sell the illiquid holdings throughout October and November, which would help bring the fund to the level at which it could reopen. Woodford's team also argued in the presentation that reopening the fund was in the best interests of its investors, and that winding it down would cost them time and money. They said a wind-down was likely to take over a year and cost investors more than a third of their assets, while carrying on repositioning the fund with a view to reopening in December would result in just a 7 per cent hit.

Woodford's sales team had carried out a poll of the company's biggest clients and found that many IFAs were still supportive of the fund manager, even after his spectacular downfall. So confident were Woodford and Newman that they could resurrect the business, they lined up a roadshow throughout November, taking in eighteen venues, where they would try to drum up support for investing in Woodford's funds. They even paid the deposits on all the hotels and events venues.

Consequently, when the pair showed up at Link's headquarters at 65 Gresham Street in London's Square Mile that Monday afternoon, they expected the meeting to be a mere formality. Within minutes, however, they realized that wouldn't be the case. Midl refused to hear their carefully planned presentation and told them that Link had taken the decision to wind down the fund and had lined up PJT and BlackRock to sell its unquoted and quoted assets, respectively. The meeting lasted just thirty minutes.

Numb with shock, and realizing that this meant the business could not survive, Woodford and Newman weaved their way through the surrounding streets, trying to collect their thoughts while avoiding the throng of commuters. Shock soon turned to anger – how could this glorified administrator effectively consign their business to the corporate scrapheap? They called Midl and demanded to continue the meeting with their lawyers present. Midl reluctantly agreed, and at 5 p.m. Woodford and Newman marched back into Link's offices and for nearly three hours pleaded with Midl and his colleagues to keep the fund going. But Link's team were unwavering. With the FCA expecting an update at 8 p.m., they called the meeting to a close at 7.55. Woodford's time was up in every sense. Woodford and Newman were once again shown the door and emerged onto the cold and increasingly deserted London streets, just a few blocks away from where Woodford's investment career had begun more than three decades earlier. A light rain drizzled over their hunched shoulders.

Woodford had always hated the 'bullshit' of London, with its groupthink culture and clubby connections. Having left for Henley as an anonymous investor in the late 1980s, he had never looked back. His renown as an investment alchemist, making fortunes for his followers, propelled him to the top of his field. The successful launch of his breakaway business five years earlier only confirmed the high esteem in which he was held. Yet in less than two years, Woodford Investment Management had gone from managing £18 billion to next to nothing. Woodford's reputation as the man who made Middle England rich was indeed, it turned out, built on a lie. It was a humbling end to the career of one of the investment industry's most celebrated fund managers.

12

Aftermath

At 8.30 a.m. on Tuesday, 15 October 2019, two dozen staff shuffled into the boardroom at Woodford Investment Management's head office, while a similar number dialled in to a conference call. Outside, in the dreary business park, a pale mist gathered as the nearby Oxford ring road hummed with morning commuters. Just five of those present – including Neil Woodford and Craig Newman – had known the night before of Link's decision to wind up Equity Income, but by now everyone was fully aware. Without warning Woodford and Newman, Link had announced to the fund's investors and the press at 7.10 a.m. that the fund was closing and that Woodford had been fired with immediate effect. Within minutes the story was splashed across the *FT's* website and led business reports on Radio 4's *Today* programme.

While all Woodford's staff appreciated the significance of the Link meeting the previous afternoon, none had expected the rug to be pulled from under them straight away. At worst, they believed, they would be given three months to liquidate the fund. The consequences were clear to everyone. The company's revenue was almost entirely dependent on Equity Income, its flagship product. It was yet to receive any money from running the Patient Capital Trust as Woodford had never met his performance targets. The smaller Income Focus fund provided some revenue, but nowhere near enough to keep the business running. All the other mandates the company ran had been taken away in the summer. Losing Equity Income was the deathblow for Woodford Investment Management.

Staff sobbed as Woodford gave another emotional speech, but

this time there were no promises to revive the business. The revenue tap had been turned off and the company simply could not survive. He told them that he would resign as manager of Patient Capital and Income Focus later that day and spend the next few months serving his notice period on the final two funds and closing operations. All staff would eventually be let go, though some would be clearing their desks that very afternoon. In many cases, those made redundant left with the minimum of just one or two months' salary as a redundancy package and were asked to sign non-disclosure agreements. It was a far cry from the lavish payouts Woodford and Newman had helped themselves to over the years.

Link insisted it had been forced to wind down Equity Income because there had been little progress in shifting the £700 million of unquoted companies in the fund. Link said if the fund were to reopen in December it was at risk of crumbling under further redemption waves and being forced to suspend again, meaning investors who were slow off the mark would be trapped once more. Woodford responded with an angry post on his website, making clear that the decision to close the fund was Link's alone and one that he 'cannot accept, nor believe is in the long-term interests of' investors. In a later, more contrite statement announcing the closure of the business, Woodford added: 'I personally deeply regret the impact events have had on individuals who placed their faith in Woodford Investment Management and invested in our funds.'

The following morning, 16 October, Link suspended trading in the £252 million Income Focus fund in response to Woodford's resignation. Fund suspensions were rare enough, and almost always happened when managers were struggling to pay off departing investors from a fund with too few liquid holdings. Income Focus had been designed to be easily tradable, though, so in this case liquidity was not the issue. Rather, Link believed Woodford's resignation would cause a run on the fund as his staunchest supporters followed him out of the door. The fund had already halved since Equity Income's suspension just four months earlier, with most of the outflow the result of Hargreaves Lansdown dropping Income

Focus from its multi-manager range. Meanwhile, Patient Capital's share price dropped 7 per cent when the market opened.

As the fallout spread, Hargreaves was yet again contaminated. Angry customers vented their spleen to the *FT*. 'They have been influential for thousands and thousands of investors who've come a cropper and waiving their fees just isn't enough,' complained Terry Mackie, who had managed to withdraw his holding in Equity Income just before the redemption gates were slammed shut. Another, who was trapped in the fund and watched in horror as his £23,000 investment withered to just £8,000, said he 'felt strongly let down' as he had 'felt reassured by the numerous Hargreaves updates' from the broker's cheerleaders, principally Mark Dampier. The Hargreaves head of research had gone to ground. He deleted numerous posts on his Twitter account praising Woodford and, for the first time in his career, avoided all calls from journalists. Hargreaves's stock was by that point down 25 per cent following Dampier and his wife's offloading of shares in the business worth £5.6 million.

Another Hargreaves customer told the *FT* that it had been Equity Income's inclusion on the fund supermarket's best-buy list, and its relentless marketing campaigns, that had persuaded him to invest in it two years earlier. 'Their articles may say "this is not investment advice" but they are written with a purpose, and the clear purpose is to encourage people like me to invest,' he said. 'Looking back, it feels like they were just writing a report based on his [Woodford's] previous good name as an investor, rather than looking into the fund and exactly what he had invested in. Shouldn't the huge amount of unquoted stocks have been a red flag for them, or at least properly mentioned in the articles?'

John McDonnell, Labour's shadow chancellor, waded in, promising to carry out a twelve-month inquiry into the finance sector if his party were elected in the upcoming general election. 'Investment platforms appear to have acted with a conflict of interest – and in many ways they are still largely unregulated,' he lamented, reserving further criticism for Andrew Bailey's FCA. 'This closure of another Woodford fund raises serious questions about whether our regulators are again asleep at the wheel.'

That weekend, scores of snared Equity Income investors contacted the *FT*'s personal finance pages to share their scorn. 'I feel like I've been scammed,' complained a thirty-eight-year-old youth worker from north London who had £2,500 of savings in the fund. 'I know I've probably lost most of that money, and I just have to shrug my shoulders and get on with life.' But the youth worker, like many other readers, did not hold Woodford solely responsible. 'The funny thing is, I don't really blame Neil Woodford for this. I feel powerless and frustrated that he's been removed from the fund as I was hopeful he could recalibrate. I fear the hit from a fire sale is going to be a lot worse than leaving him in there.'

A common feeling among the aggrieved investors was that it was Woodford's mess and he should be allowed to clear it up, rather than Link – a company they barely knew existed until just a few months before – taking the matter out of his hands. They were concerned about the fees BlackRock and PJT would extract from the fund for their role in winding it up. 'I would much prefer Woodford to sort things out as he has skin in the fund both financially and in terms of saving his reputation,' said Julian Thornett, another investor in the fund. 'In the case of a third party selling the lot and lining their pockets in the process, only their profit motivates them – crystallizing other people's losses does not hurt.'

Just over a week after Woodford resigned as manager of Patient Capital, the trust's board announced it had lined up Schroders, the blue-blood City fund manager, to replace him. Shareholders reacted with glee, pushing the stock price up 30 per cent – though it was still less than half its value at the start of the year, and a third down on when Woodford had cashed out in July. Investors in the fund said they hoped Schroders, which had been managing investment trusts since 1924, would take a more rigorous approach to risk management and stock selection. But analysts warned that despite the spate of write-downs the fund had already suffered that year, more were likely to follow once the incoming manager took a closer look at the underlying investments. Investors would also notice the new charging structure Schroders negotiated. Rather than giving up a fee if it failed to hit a performance target, as Woodford had done, the new manager would pocket up to 1 per cent of the assets each year, regardless of how well it performed. It was a standard fee model for the investment trust industry. Woodford's attempts at upsetting the status quo on charging had failed.

Those Eeyoreish analysts who warned more bad news was in store for Patient Capital investors were proved right just days later when Link once again marked down the value of Industrial Heat, the controversial cold fusion company that had attracted investment from Brad Pitt and Laurene Powell Jobs. Link said it devalued the loss-making company owing to a 'delay in its operational progress'. As a result, the business, whose value Link had marked up by 357 per cent just a year earlier, had since been cut back by 83 per cent. Link's valuation process was being shown up for the shambles it was. The trust's share price fell once more, while the reduction in the fund's net asset value caused it to trip over the 20 per cent borrowing limit it had in place with Northern Trust.

Having mostly treated Woodford's business with kid gloves since its launch five years earlier, the Financial Conduct Authority belatedly decided it needed to take control of the situation. It had been castigated by politicians, consumer rights activists and the press for its supine approach to dealing with the fund manager and his increasingly cavalier methods of running his portfolios. Bailey was also still in the frame for the Bank of England role and he needed to demonstrate that the regulator was on top of its latest crisis. The FCA continued to probe authorized corporate directors and began looking at the various multi-manager funds that were still exposed to Equity Income. At least fifteen products offered by wealth managers and brokers, holding £15 billion of savings, were invested in the defunct fund. Hargreaves accounted for six of the funds and more than a third of the assets, while products from wealth manager Quilter and several smaller offerings were also invested. The regulator worried that liquidity fears over Woodford's fund would spread to the other products and investors would bolt, leaving those remaining with unsellable holdings in Equity Income.

The FCA's belated attempts at showing it was in control of the situation proved enough for Bailey to achieve his ambition. The Conservatives swept to victory in the general election and a week later, on 20 December, chancellor Sajid Javid announced that Bailey would take over from Mark Carney as governor of the Bank of England at the end of January. A year older than Woodford, Bailey began his career at the Bank of England in the mid-1980s when Woodford was cutting his teeth in the City. During Woodford's short spell at Eagle Star, the two worked on opposite sides of Threadneedle Street. As poacher and gamekeeper, the pair rose through the ranks of their long-term employers, Invesco Perpetual and the Bank of England, and became stars within them. At similar junctures in their careers, they each left comfortable roles to try new ventures, with Bailey becoming the first chief executive of the Prudential Regulation Authority a year before Woodford launched his own investment business. But at the point where Woodford's career was in free fall, Bailey's reached its peak.

As Bailey prepared to take on one of the biggest jobs in global finance, Woodford and Newman were in the advanced stages of winding up the company they had launched with great pizazz just a few years earlier. Most staff had been laid off and the business abandoned its Oxford offices. The handful of workers kept on to close the company down and ensure the last two funds transferred to the new managers without a hitch were working from home. Link had by now decided to hand over the reins of Income Focus to Standard Life Aberdeen, the UK's largest listed investment group, but the managers entrusted with turning the fund round had failed to beat the FTSE All-Share over the previous five years. Link, Standard Life Aberdeen and Northern Trust, the custodian, all agreed to waive their fees for the first few months, yet investors would still be saddled with the costs of the new fund managers remodelling the portfolio to their own liking.

While most business commentators were calling the end of

Woodford's career, the fund manager had other ideas. In December Woodford and Newman flew to China to meet investors interested in backing young British companies. The Tories' victory at the general election had made Britain's departure from the EU a foregone conclusion. It was the opportunity Woodford had been waiting for. Now there was certainty about Brexit, he believed the pent-up demand from overseas investors to buy UK businesses would be unleashed. He hoped to convince Chinese investors he had got to know over the years, companies that had put money into some of the same university spin-offs as he had, to fund a new venture he had in mind that would invest solely in British start-ups. China Construction Bank, for example, the world's second largest lender, had been persuaded to back Woodford's two favourite unquoted companies, Oxford Nanopore and Immunocore. It was clear that, despite the disintegration of his business owing to his investments in unquoted companies, this was still an area Woodford wanted to pursue.

On 28 January 2020 the scale of the losses for the approximately 400,000 investors trapped in Equity Income started to become clear. Woodford no longer had any involvement in the moribund fund but his management of it still ate into their life savings. Link revealed that BlackRock had managed to shift the three-quarters of the fund's assets that it had been instructed to dispose of. These were stakes in the biggest listed companies, which were the easiest to unload while receiving a fair market price. This enabled Link to pay back investors an initial instalment on their holdings in the fund. In theory, this was the first milestone for the fund's investors on a long road to moving on from the whole debacle. It should have been cause for some relief. However, the payment crystallized their losses, the money they were getting back being 20 per cent less than they would have received had they taken it out before the fund was suspended in June.

And worse was to come. The remaining quarter of the portfolio was much harder to sell. PJT still had made little progress in disposing of the remaining £700 million of large stakes in unlisted and small businesses left in the fund. Losses on that portion of the portfolio were likely to be much higher – meaning investors could in theory lose up to 45 per cent of their trapped savings. Link provided no time-scale on how long the sale of the illiquid assets would take, but analysts speculated that the process could drag on for at least another year. One investor in the fund told the *FT*: 'On one hand, it's deeply disappointing to face further delays in getting my money back; on the other, it's not at all surprising. For me it's only a few thousand pounds – if it was my life savings, I would be up in arms.'

To rub salt into the wounds, Proton Partners – which had since renamed itself Rutherford Health – called in another £7.5 million from Equity Income as part of the £80 million commitment Woodford made to the cancer therapy company a year earlier to encourage it to go public. The managers of the business recognized there would soon be little left in the fund so were making sure they secured what they were due. In fact, a total of £22.5 million was still owed to various companies Woodford had made promises to and the payments would be coming out of the fund before investors received their own reimbursements. As if that was not bad enough, the fund's investors were also having to pay wind-up costs, which had grown to £5 million since Link sacked Woodford three months earlier. Link expected these to rise to £10.3 million over time. Woodford IM had already taken £8 million in fees for the four months it managed the fund between June and October. The captive fund investors were having to wait until everyone else had taken a bite before they would see any more of their money.

Two people who had certainly had their fair share over the years were Woodford and Newman. In the five years they ran the business into the ground they extracted at least £75 million in total from it in dividends. Woodford's share was two-thirds of the pickings, amounting to £50 million, compared to Newman's £25 million. The payouts ensured both men were well stocked with sports cars and could continue to indulge their weaknesses for luxury properties and expensive pastimes. But the true level of their appropriation from the business was actually a fair amount higher. In 2016 the pair remodelled the business from a legal point of view, turning it from a partnership into a limited company. They always insisted there were no personal tax advantages to the move, but it did mean that there were six months of unreleased financial accounts for the business during the transition. People close to the company say that in that period they took a similar amount out of the business as they had done in the six months on record – which would bring their combined hoard closer to £90 million.

The Woodford wreckage could not have come at a worse time for the Financial Conduct Authority. Andrew Bailey had been desperately trying to make himself out to be the natural successor to Mark Carney at the Bank of England, while the regulator could not shake off the lingering stench of incompetence that had become more powerful with the collapse of London Capital & Finance. Woodford's fall from grace could have been averted had the watchdog heeded red flags earlier and not outsourced regulatory oversight to Link. The FCA was far too eager to allow Woodford's partners to set up the new business, waving through the application in record time despite the fact the stock picker was at the centre of a huge ongoing investigation while at Invesco Perpetual. This in itself should have given the regulator pause to consider whether there was enough challenge within Woodford's new business to prevent similar missteps. At only one point did the FCA push back on the business plan, and that was to impose Link – or Capita, as it was then – as the authorized corporate director, despite the regulator having chastised the administrator for the role it had already played in two fund scandals. It was as if the FCA believed that, because Link and Woodford had both been through the regulatory wringer, they would each be more cautious this time round and influence the other to take fewer risks. They could not have been more wrong.

The FCA then failed to pick up on several warning signs throughout the five years Woodford IM was up and running.

When Nick Hamilton and Gray Smith, two of the four founding partners, left the business acrimoniously within a year and reported their concerns to the regulator in lengthy exit interviews, the FCA failed to act. The regulator continued to trust that Link would keep Woodford on the straight and narrow, even after it had allowed the fund manager to breach the trash ratio limit on two occasions in early 2018. And when the FCA found out that Woodford had arranged complex schemes to wheedle his way out of the self-imposed liquidity trap – such as the Guernsey listings and the Patient Capital asset swap – without Link giving it notice, the regulator again did nothing.

The evidence that came to light as part of the Treasury Select Committee's probe revealed a docile watchdog that, despite growling, did not bite. It was too ready to entrust authorized corporate directors like Link to carry out day-to-day oversight of investment funds, which meant it had little understanding about what was going on in the industry. A Freedom of Information request by the *FT* showed the FCA had no central database to monitor when funds suspended trading, so it could not keep track of how big a problem this was among the 3,200 investment funds that savers relied on it to police.

By coincidence, at the same time the Woodford scandal was unravelling, the FCA was due to publish a report into the series of suspensions of UK property funds immediately following the Brexit referendum three years earlier. The funds were invested in bricks-and-mortar assets, such as shopping centres and office blocks. As investors became spooked that the UK property market would take a hit after the vote, they tried to withdraw their money and the fund managers were unable to sell the assets quickly enough to meet the redemption requests. The regulator was already in the process of looking into the problem of open-ended funds investing in hard-to-sell assets at the point when Equity Income was felled by the same flaw. The FCA delayed its report into the property funds until late 2019 to consider its initial findings from the Woodford debacle.

The report found that Equity Income investors 'were not aware of, or did not appear to understand, the liquidity risk to which they were exposed'. It also said they had little knowledge of 'the impact this [liquidity] risk might have on their ability to realize their investments on demand'. It was as close to a rebuke as the regulator was willing to give. The report also unveiled a range of safety measures that property funds would need to implement within a year, including increased disclosure to investors, additional over-sight from depositories and for fund managers to have strong liquidity risk contingency plans in place. It also introduced a safety net in the form of an instruction that funds must suspend trading if more than 20 per cent of their assets were deemed hard to value by the fund's independent valuer. Though the new rules related only to property funds, the FCA said it would consider rolling them out more broadly to other investment products.

While the new measures were cautiously welcomed by those in the industry, they failed to tackle some of the more fundamental problems the Woodford saga exposed. Chief among them was the issue, highlighted by Mark Carney, where investors thought they could treat certain funds like ATM machines when in fact they were investing in assets that were impossible to shift in short order. The FCA also failed to tackle deficiencies in the system that even Bailey identified during his testimony in Parliament, such as funds skirting the trash ratio rule by announcing that unquoted compa-nies planned to list within a year. The Guernsey listings also exposed a gaping loophole the FCA failed to close.

Link's failure to keep Woodford in line tarnished the reputation of authorized corporate directors as a whole. The FCA's probe into the little-understood cottage industry was aimed at working out whether the flaws were Link's alone or fundamental problems in the whole governance set-up. A person who knows the sector well believes Link was simply the wrong company to work for Wood-ford, with his inclination to stretch the rules, which made the decision for the FCA to force Link onto the new business all the more bizarre. 'Link has one model and one model only, which they stick to no matter the client,' the industry expert says. 'But Link is commercially driven, and they take on anyone, whatever their requirements. Woodford was simply too big and complex for Link's process-driven approach. The FCA, as much as anyone, should have known this.'

Link allowed Woodford to breach regulatory limits and, to the regulator's dismay, failed to notice conflicts of interest over the valuation process of unquoted companies. Once Link took more control over pricing these businesses, their values soared then plunged, revealing a chaotic and poorly planned system. The results were devastating for the liquidity levels of Woodford's portfolios. Link's failure to keep the regulator in the loop on the Guernsey listings and Patient Capital asset swap appeared sloppy at best. Though Link was not formally required to inform the FCA, the creative ploys were warning signs Woodford's fund was in trouble and which the regulator should have been made aware of. The company's process-driven approach also meant it suspended Equity Income in June without trying to reach a compromise first. Newman had long suspected that Link was not up to the job and in 2017 commissioned some research into the sector to assess what other providers could offer. The report was scathing about Link's proficiency and suggested several other companies could do a better job. But Newman chose to stick with Link, not least because its fees were among the lowest in the market. It would be a decision he would come to regret bitterly.

As part of its industry review, the FCA said it would consider introducing different redemption terms for large and small fund investors to avoid risks of institutional clients like Kent County Council trying to pull hundreds of millions of pounds in one go and sparking a fund implosion. The various steps taken by Kent through its five-year association with Woodford IM revealed a body with its own governance deficiencies. The decision to invest fully in the fund and become one of its biggest investors, rather than choosing to go for a separate mandate, tied Kent's hands behind its back from the start. Nick Vickers, the local authority's

finance director, also rejected offers to restructure the arrangement in the months leading up to Equity Income's suspension,
which would have given the council more flexibility when it chose
to withdraw. In the end, Kent's miscommunication with Link when
the eventual decision was made to fire Woodford lit the fuse on
Europe's biggest investment scandal for a decade. Kent generally
had a good reputation among local authorities and was especially
liked by Conservative national governments. But it failed to learn
lessons from its dealings with risky Icelandic banks a decade earlier. Once again it had endangered the retirement savings of
hundreds of thousands of local government workers.

When Hargreaves Lansdown's aggressive marketers negotiated
the biggest discount on offer for its clients to invest in Woodford's
funds in return for heavy promotion of the products, they hoped to
tie the two popular brands together and draw in the stock picker's
hordes of devotees as new customers. Woodford's new venture was
the most eagerly anticipated launch in British fund management
and Hargreaves hoped to ride on its coat-tails. The trouble was,
the plan worked too well. The years of personal endorsements for
Woodford by Hargreaves spokesmen – from co-founder Peter
Hargreaves to cheerleader-in-chief Mark Dampier and head of
investments Lee Gardhouse – created an unhealthily close relationship between the two companies. This was intensified by the
inclusion of Woodford's funds on the highly persuasive best-buy
lists all the way to Equity Income's suspension, despite their shocking performance for the final two years. The heavy investment into
Woodford's vehicles by Hargreaves's multi-manager funds created
even tighter ties between the two businesses, which eventually
began to suffocate the fund supermarket.

As Woodford's company eventually imploded, close to 300,000
Hargreaves customers were caught in the suspended Equity
Income, with tens of thousands more having made big losses following Hargreaves's recommendations and investing in his other
funds. These DIY investors seeking somewhere to park their

savings trusted the Hargreaves brand to point them in the right direction. So when it was revealed as part of the Treasury Select Committee evidence that Dampier and his fellow investment analysts at Hargreaves had felt uneasy about Woodford's stock-picking ability for at least eighteen months before Equity Income's suspension but had given little indication to their customers, that trust evaporated. Added to that, Dampier and Gardhouse combined sold millions of pounds' worth of shares in their own company in the days leading up to Equity Income's suspension, when it was clear to those closest to Woodford's business that it was in danger of running aground.

The damage was irreparable. During nearly forty years, Hargreaves Lansdown grew from its humble beginnings in a spare bedroom in Bristol to become a FTSE 100 company and Britain's largest investment wholesaler. Its stunning rise was built on making it easier for savers to invest in funds and convincing its customers that it was looking out for them. In doing so, it had created one of the strongest consumer brands in UK finance. But overnight that went out the window. Suddenly law firms up and down the country began to advertise to aggrieved Hargreaves customers, trying to build class action lawsuits against the business. In one advert, posted on Facebook in November 2019, a law firm tried to drum up interest using a photo of a pensive twenty-something hipster, complete with thick beard, top-knot hairstyle and denim shirt. 'We're investigating possible claims for those who invested in Woodford funds through Hargreaves Lansdown and have lost money after the closure of its Equity Income fund,' the ad read. 'Approximately one in four customers may be affected.' It showed the victims came from all walks of life, not just those close to retirement with weighty savings pots. Thousands of Hargreaves customers signed up with the litigation specialists in the hope of recouping some of their losses.

Hargreaves's failings also tarred best-buy lists in general. Investors who relied on what they believed to be carefully researched lists of the funds with potential to outperform the market were shocked to discover that in some cases the selections were based more on the level of discount the fund manager was prepared to offer. In late 2019 the *FT* commissioned a study by research group Fundscape into the quality of funds promoted on best-buy lists. It found that actively managed UK equity funds recommended by Hargreaves and two other distributors – Bestinvest and Charles Stanley – on average lagged much cheaper tracker funds over the previous three years.

The FCA had looked at the lists on several occasions, and it had given them a clean bill of health during its last market-wide probe in March 2019. That report highlighted how important the lists were, with a fifth of investors relying on them. It also found that inclusion on the list led to an average of £5.9 million flowing into the funds each year – but for high-profile funds like Woodford's, the figure was in the hundreds of millions. In the immediate aftermath of Equity Income's suspension, when Andrew Bailey was desperately trying to appear to be in control of the situation, he announced the regulator would once again look at how brokers were using best-buy lists. In February 2020 the FCA wrote to the chief executives of fund supermarkets to tell them that, when creating such lists, they should do so with impartiality. They should avoid giving preference to funds with the biggest discount and make sure the research teams putting the lists together were independent. The regulator also said that the platforms should have clear processes to pick, monitor and remove funds from the lists, and inform customers how decisions are made. Hargreaves responded by scrapping its now much-maligned Wealth 50 list and replacing it with a new Wealth Shortlist, which would be presided over by an independent panel. The broker's customers – and their lawyers – will be watching closely to see if this turns out to be a more transparent approach or merely a rebranding exercise.

The Woodford scandal had less impact on St James's Place, the wealth manager whose £3.7 billion enabled the investor to set up on his own. For most of the eighteen years SJP backed him – including his time at Invesco Perpetual – Woodford was the model investment manager. His countercyclical bets paid off handsomely and his commitment to unloved but profitable businesses kept SJP's well-to-do clients happy with regular income. But the final few years were an unmitigated disaster. When even Mark Dampier had doubts about Woodford, SJP continued to believe he had not lost his ability to pick stocks; rather, he was just stuck in a rut of bad fortune. The wealth manager had been canny and insisted its clients' funds were managed in a separate pot to Woodford's main funds, ensuring it would not be caught in the fund manager's liquidity trap. It also recognized very early on that Woodford lacked the skill or expertise to pick out tech start-ups, so SJP's investment committee had restricted him to invest in only large and mid-size British listed companies. When SJP did eventually whip away its business, Woodford should not have been surprised, given how ruthlessly the wealth manager had ended its long relationship with Invesco Perpetual five years earlier.

Woodford's downfall coincided with damaging revelations of the extravagant rewards offered to SJP's advisers for meeting tough sales targets. Yet the wealth manager's clients did not seem to care. SJP's assets actually grew by nearly a quarter throughout 2019 and it said it would clamp down on its much criticized 'cruise and cufflinks' rewards programme. Andrew Croft, the group's chief executive, had his own bonus docked from £498,000 to £310,000 by SJP's board, which said it had 'reflected upon key events that arose during the year, including certain criticisms aimed at the business and the decision to transfer mandates from Woodford Investment Management'. The directors did not clarify whether they felt the firing of Woodford was a good or bad development.

Dampier was not the only tub-thumper for Woodford over the years – he was just the loudest and gave the most sycophantic personal endorsements. Scores of other prominent investment commentators praised the celebrity stock picker throughout his good times in Henley and fell over themselves to recommend that Invesco Perpetual customers switch to his new venture. Financial advisers up and down the country also gleefully persuaded their clients to follow the great investing guru. The IFAs had become smitten with Woodford during his years of enviable performance at Invesco Perpetual and many enjoyed rubbing shoulders with him during the champagne-fuelled jollies that accompanied the Henley regatta. Woodford was as close to showbiz as the investment advisory market got.

The financial press also helped burnish Woodford's credentials as 'Britain's very own Warren Buffett' and 'the man who can't stop making money'. He had survived the first two major market crashes of the new millennium, each time digging his heels in and refusing to follow the crowd. Unlike typical buttoned-up fund managers, Woodford was not afraid to speak his mind in interviews. His frequent tirades against the bosses of the companies he invested in made for great stories. Woodford's love of fast cars, blingy watches and Led Zeppelin's music gave him a rock-star image that was rare in the staid world of finance. His escapades inside and outside the office were covered far beyond the business pages. Journalists would furiously compete for interviews with Woodford and flock to his annual press gatherings, hanging on his every word. The businesses he invested in also received outsized press interest because of his association, with headlines beginning 'Woodford-backed company . . .' appearing daily. But when his career turned for the worse, the press was on hand to bring him down much quicker than they had built him up.

While the cast of players in Neil Woodford's spectacular rise and crashing fall are numerous and varied, the starring role goes to the eponymous anti-hero himself. Woodford's emergence as the country's best-known stock picker during his twenty-six years at Invesco Perpetual was based on making three significant counterintuitive calls – investing in cigarette makers when all other stock pickers were put off by the potential for destructive litigation, avoiding tech stocks in the run-up to the dotcom crash and skirting banks leading up to the financial crisis. The adulation Woodford received after coming out on the winning side of these bold bets only bolstered his already heightened self-confidence in his investment abilities. By the time he left Henley, he was dripping with hubris.

The decisions made at the start of his new venture in Oxford would set it on a road to ruin five years later. Naming the business after Woodford himself meant it was always going to be a one-man show, with his authority ruling supreme. This helped create a culture where anybody who stood up to Woodford and his sidekick Newman had little future at the business. The lack of challenge on regulatory issues was deeply unhealthy. The pair cemented their authority by extracting the profits for themselves each year in multi-million-pound dividend payments, while paying staff fixed salaries. Woodford ensured loyalty from the board of Patient Capital by recruiting executives whose own businesses relied on his support. Woodford was heralded as the doyen of fund managers on promoting sound corporate governance and executive pay restraint. But these principles were forgotten when it came to managing his own business and personal bank account.

Even though part of the reason Woodford set up his own business was that he wanted to invest more in private companies, the new venture heavily courted retail investors, many of whom had little knowledge of or appetite for investing in such risky outfits. Equity Income was designed to mimic Woodford's staggeringly popular High Income and Income funds at Invesco Perpetual in order to prise away as many of his former followers as possible. But as the cash poured in during the heady first couple of years, Woodford wrote scores of hefty cheques to poorly researched private companies, whose tribulations would ultimately contribute to his collapse. When the tide eventually turned and investors began demanding their money back, causing the inevitable liquidity trap, rather than taking drastic action sooner – such as swallowing a loss on sales of some private businesses to balance the books – Woodford was defiant. He refused to sell his prized start-ups, even as the businesses got closer to breaching liquidity limits. The tighter the predicament, the firmer Woodford's resolve became. He had ridden out two career-threatening crashes – this one would be no different, he believed. As the net closed in, Woodford, with fewer and fewer options, tried whatever he could get away with – not least the Guernsey listings and Patient Capital asset swap.

Ultimately, Woodford's biggest failing was his inability to pick strong companies and hold on to them. His stock-picking prowess had been what propelled him to stardom – but it let him down badly during his years running his own company. Some industry analysts had long suspected that, while he was good at making big sector calls, he struggled to identify individual performers within industries, especially start-ups. This meant that when it came to unquoted companies, for every potential winner – such as Oxford Nanopore, whose DNA analysis technology was the first to sequence the Covid-19 virus – there was a stack of duds. Even in listed companies, where Woodford spent most of his career invest-ing, his record in the final few years was awful. An analysis by Stockopedia, an investment data provider, found that of the seventy-two companies Equity Income held in 2016, just nineteen had produced a positive return by the time the fund closed in October 2019. Of those, Woodford had sold all but four. Of the fifty-three companies that lost value during that time, Woodford sold only thirteen. He had made the classic investor mistake of keeping hold of his losers while selling his winners.

The unquoted holdings Woodford left in Equity Income proved fiendishly difficult to shift. PJT struggled to attract enough interest for six months in the £700 million basket of private companies. But one ray of light for the trapped investors was WG Partners, a bou-tique investment bank that specialized in science ventures. It made a serious commitment to buying fifteen companies, worth around £500 million. These were the cream of the crop, including Oxford Nanopore and Benevolent AI. WG entered exclusive talks with PJT over the sale, but negotiations collapsed in February 2020 after WG failed to stump up the cash by the agreed deadline. PJT's sale process was right back where it started.

The failure of the WG deal caught the attention of Woodford, who had just turned sixty and had kept his head down since his business unravelled. Several investment groups that had previously shown tentative interest in buying the unquoted holdings began calling Woodford at his Cotswolds country pile. They wanted to get his views on the businesses and what he thought they were worth. Sensing appetite in the market, Woodford and Newman began contacting several wealth managers and institutional investors, pitching the idea of a phoenix fund, aimed at deep-pocketed investors, certainly not the retail investors who were trapped in Equity Income. The idea was to raise capital for a new vehicle that could buy back the unquoted holdings on the cheap, which he would manage for his new wealthy backers. Woodford and Newman were planning their comeback – but his former investors would be losing out once again.

Eventually PJT and Link managed to find a buyer for nineteen of the unquoted holdings, raising £224 million in a sale to a specialist American investment group called Acacia Research in July 2020. But there was another sting in the tail for Equity Income's trapped investors as Acacia managed to flip several of the holdings within days and make tens of millions in profit – gains Equity Income's investors had missed out on. In September 2020, Link revealed that the trapped investors were unlikely to receive all their money back for at least a year.

Nearly twenty-five years after graduating from Maidenhead Grammar School, Nick Stein, Woodford's former classmate, became aware of his childhood friend's stellar professional reputation. The pair had lost touch since going to separate universities. Stein had had the type of career his old friend Woody had at one time dreamed about. He joined the RAF, eventually becoming a flying instructor. Over fifteen years, he served in the Falklands and the Gulf, provided famine relief in Ethiopia and supported UN peacekeeping missions. After leaving the forces he became a commercial pilot. In 2003, while Stein was taking part in a flight simulation, another pilot told him about how he had invested most of his pension with an incredibly successful fund manager called Neil Woodford who worked at Invesco Perpetual.

Stein did some research, consulted his IFA and decided that he too would join the crowd of retail investors entrusting their savings with Woodford. 'I invested quite a lot of money with him – not just because he was an old mate who I respected, but because I agreed with his approach,' recalls Stein. For several years, his former fellow prefect delivered the goods. So much so that, when Woodford set up his new venture more than a decade later, Stein once again invested in his funds. The pilot was especially taken with Patient Capital, which he believed made a lot of sense, and was happy to invest some of his savings for the long term in the hope that one or two of the ventures paid off. He invested several thousand pounds in the funds – not his life savings, but money he had put aside to make his retirement more comfortable. Instead, Stein has become just one of the hundreds of thousands of British savers who are nursing heavy losses from Woodford's spectacular downfall. 'I would love to sit down and grab a beer with him,' Stein says. 'I just want to know what went wrong.'

Not all Woodford's victims have got off so lightly or are as charitable. Pauline Snelson, the bed-and-breakfast owner in Devon, has had her quality of life irrevocably ruined by Woodford's reckless management of her savings. Having entrusted him with £50,000, she has had to accept that she will be lucky to see half of it back and will be working for many years to come. 'I have no prospect of retiring thanks to him. I'm sixty-seven and completely pissed off with it,' says the usually reserved grandmother of three. 'I can't understand how he's got away with it. It's unbelievable.'

Snelson's partner, Fred Hiscock, invested £25,000 with Woodford after losing money trying to play the stock market himself. He read about Woodford's avoidance of tech stocks in the dotcom bubble and of banks in the run-up to the financial crisis. He believed the fund manager was shrewd and had a comforting long-term outlook. Hiscock was also drawn to Woodford's funds as he wanted to invest in businesses that were doing good in the world. He especially liked the fact that Woodford backed companies that focused on finding cures and therapies for strokes and cancer, two conditions he had personal experience of. But his years of investing in Woodford's funds have changed all that. 'I thought he knew what he was doing, but he clearly didn't do any due diligence on these companies,' Hiscock says. 'The guy's a gambler. He was lucky in the past, but not this time. And we're the ones that are suffering.'

What has been especially galling for Snelson and Hiscock is the daily reminder of the fortune Woodford amassed while mismanaging their money. Just a few streets from Snelson's B&B in Salcombe, which she struggled to keep going through the coronavirus lockdown, is the luxury six-bedroom holiday home Woodford bought for £6.4 million in cash in 2017. Since then Woodford has added an expensive hot tub and bought a huge yacht in the bay. 'The worst thing is living here and knowing he has that multi-million-pound house just minutes away. I pass it every day,' Snelson adds. 'He's sunning himself down there at the moment with his yacht out.

'I'm a believer that people who do things like that get their comeuppance. That's how I get on: I believe that he will get his in the end.'

Acknowledgements

This book's genesis was a frenetic week in June 2019 when Neil Woodford's empire imploded and his unravelling career became the biggest British business story of the year. The *Financial Times* covered every angle of this fascinating tale of hubris and failure. My first thanks go to Peter Smith, my boss at the time, who commanded the *FT*'s coverage of the scandal and worked alongside me on a string of scoops throughout 2019. Our stories were complemented and enhanced by diligent reporting from colleagues across the *FT*, in particular Kate Beioley, Chris Flood, Siobhan Riding, Attracta Mooney, Caroline Binham, Kadhim Shubber, Robert Smith and Jamie Powell. All of us were cajoled/pressganged by our editors – primarily Tom Braithwaite, Matthew Garrahan, Richard Blackden and Sharlene Goff – whose insatiable appetite for more stories and daily demands of 'what's tomorrow's splash going to be?' knew no bounds. Thanks also go to Lionel Barber, the *FT*'s then editor, who spotted the significance of this story months before it broke and made sure everyone in the newsroom knew it was a priority. No pressure.

There are plenty of other colleagues upon whom I have relied while writing this book. I am grateful to Patrick Jenkins, James Lamont and Tobias Buck for their encouragement in letting me pursue this project and for giving me the bandwidth to do so. I am also indebted to Jonathan Guthrie and David Oakley, who have covered Woodford closely at various points in his career and read early drafts. Their insights and feedback were invaluable. Nigel Hanson, the *FT*'s in-house lawyer, helped me through some hairy moments in summer 2019. I would also like to place on record my thanks to two unsung heroes of the *FT*, Peter Cheek and Bhavna Patel, who run the library and provide a vital research service that underscores much of our reporting.

Throughout this book I have referenced sources of significant stories or interviews outside the *FT*'s coverage. One journalist in particular, Daniel Grote of *Citywire*, was responsible for uncovering many of the Guernsey manoeuvres. I have also relied on several books to provide historic context for earlier periods of Woodford's career. David Kynaston's comprehensive City of London series is the first port of call for anyone interested in the Square Mile in the 1980s. Bill Kay's *The Big Bang* is an accessible contemporaneous account of the period. I am especially grateful to Bill for reading early chapters and being generous with his feedback. Iain Martin's *Crash Bang Wallop* offers a useful thirty-year perspective on the seismic changes brought on by the Big Bang. *Science, the State, and the City*, by former *FT* editor Geoffrey Owen and Michael Hopkins, is an authoritative study of the problematic marriage between Britain's investment sector and its biotech industry.

Much of this book is based on interviews with scores of people who worked with or have been close to Woodford over the years. Some were happy to be quoted on the record, but many others understandably preferred to stay anonymous. I would like to thank all those who gave up their time to speak to me and share their insights – in particular, Cllr Barry Lewis of Kent County Council went above and beyond – but most importantly, I am indebted to the victims themselves, especially Pauline Snelson and Fred Hiscock. Thank you for sharing your story – I hope you will be able to have the retirement you planned and worked so hard for.

My agent, Toby Mundy of Aevitas, was instrumental in devising this book. My editors at Penguin Random House, Lydia Yadi and Celia Buzuk, offered fresh perspectives on early drafts, which greatly enhanced the final manuscript. Martin Soames of Simons Muirhead & Burton asked important questions and provided lawyerly reassurance. This book was much improved by Trevor Horwood's tight copy-editing and meticulous fact-checking. I am also deeply grateful to my father, John Walker, for interrupting work on his own latest book to read through the manuscript and pick me up on the finer points of public administration.

Finally, I would like to thank my wife Sarah, without whom this would never have been possible, and my sons Arthur and Albie, who provided much-needed distraction in the long months of writing and editing during lockdown. This book is dedicated to them.

Index

Woodford IM indicates Woodford Investment Management.

PENGUIN PARTNERSHIPS

Penguin Partnerships is the Creative Sales and Promotions team at Penguin Random House. We have a long history of working with clients on a wide variety of briefs, specializing in brand promotions, bespoke publishing and retail exclusives, plus corporate, entertainment and media partnerships.

We can respond quickly to briefs and specialize in repurposing books and content for sales promotions, for use as incentives and retail exclusives as well as creating content for new books in collaboration with our partners as part of branded book relationships.

Equally if you'd simply like to buy a bulk quantity of one of our existing books at a special discount, we can help with that too. Our books can make excellent corporate or employee gifts.

Special editions, including personalized covers, excerpts of existing books or books with corporate logos can be created in large quantities for special needs.

We can work within your budget to deliver whatever you want, however you want it.

For more information, please contact
salesenquiries@penguinrandomhouse.co.uk